GORTON TANK
Late 1950s

Redrawn by David Gosling from BR Drawing 14801 - C

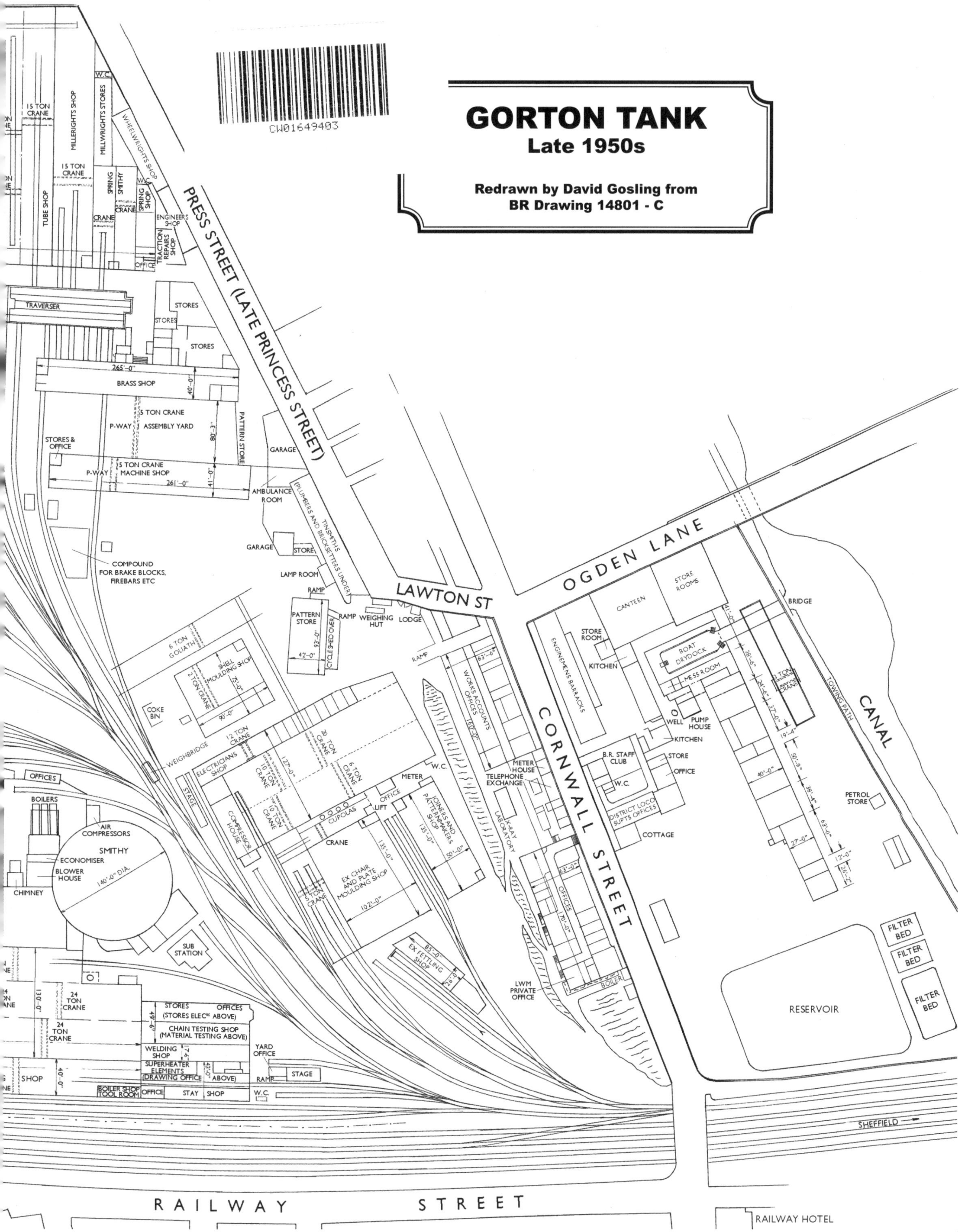

2021

GORTON TANK

A Pictorial Review of Gorton Locomotive Works
Manchester

1847 – 1963

Designed by Ian Pope
British Library Cataloguing-in-Publication Data. A catalogue record for this book is available from the British Library
ISBN 13: 978 1 911038 87 0

Lightmoor Press
Lightmoor Press is an imprint of
Black Dwarf Lightmoor Publications Limited
144b Lydney Industrial Estate, Harbour Road,
Lydney, Gloucestershire, GL15 4EJ
Printed in Poland www.lfbookservices.co.uk

GORTON TANK

A Pictorial Review of Gorton Locomotive Works Manchester

1847 – 1963

courtesy J. H. Hillier

author's collection

DAVID GOSLING

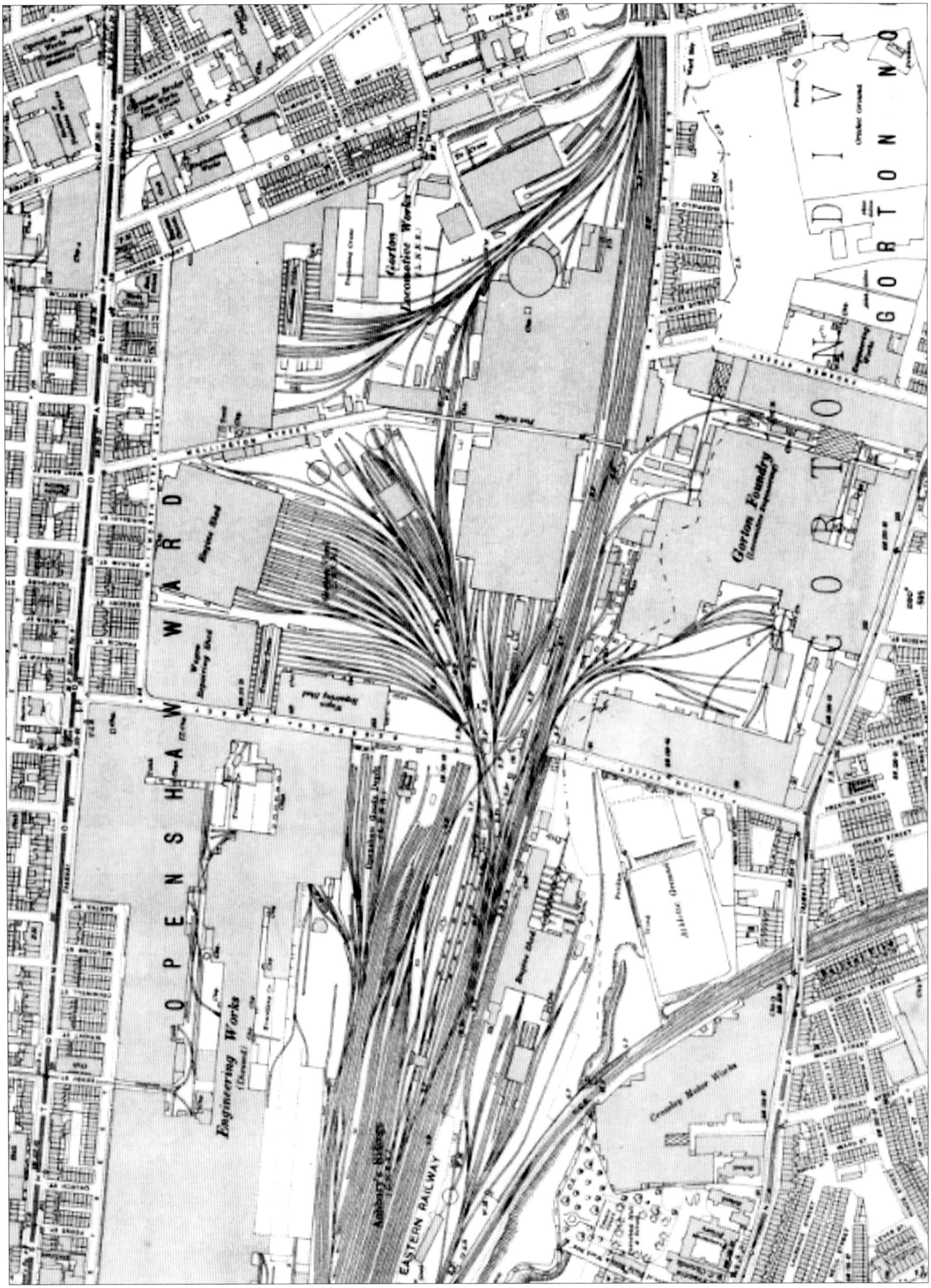
OPENSHAW WARD
GORTON
DIV
Gorton Foundry
Engineering Works
Gorton Locomotive Works
Engine Shed
EASTERN RAILWAY
Crossley Motor Works

CONTENTS

FOREWORD

It has been both a privilege and a pleasure to have been asked to write the Foreword to Dave Gosling's history of Gorton Works. Over many years I have researched material relating to the locomotives of the Great Central Railway, its antecedents and successors. Such work has brought me into contact with Gorton Works – the famous 'Tank' – but never close enough to learn how the place was formed, how it developed, the functions of the various sections and the men and tools that made it all tick.

Dave Gosling got to know 'The Tank' as a young man. Clearly a dedicated employee, he formed close bonds with the works, the men and its myriad of products. His work knows no bounds: despite being an expatriate for several years he has beavered away aided and abetted by his many contacts and bolstered by his determination to write the definitive history of this, his *alma mater*.

We live in an age when railway books abound and seldom does a month pass without new titles appearing on the shelves. Sadly, many such publications are mere pot-boilers, a mere few tick all the boxes; fewer still stand as 'definitive.'

Gorton was not a Crewe, Swindon or Doncaster, but its locomotive engineering was second to none. Why else would a man of Gresley's stature entrust production of such vital components as cylinders for his magnum opus – his 'A4' and others besides to Gorton?

I commend Dave's work to railway enthusiasts, students and historians. This is a magnificent piece of research and it deserves a place in the pantheon of locomotive development and history.

Eddie Johnson, Burnage, Manchester, December 2020

A panoramic view from the top of the coaling tower taken in the 1930s and looking eastwards over the works and the Manchester to Sheffield main line. The whole scene oozes the railway industry and its infrastructure. The dark building on the right is the LM&SR Belle Vue sheds, further along can be seen Beyer, Peacock's works. The four-track main line heads towards Guide Bridge and beyond. Immediately in front of the coaling tower are the wet ash pits with four locomotives probably being attended to over the pits. To the left of the ash pits are three rows of coal wagons as they queue up to the hoist of the tower and feed the bunker. The roads on either side of the ash pits are for ash disposal wagons. Priory Junction with the four rail bridges that lead in and out of the works and running sheds and carriage and wagon shops are beyond the pits, with Priory Junction signal box on the south side of the main line. Further east are the five bays of the erecting shop and wheel shop to the left of No. 5 bay. The light coloured long horizontal building in the distance is the steel/bar store. The gradual upward sloping structure in front of the steel store and leading upwards behind the wheel shop is the birdcage. The white area to the left of the ash pits is the sand drying facility.

courtesy John Ryan

INTRODUCTION

Gorton Locomotive Works, known as Gorton Tank, or, to those who lived in the immediate area simply as 'The Tank', was never a very large works, It did not enjoy the fame or charisma of such locomotive workshops as Crewe, Swindon, Doncaster, Darlington or Eastleigh, and therefore very little has been written about it comprehensively, good articles have been written in various railway magazines over the years on Gorton, but nothing has been delved into its 'heart and soul' as a locomotive works. With this in mind I decided to produce this pictorial historic review of the works and how it developed and put Gorton Tank in its rightful place as one of the finest locomotive workshops in the country in its day. This book is a review of the actual locomotive works, not simply of their products.

First conceived by the Sheffield, Ashton-under-Lyne and Manchester Railway (SA&MR) in 1845, work commenced on the construction of the 'Depot' (as it was called on the architects drawings) in 1847 and, became a working entity in 1847/8, the work shops were designed to repair and build both locomotives and carriages and wagons. By the time the works was completed the SA&M had changed its name to the Manchester, Sheffield & Lincolnshire Railway (MS&LR). This had come about by the amalgamation of the SA&MR with several other railway companies, mainly in the Yorkshire area, also others railways east of the Pennines. The new workshops were designed by Richard Peacock.

Prior to Gorton 'Depot' being constructed, locomotives and rolling stock had their repairs carried out further out of Manchester at Newton, Hyde in Cheshire, adjacent to the SA&MR line. The facilities here were quite rudimentary and consisted mainly of wooden buildings, theses buildings were inadequate for their intended purpose. New and much larger premises for maintenance to rolling stock would soon be needed.

The MS&LR later changed its name in 1897 as a result of its new main line from the North of England to the capital in 1899. The driving of this line into London became known as the London Extension. Up until then, the MS&LR was a cross-country railway stretching east to west from Lincolnshire and Yorkshire, across the Pennines into Lancashire and Cheshire. Now, with its main line into the capital it had to have much grander name, the Great Central Railway (GCR).

In later MS&LR days it was becoming obvious that some expansion of the works would be needed to cater for the extra locomotives and rolling stock required by the expanded company. Over the decades of the nineteenth century the works had gradually increased in size so that by the early 1900s they had almost assumed the capacity to carry them through to closure in 1963.

With the grouping of the 'Big Four' in January 1923, the GCR became part of the London & North Eastern Railway (L&NER), a company second only to the London, Midland & Scottish Railway (LM&SR) in size.

As the main locomotive works of both the MS&LR and GCR, Gorton without a doubt had enjoyed its best years. The works at this time in its history, under its company's Chief Mechanical Engineer, John George Robinson and his first-class team, produced some of the most successful and graceful locomotives in the country, the 'Jersey Lily' 4-4-2 Atlantics, the 8K 2-8-0s and the D10/11 4-4-0s and his 'Pacific' 4-6-2T suburban passenger tank locomotives to mention just a few. Now, as part of the newly formed L&NER, Gorton Tank lost a lot of its prestige. The main locomotive workshops now under the ownership of the L&NER were chosen to be the former Great Northern Railway workshops at Doncaster and the former North Eastern Railway shops at Darlington.

Most new engine design and construction was now to be carried out at Doncaster and Darlington. Gorton was starting to play second fiddle, new locomotive build was very limited, Gorton Works then concentrating on repairs, mainly to its own ex-GCR fleet but other L&NER group locomotives started to come to Gorton for attention as time passed.

With the formation of the L&NER, a new Chief Mechanical Engineer was needed to be appointed. J. G. Robinson was approached to fill this position but 'John G.', by this time in his mid 60s and approaching retirement, declined. He recommended that the young Herbert Nigel Gresley was the man they should appoint as the new Chief Mechanical Engineer. John G. Robinson retired his position on the formation of the 'Grouping'.

Nothing more needs to be said about the work of Nigel Gresley (later Sir) and his outstanding work both with the GNR and later the L&NER. His untimely death at 65 years old came as a shock to the railway world.

Gorton's last steam locomotive new build was ten of the successful Thomson 'B1' 4-6-0s, the last being No. 61349 in 1949. On January 1st 1948 the L&NER was no more, the railways of Great Britain were nationalised and became known as 'British Railways' (BR). The L&NER under BR was split into two 'regions' the Eastern and the North Eastern Regions. Gorton works fell now into the hands of the Eastern Region. With the impending electrification of the Manchester to Sheffield main line with lines to Wath upon Dearne (a project that had started before the Second World War under the L&NER but was put on hold during those hostilities) Gorton works was entrusted by BR to build the 'EM1' and 'EM2' Class of electric locomotives. The 'EM1's being built to the design of the prototype locomotive designed by Sir Nigel Gresley which was built at Doncaster in 1941. This prototype was the famed *Tommy* No. 6701 (later BR No 26000). Fifty-six Class 'EM1' locomotives and seven Class 'EM2' locomotives were built at Gorton. These two classes of locomotives became the last new locomotives to be built there. The 'EM1' Class was built for mixed traffic purposes and the 'EM2's for passenger work.

By the very late 1940s Gorton started cutting up life-expired steam locomotives in addition to carrying out repairs. By the middle of the 1950s increasingly large numbers started to be scrapped and cut-up there. Many locomotives stood in the works yards with large 'X's painted in white on their sides indicating that they were waiting for their fate under the cutters torch.

The last locomotive to leave the works erecting shop after a Major/General overhaul was a Stanier Class '8F' 2-8-0 No. 48520 at the end of April 1960. Very shortly afterwards the very last steam locomotive, a Robin Riddles designed BR Standard Class '9F' 2-10-0 No. 92161 left the erecting shop following an unscheduled repair, this was followed soon afterwards by EM2 Class electric locomotive No. 27001 *Ariadne* after a light repair and the erecting shop doors closed, leaving it empty of locomotives.

Gorton 'Tank' closed officially on the 31st May 1963. Demolition of the site commenced in 1964 and made way for the new Smithfield wholesale fruit and vegetable market. A few scrapped locomotives remained in the works yard after the works closed for a very short time waiting for them to be removed to other disposal points for cutting up.

Why the name 'Gorton Tank' ?

Over the years 'Gorton Tank' was thought to have obtained the name after a water storage tank on a tower (presumably on top of the roundhouse clock tower). This is not the case. The reason behind the name dates back from the time when permanent way track sleepers were treated with creosote as a preservative at Gorton. This process was done by placing the sleepers in large 'tanks' of creosote. Many railway depots carried out the same process of preserving sleepers and, assumed the same name, Longsight Tank and Newton Heath Tank being examples. Gorton Tank carried the name 'Tank' to the very end of its days whereas other depots lost their 'tank' identity over time.

The top of Gorton's roundhouse clock tower never had a water tank installed, the feature on the roof was purely ornamental with a ventilation and flue chimney. The only water tank of any size at Gorton Works was installed on top of the C&W works building tower in 1881.

Photographs

Over the years, I have managed to acquire quite a considerable amount of photographs pertaining to Gorton works, many of these are included in this book where they are of importance to its content. For a relatively very small number (one or two) I have no knowledge as to who the photographer was and so they must remain as unknown but I do give full tribute to their excellent and very much appreciated efforts. I have though spent many hours researching and sending numerous emails trying to locate their sources. Sadly, I have been unable to further contact a few people who have contributed a number of photographs that gave me permission to publish them, maybe they have moved on over the twelve years or so since I initially gave thought to researching Gorton Tank. I do though hope that they read this and see that their contributions have helped in making this work as comprehensive as it is. It is sad to think that some of those who have contributed them all of those years ago may no longer be with us, I am sure that they would have approved and enjoyed the outcome of their efforts.

Gorton Tank and Beyer, Peacock & Co.: A clarification

It is just over fifty-five years since Gorton Works shut down and there is starting to be some confusion that the Gorton Locomotive Works (Gorton Tank) and Beyer, Peacock Ltd (Gorton Foundry) was one and the same establishment, this especially so to the less informed and younger generation of railway enthusiasts.

Gorton Locomotive Works and Beyer, Peacock Ltd Locomotive manufacturers were two totally different entities:

Gorton Locomotive Works (Gorton Tank) being a locomotive works building and repairing locomotives and rolling stock for the railway owning company, i.e. The MS&LR, GCR, LNER and BR. Gorton Tank was on the northern side of the Manchester to Sheffield railway line.

Beyer, Peacock Ltd (Gorton Foundry) was a public limited company, building and supplying new locomotives for many railway companies both within Great Britain and Overseas as a profit making business. Beyer, Peacock was located directly opposite Gorton Tank on the south side of the Manchester to Sheffield railway line. An excellent book has been written by R. L. Hills and D. Patrick titled *Beyer, Peacock: Locomotive Builders To the World* a well worthwhile read.

Abbreviations used in this book:

SAuL&MR	Sheffield, Ashton-under-Lyne & Manchester Railway
GCR	Great Central Railway
MR	Midland Railway
L&NER	London and North Eastern Railway
BR	British Railways
LM&SR	London, Midland and Scottish Railway
LMR	London Midland Region
GER	Great Eastern Railway
ER	Eastern Region
MSJ&AR	Manchester South Junction & Altrincham Railway
CLC	Cheshire Lines Committee (Railway)
MLS	Manchester Locomotive Society
SLS	Stephenson Locomotive Society
GCRS	Great Central Railway Society
BP	Beyer, Peacock and Company
BRSA	British Railways Staff Association
L&Y	Lancashire & Yorkshire Railway
YEC	Yorkshire Engine Company
MS&LR	Manchester Sheffield and Lincolnshire Railway
VUL	Vulcan Foundry Co. (later Limited)
LD&ECR	Lancashire, Derbyshire & East Coast Railway
I.L.E	Institute of Locomotive Engineers
MOSI	Manchester Museum of Science and Industry

ACKNOWLEDGMENTS

There is no way that this book could have been written without the assistance of quite a number of individuals and organisations. Where do I start ? That is not too difficult. The first two people that comes to mind are Eddie Johnson and Terry Holtby. Eddie has given me so much invaluable help over quite a period of time. Both in advice and furnishing me with material, especially on the locomotive side. I have been welcomed into his home many times and spent a lot of time sifting through and perusing over his large amount of material (and enjoyed his good wife's tea, coffee, cake and biscuits!) and also thoroughly enjoying his company. Second in mind comes my good friend and fellow ex-Gorton Tank employee Terry Holtby. Terry has also been invaluable in my research, his photographic memory has been most helpful, where my memory has lapsed, Terry has taken over and jogged my brain cells back into life. We have enjoyed many a conversation on The Tank, sometimes well after midnight discussing all sorts of Gorton Tank stuff. A large thank you also to the Manchester Locomotive Society (MLS) for all their assistance and to Paul Shackcloth for access to their large photographic collection, Many of the MLS images are from deceased members, with a number of them by unknown contributors in the collection. Thank you to Nick Howell and Chris Tasker, also to Tony Zajac. It is always a pleasure visiting the MLS on a Wednesday at Stockport railway station and sharing railway stuff in general with fellow members. Many thanks to John Hillier, John, the son of the last works Manager John T. Hillier has given me permission to use his father's personal material to assist with the book, Mr Hillier Senior's article on the handing over Class 'D11' 4-4-0 locomotive *Butler Henderson* to the Clapham Transport Museum in 1962 fully captures the essence of that era. John is very well known for his long association with the preserved ex LM&SR locomotive, BR Class '6P' 4-6-0 No. 45996 *Bahamas* with the Bahamas Locomotive Society and the Dinting Railway Centre. I have had the honour of being invited onto the locomotive and travelling behind it. The National Archives at Kew, who went out of their way with help in my research on the 'Tank' in the Great Central era. I must also mention Taryk Welburn and Andy Croxton at the NRM who have had to suffer my constant pestering. I can imagine them rolling their eyes every time I emailed or telephoned them. Thanks for your valued assistance, also to Justin Hobson the Imaging Licensing Executive of the combined Science Museums. John Pitman and David Kitching for their assistance with information on the Canal Depot's narrow boats. Emma Burgham at the Manchester Museum of Science and Industry (MOSI) for her help with their photographic collection in sifting through the Gorton locomotive cylinder collection. John Duncan, an ex-Gorton man, John started at Gorton in the late 1940s as an engineering apprentice, and, being a railway enthusiast took quite a number of photos from that period which he has permitted me to use. I worked with John in the late 60s at Reddish Electric Traction Depot. He is probably better known in railway circles for his activities concerning the Oliver Bulleid 'West Country' Class Pacific locomotive No. 34092 *City Of Wells* at Carnforth. For my wife, Jeanine, converting our dining room into an office, conservatory and then the kitchen table was not part of her grand scheme of things when we moved into our house in Glossop. Being sympathetic to a cause can have its limits but, her patience has been outstanding. For my brother Peter, another ex-Gorton Tank employee, who, though not a railway enthusiast as such, encouraged me to 'go for it' when I first mentioned about starting a history of Gorton works a number of years ago. My brother in law, the late Harold Faulkner and my late sister Jean for their encouragement. Harold was an ex-Gorton locomotive fireman – he once fired No. 60103 *Flying Scotsman* out of Gorton – who when I was about twelve or thirteen years old gave me my first in-depth railway book *The Gresley Pacifics of the LNER*. This was a book that I could not put down, and expanded my interests in railways from just being a trainspotter with my Ian Allen ABC combined volumes to wanting to work at Gorton Tank two or three years later. My late father, Albert Gosling; he also worked at Gorton, both within the works and also the canal depot. For my 21st birthday he bought me 'part one' of George Dow's famous trilogy *Great Central*, another book I could not put down. When we were talking railways and mentioning John G. Robinson's name, he always referred to him simply as 'John G. and Robert Thompson, as 'Robert Thom' and not by his initials as some were prone to do (R.A.T.).

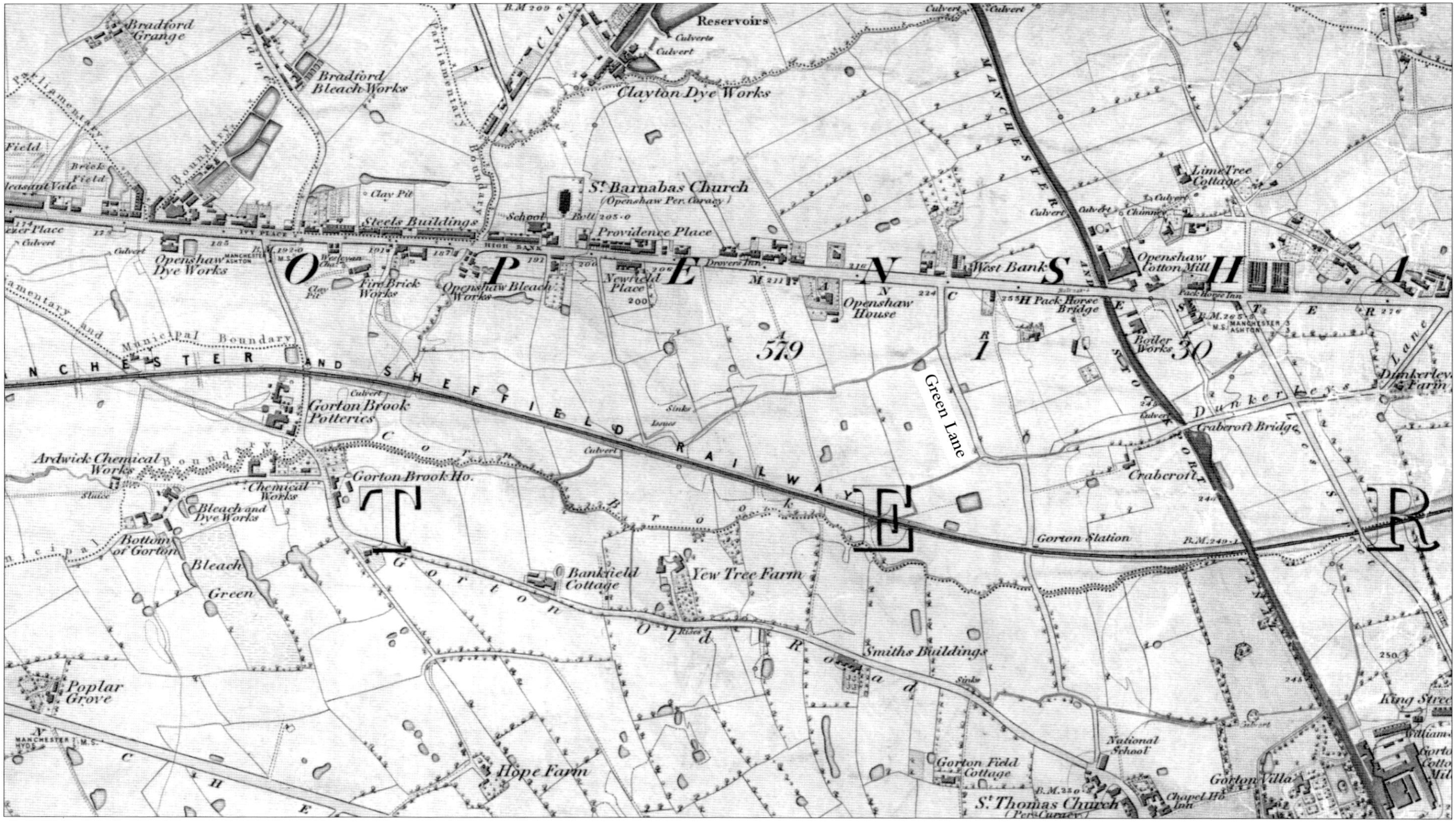

The above map, an extract of the 1848 Ordnance Survey 6-inch sheet (surveyed in 1845), shows the Sheffield, Ashton-under-Lyne and Manchester Railway cutting across the centre of the page, it being a single track line at this time. The Stockport Branch of the Ashton Canal (shaded dark) runs from the top centre of the map to the bottom right side of the map. Gorton Depot (Gorton Locomotive works) as originally built in 1847 to 1851 travelled westwards from the side of the canal at a point to the left of Crabtree Bridge to Green Lane then south down Green Lane to Gorton Station, then back east along the main line back to the canal. This area that was to be the new railway workshops was mostly fields and pasture land at the time of construction and covered an area of approximately twenty acres, with approximately nine at the canal depot and cottages. This railway station was relocated further east closer to the canal at about the time when construction of the works commenced in 1847 leaving just a level crossing. When the construction of the works started Green Lane became more established as a thoroughfare and as rail traffic increased a bridge was built over the railway. Unfortunately, no drawings appear to be in existence of this first station. Crabcroft Bridge was later to be named Ogden Lane Bridge. Dunkerleys Lane later became Ogden Lane. A very small hamlet, probably just a few dwellings called Crabcroft was located approximately where the main entrance to the works was later to be built. Note: Green Lane followed the general direction of what was later to be known as Wellington Street, and later still as Widnes Street. The land to the left of Green Lane was later taken up by the works up to Bessemer Street. On the south side of the railway, the joining lane passed over the Corn Brook and led to St. Thomas Church and the National School there, where, it joined several other lanes and later joining what was to become Hyde Road.

CHAPTER ONE
GORTON AND OPENSHAW 1841-1851

The Sheffield, Ashton-under-Lyne & Manchester Railway becomes the Manchester Sheffield & Lincolnshire Railway and Gorton Works is built
The Census of 1841 put down Gorton as having a population of 2,423
Openshaw, being a somewhat smaller area, had a population of 2,283
This population in the near future was to increase at a rapid pace...

Prior to the commencement of construction of 'Gorton Depot' in 1846, the Gorton and Openshaw area was at that time out of Manchester's City boundary. Manchester's built-up urban areas to the east of the city at this time only went out as far as Ancoats and Ardwick, John Ashbury's large Railway Carriage and Wagon Works stretched from Ardwick and into Lower Openshaw on the northern side of the then Sheffield, Ashton-under-Lyne & Manchester Railway (SAuL&MR).

The Gorton and Openshaw areas were mainly rural with the main but small industries being a few chemical works, a boiler works, dye and bleach works, a pottery works and fire brick manufacturers, all no doubt supplying materials to the few cotton mills that dotted the surrounding areas. The remainder of the areas consisted of small farms, hamlets and open fields. The main road through Openshaw eastwards from Manchester was called Ashton Lane, later called Ashton Road, and later still Ashton Old Road, this was 'turnpiked' in 1731, it was along this road that most of the development of Openshaw had grown. The main road eastwards through Gorton from Manchester was 'Manchester Hyde Road' known later as just Hyde Road, which had become a turnpike in 1818.

Just to the north of Ashton Lane (Ashton Old Road) bordering Openshaw and Clayton running eastwards in the same direction from Manchester to Ashton-under-Lyne was the Ashton Canal. At Ashton-under-Lyne the canal joined the Huddersfield Narrow Canal and the Peak Forest Canal at Ashton's Portland Basin. Back in Clayton, to the north of Openshaw, the Ashton Canal had a branch that led to Stockport, this section was officially called 'the Stockport Branch of the Ashton Canal', commonly known more simply as the 'Stockport Canal' and was to play a role in the construction of the locomotive works.

Up until the early 1840s Gorton and Openshaw were destined to become part of Lancashire's giant textile industry, another district that would have a skyline dotted predominantly with cotton mills, much the same as other Lancashire areas. By the early to middle 1840s one man would change all that: Richard Peacock, who was soon to turn Openshaw and Gorton into one of the early great railway engineering centres of the world along with his future business partner Charles Beyer.

The map opposite shows the Gorton and Openshaw areas in the mid 1840s and displays the predominantly rural area. The main industrial features being the SAuL&MR line and the Stockport Canal. The construction of Gorton Works had not been started as yet.

As previously mentioned, during the very early 1840s the SAuL&MR had their railway work shops at Newton near Hyde in Cheshire, here repairs were carried out to the company's rolling stock. The locomotive engineer of this period of time had come from the Great Western Railway, where, he had worked under the renowned Daniel Gooch, and no doubt gained a vast amount of experience from him. The gentleman in question was the very young and, extremely capable Richard Peacock, Initially his position on commencing with the SAuL&MR was recorded as 'Engine Driver No. 1'. Richard Peacock was very soon given the responsibility for all matters concerning locomotives and rolling stock.

As construction and expansion of the SAuL&MR continued on its way eastwards towards Woodhead, so did its infrastructure. Fairfield Station was up to this time the first station out of Manchester, being open from the very start of services. Doubling of the tracks took place on this section in 1842-1843.

Gorton Railway Stations

As seen on the map opposite, the SAuL&MR line shows a railway station mid way across the map. Very little is known of this station. It is quite likely that this was a very temporary structure no doubt constructed of wood and opened on the 23rd May 1842. The station probably served more so as the gate keeper's post for the level crossing that was installed there than it did for passengers. The level crossing joined Green Lane (Wellington Street – later Widnes Street) on the north side of the railway line to the lane leading to St. Thomas' Church on the south side.

In 1842 the first 'permanent' brick built passenger station at Gorton was built on the east side of what was later to become Chapman Street on the south side of the railway line (Chapman St joined Cornwall St at this point) and the Stockport Canal being at the east end of the station. A public house was built very close to the railway station and was named the 'Cornwall Inn', later to be called the 'Railway Hotel'. The Stockport Canal crossed over the railway via a brick built aqueduct.

At this very early period in time, the Stockport and Ashton Canals had a packet service vying for passengers on this section of canal and into Manchester as there were very few roads and it was a safer way to travel. The railway station at Gorton was now a staging place for boat passengers to travel to destinations further afield. The hotel at the side of the railway station would have been a warm welcome for thirsty 'transit' passengers.

By 1844 it was becoming obvious that serious thought had to be put into finding much larger workshops than those presently at Newton near Hyde in Cheshire for the locomotive and carriage and wagon repairs The workshops there were rudimentary and totally inadequate. In 1845 Richard Peacock was asked to look for a suitable site where permanent large workshops could be built. Peacock looked closer to Manchester where there would be the necessary manpower with the engineering skills required by the budding railway industry.

Peacock selected land in Openshaw, about two and a half miles to the east of Manchester city centre. It was here that the land and railway line were both at the same ground level as the land to this point out of Manchester was lower than the railway which had to be elevated above ground level for the first two miles out of Manchester. The land also was far enough out of Manchester not to be subject to the high taxes that would be applicable in the city, also it was close to the Stockport Canal which would be able to bring in necessary materials for construction of the works, and, give an ample supply of water for the works and for domestic purposes.

The land in this part of Openshaw was owned by a George Cornwall Legh of High Legh, near Knutsford in Cheshire. Legh was born in 1804 and was MP for Cheshire North from 1841 to 1868 and Mid Cheshire from 1868 to 1873. The Cornwall Legh

George Cornwall Legh
30th August 1804 – 16th June 1877
Member of Parliament for Cheshire North 1841 to 1868
Mid Cheshire from 1868 to 1873
By kind permission of Manchester Art Gallery

Richard Peacock
9th April 1820 – 3rd March 1889
Locomotive Superintendent of the Manchester Sheffield and Lincolnshire Railway from 1847 to 1854
Richard Peacock is buried in the family mausoleum in Brookfield Unitarian Church graveyard, Hyde Road, Gorton, Manchester
author's collection

family origins go back to the 13th century, all centred around High Legh near Knutsford in Cheshire.

Cornwall's name lives on in Openshaw with Cornwall Street, There was also a public house on Ashton Old Road bearing Legh's name but this has since been closed down (The Legh Arms).

The lead up to the works

On the 17th November 1841 the Sheffield, Ashton-under-Lyne & Manchester Railway ran its first trains into and out of Manchester towards Guide Bridge and Ashton, out as far as Godley. The SAuL&MR was now a going concern. Through trains to Sheffield would not run for another four years until the first of the two bores of the Woodhead Tunnel had been completed and opened. At this period of time (1841) there was no significant railway station at Gorton.

The directors of the SAuL&MR met in London on the 4th March 1846 at the Morley's Hotel near Trafalgar Square and approval was given to purchase land for the locomotive workshops. Twenty acres were purchased from George Cornwall Legh. The land purchased bordered the Stockport Canal from the railway aqueduct at Gorton Station northwards to Dunkerley's Lane at Crabtree Bridge (Ogden Lane), and westwards to Green Lane, what was later to be Wellington Street and which later still changed to Widnes Street, and then south bordering the main railway line. Peacock was given the task of planning and designing the works. Contracts were given to Barber and Worthington on the 16th May for earthworks at 8d per cubic yard and to Chadwick and France for building and civil works for almost £27,000. The architectural work was awarded to Matthew Ellison Hadfield of Sheffield, the same architect that was commissioned for Dinting Vale and Broadbottom Vale viaducts.

Towards the end of 1846 and into 1847 planning and construction of the works commenced. The Stockport Canal was very busy at this point in time with its normal everyday business of taking supplies to the local industries and shipping out their finished products. The canal was also useful for delivering materials for the works and thus its bank would have been one of the first areas cleared for development. The MS&L built a canal depot just to the south of Crabtree Bridge (later Ogden Lane Bridge) on the canal's western bank. The lane from Ashton Lane (Ashton Old Road) would also have been put to good use. Tracks were laid alongside the main line directly adjacent to the works site to enable construction materials to be off-loaded from the main line. The depot was first put into some sort of practicable use at the end of 1847. Gorton Depot was now 'on the map'. One hundred and forty cottages were built on the canal depot site for the locomotive works employees and their families, and a reservoir for the depot large enough to hold approximately one month's water supply led directly from the canal to the locomotive and carriage & wagon works. At about the same time that the SAuL&MR became the MS&LR through its amalgamation the canal company was purchased.

A lane between the canal depot and the works soon became necessary as development progressed. This was later upgraded to become Cornwall Street (in recognition of George Cornwall Legh). Cornwall Street was to run between Ashton Old Road to the north and Chapman Street on the south side of the main line (in Gorton), This lane joined Dunkerleys Lane (originally Ogden Lane) near Crabtree Bridge (Ogden Lane Bridge).

The spare land situated between the canal complex and the locomotive works covered approximately six acres. This spare land would soon be utilised as the works expanded under the

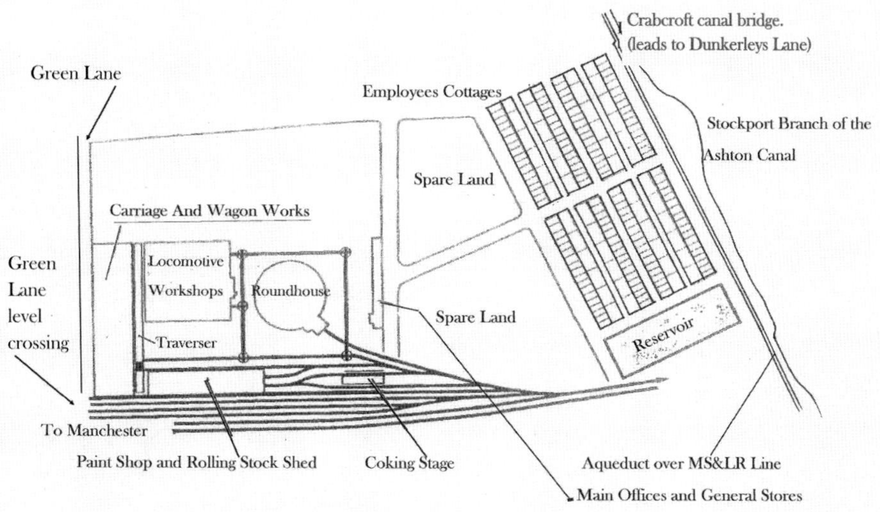

Gorton Depot (Gorton Locomotive Works)

The above sketch shows the layout of the locomotive works and canal depot with the staff housing as completed in 1851 (the canal being to the right of the cottages and reservoir). The canal aqueduct mentioned was later replaced due to the MS&LR track quadrupling in 1905 by a cast iron trough type aqueduct. *Based on G. Dows drawing in Great Central Part 1.*

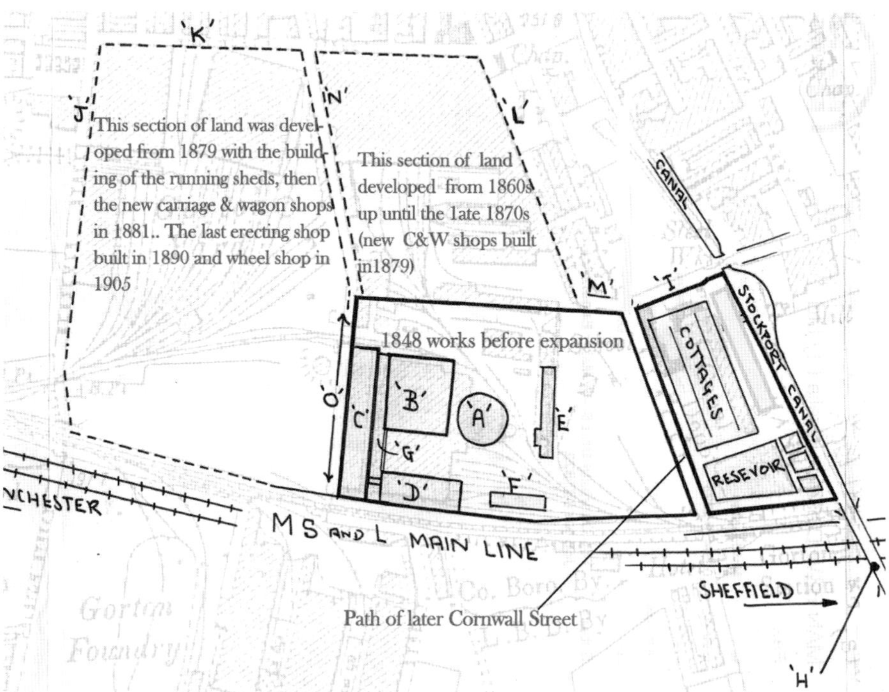

This sketch depicts the area (lined out in bold) of the works area in 1851 as compared to the works boundaries (dotted lines) of the completed Locomotive and Carriage & Wagon works in 1963. The buildings were: 'A' The Roundhouse; 'B' Locomotive Workshop Complex; 'C' Carriage & Wagon Works (Wagon Shop on lower floor, Carriage Shop on upper); 'D' Paint Shop & Stock Holding Shed; 'E' Main Offices & Stores; 'F' coking stage/ shed; 'G' traverser (for transferring rolling stock to the various departments/workshops); 'H' Stockport Canal Aqueduct; 'I' Canal Depot (reservoirs, settling ponds, employees houses and canal dock); 'J' west boundary - the running sheds; 'K' northern end of the works; 'L' eastern boundary of the works; 'M' main entrance to the works in later years (off Lawton Street); 'N' route of Widnes Street (Green Lane on the 1840s map) which divides the Locomotive Works from the running sheds and C&W Works; 'O' elevated overhead section (bridge) of Widnes Street, this was a footpath only access over the erecting shop and main line and followed the line of Green Lane. This was constructed in 1890 on completion of the erecting shop and is described in more detail in later chapters. Note: Lines L & N show the expansion of the works from the 1860s to 1879 whilst lines J & K show the expansion of the works from 1879 to closure.

author's drawing

new Locomotive Superintendent W. G. Craig following Richard Peacock's retirement.

The architects drawings gives the name of the works as 'Gorton Depot'. but Gorton Works was actually in the parish of Openshaw. The most probable reason it assumed the name of Gorton Works and not Openshaw Works is that it followed on from the name of the first 'Gorton' Railway Station of 1842 which had its booking/ticket office on the Gorton side of the MS&LR main line. The later station, opened in 1905, was named 'Gorton and Openshaw'. It was built as a consequence of the main line being quadrupled and had its booking/ticket office on the Openshaw side of the main line.

The original works buildings remained intact, though altered and extended extensively and utilised for different purposes, up until the very end of the works existence in 1963.

The Roundhouse

This building had an internal diameter of 140 feet. The turntable which was 40 feet in diameter had two running lines on the table instead of one as is usually the norm. The tracks ran side by side and the table revolved around a large central cast iron column that extended to the top of the building and supported the roof. On entering the shed a loco would run onto the right hand side line, turned and then run onto its allocated road. On leaving the roundhouse the loco would run onto the left hand side on the table. The roundhouse had seventeen roads, all with pits, all offset at an angle to match the table layout. With this arrangement, two locomotives could be turned at any one time, one entering, and one exiting the shed, (see plan), locomotives could be turned in approximately one minute by three men.

With the central column arrangement, there was no need for any other supports for the roof and locomotives were free of any obstructions near them which eased maintenance. Each loco had around 1000 square feet of free working space around them. Locomotives entered the roundhouse going forwards, this to give ease of maintenance for tube cleaning.

The roundhouse was quite an impressive building, with an ornamental portal into the shed and a clock tower built onto to the portal side. The tower was 'capped' with a pergola style of roof and finial. The tower had a clock which was five feet in diameter on each of its four sides.

The Roundhouse was to have a

continued on page 19

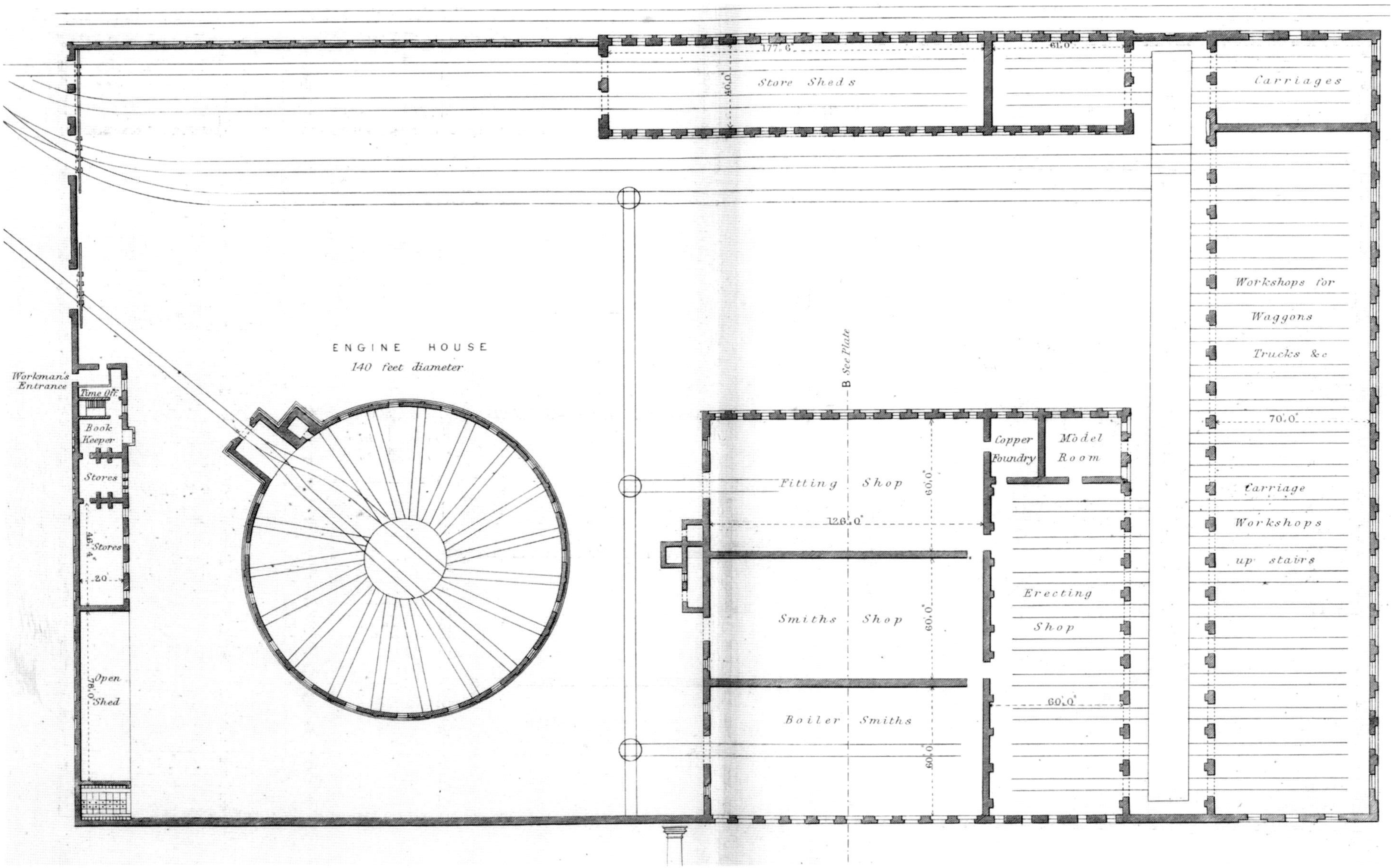

The architects drawing for the plan of what was then termed 'Gorton Depot'.

The architect was M. E. Hadfield of Sheffield. The plans were drawn up to Richard Peacock's ideas in 1846 for what was at that time the Sheffield, Ashton-under-Lyne & Manchester Railway. The architects are still in business in Sheffield today under the name Hadfield, Cawkwell, Davidson.

The Roundhouse (Rotunda) – general front view
The architects drawing (opposite) shows the building as having eighteen roads. This was changed to seventeen roads probably due to the shortest road being a hindrance for the furnace locomotive firebox lighting up area. As mentioned, locomotives entering the Roundhouse entered via the right-hand side road and exited via the left-hand road. Note: the chimney outlet for the furnace was from an ornamental outlet at the top of the tower.

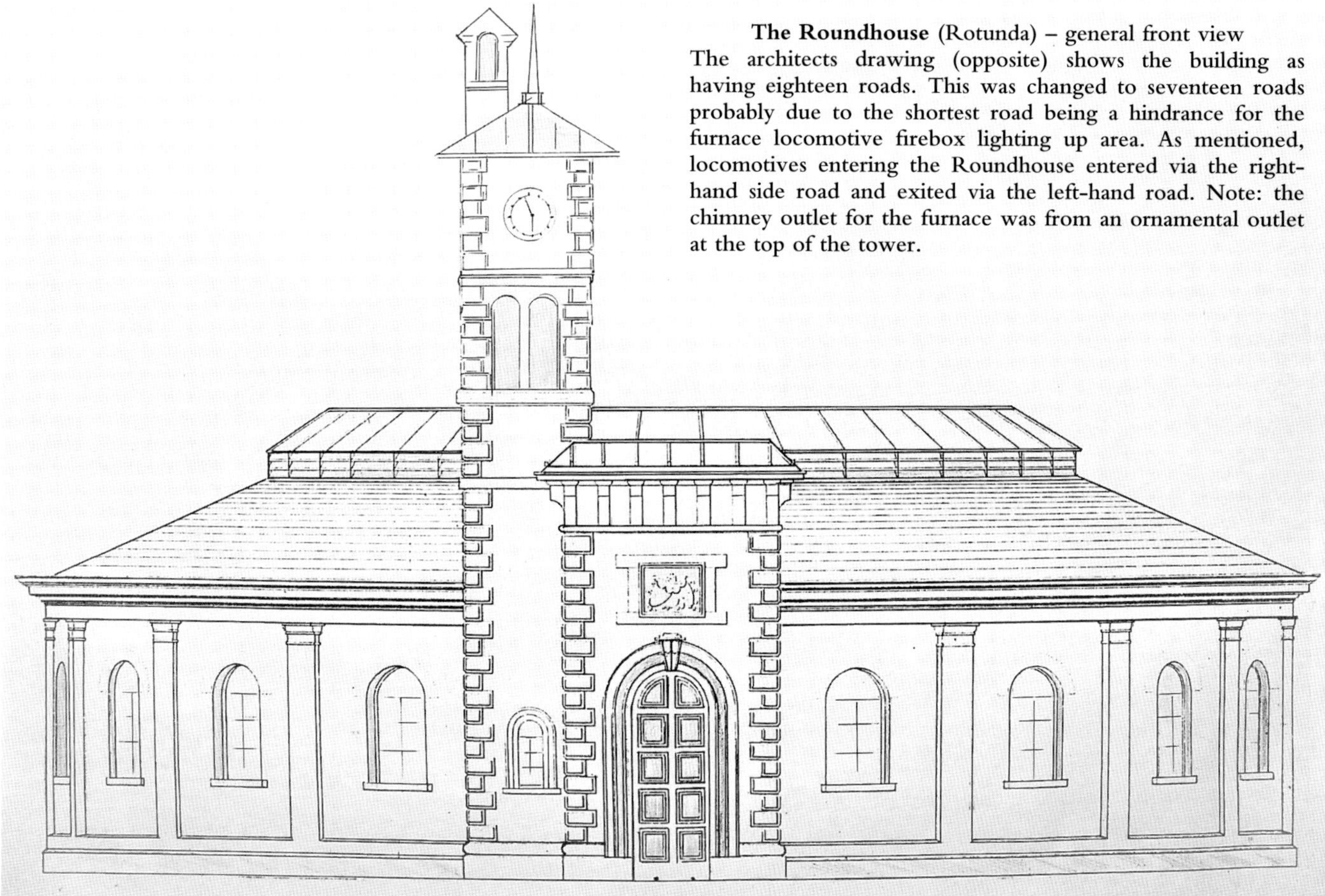

This view is looking west onto the Roundhouse. The clock (on all four sides) was five feet in diameter. Regrettably the pergola-shaped capping with its finial was dismantled early in World War Two. The roof was altered to be flat with a wall around the outside of it to make the tower top a good lookout post for the Home Guard looking for any approaching enemy aircraft.

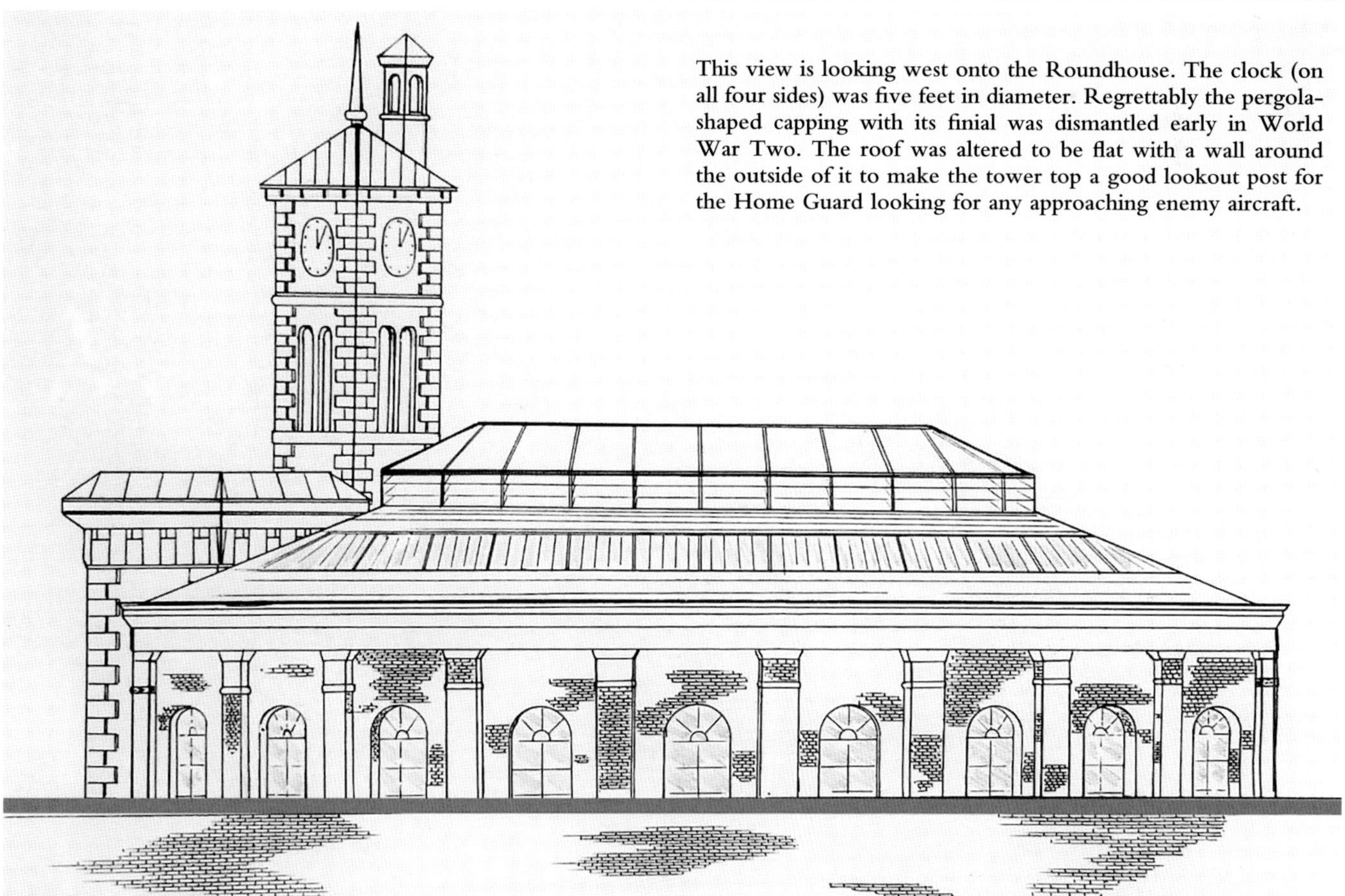

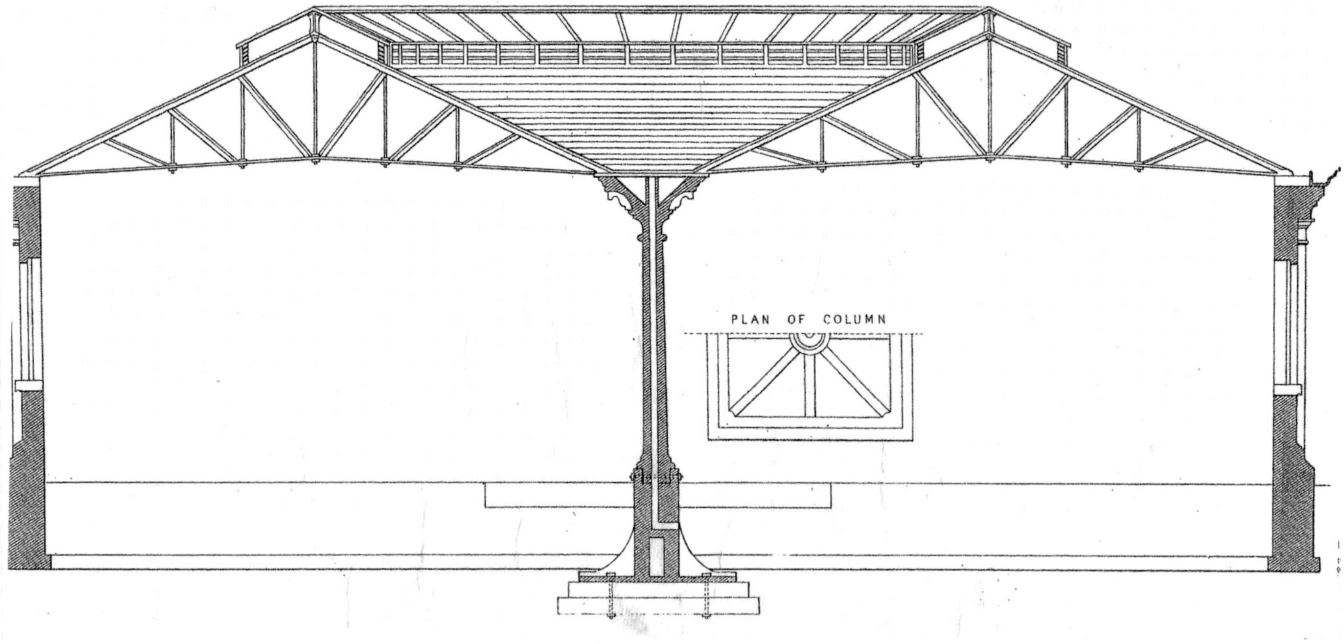

Cross-section of the architect's drawing of the Roundhouse. Note the very heavily constructed central column base on its equally sound foundations. The column base was separate to the main column and bolted together at track level. The column was hollow to act as a drain pipe for the roof to run off rainwater. Note the turntable pit large enough to accommodate the 40 foot diameter two-road turntable.
National Railway Museum

Quarter section of roofing members and the portal with the clock tower. The base of the tower housed a furnace that was used for lighting and firing up the locomotives. The small rectangular section in the base of the tower was the chimney for dispersing the fumes through the roof outlet chimney at the top of the clock tower.
National Railway Museum

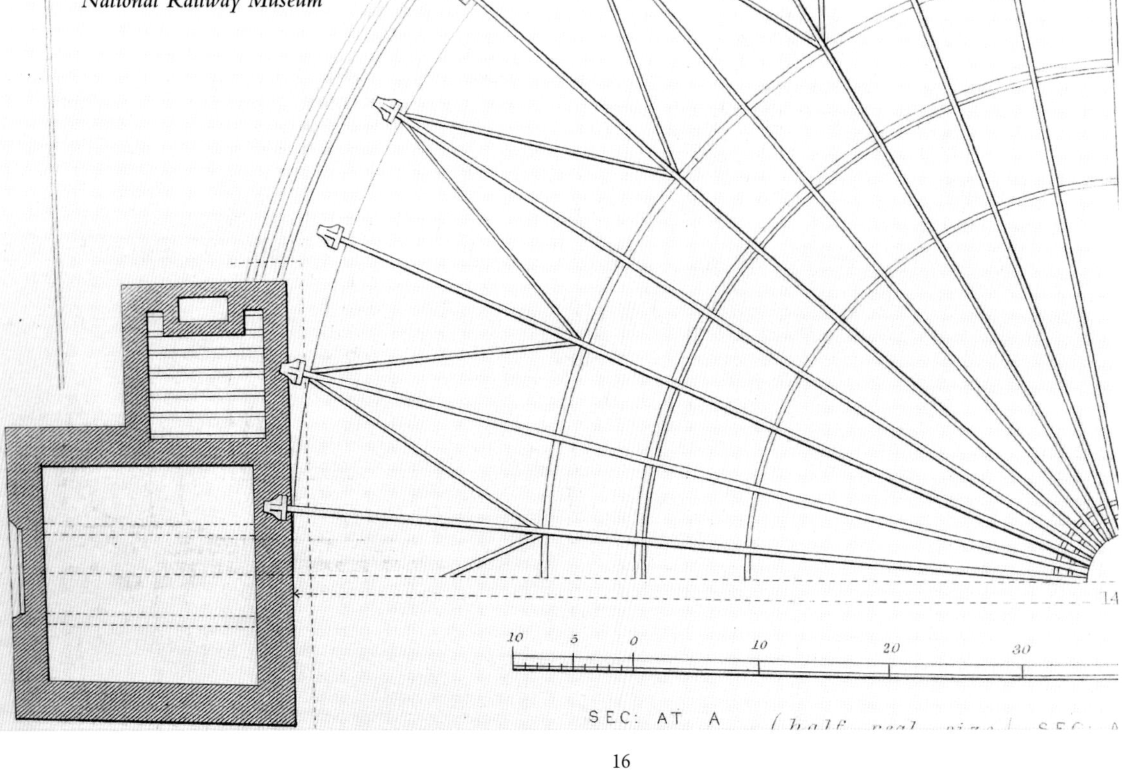

Looking west onto the main workshops, back to the Roundhouse. In view on the right is the boiler shop. The larger building to the left is the Blacksmiths Shop with the boiler/engine room with chimney in front, this being a single story building. The larger doors were rail access for rolling stock to enter and exit the shops. The two smaller doors being the engine room entrance. *National Railway Museum*

Again looking west from the same location a little to the left of the drawing above. The building to the left is the Fitting Shop. The boiler/engine room to the right. The long horizontal roofline is the Erecting Shop. *National Railway Museum*

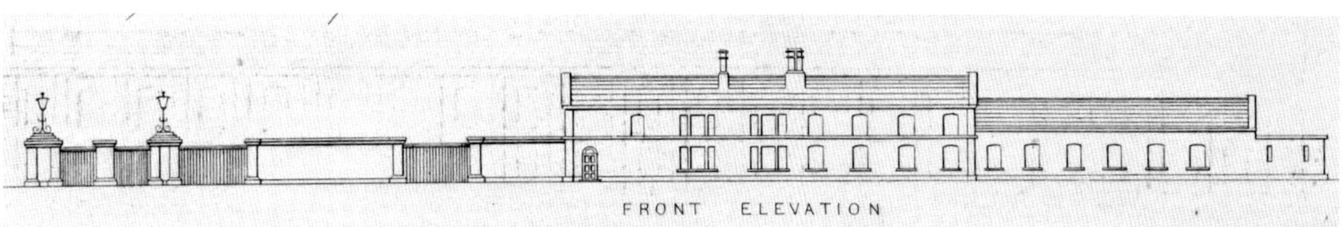

From the same architects drawings, the main entrances from the railway to the workshops, the offices and the main stores (the single storey portion of the building. This would in all probability be the front of the complex, no doubt being considered the postal address today. Whether the two ornamental lamps were fitted to the running lines into the Paint Shop and spare stock holding shed is not known. The buildings though follow a very strong resemblance to an early photograph, see page 32. This is viewed looking west, having ones back to what would later become Cornwall Street.

Main Buildings

Transverse section of the paint and rolling stock holding shop. *National Railway Museum*

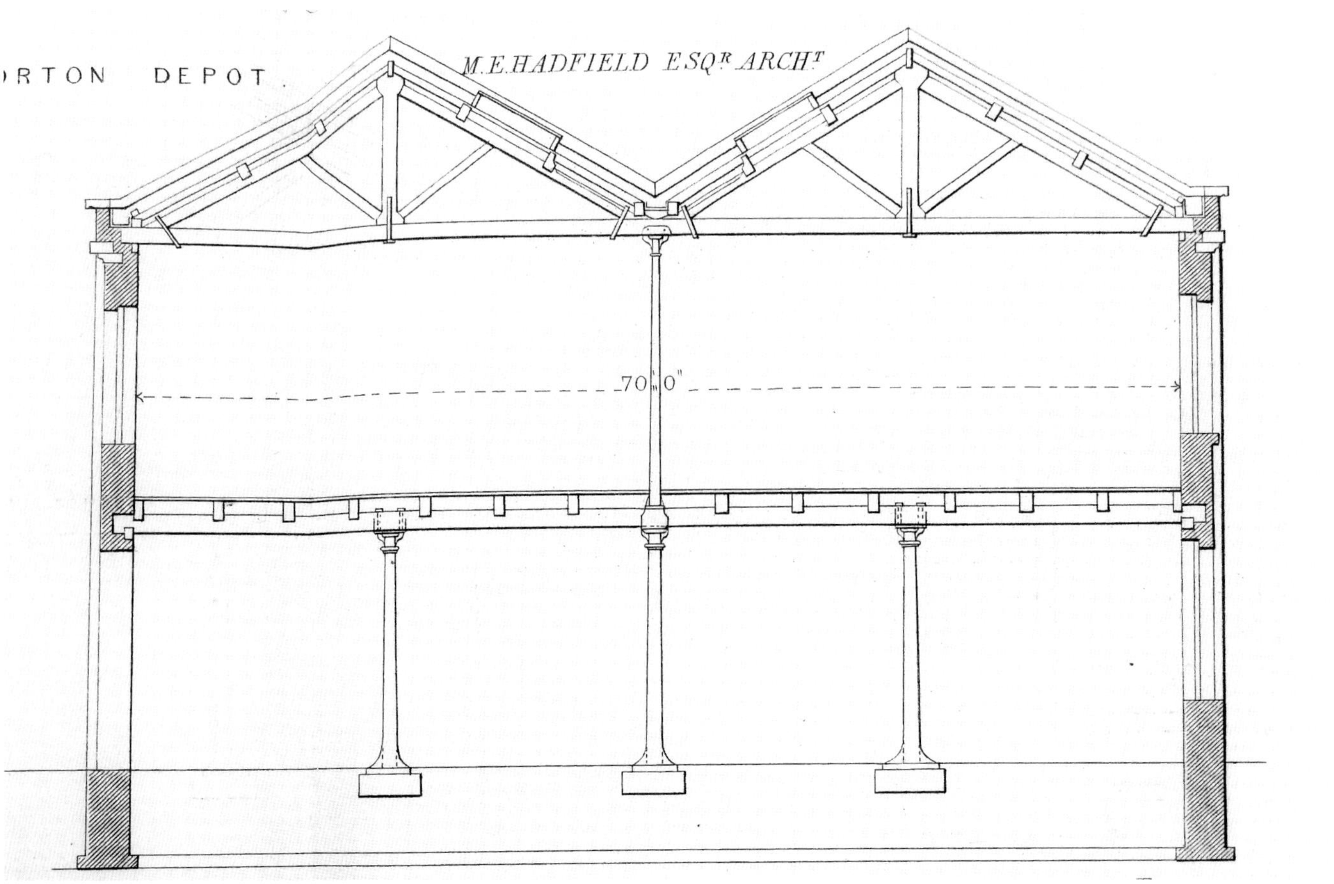

A section of the Carriage and Wagon Shops. The upper floor was for carriages and the lower for wagons, trucks, etc. When the shop was converted into an erecting shop the upper floor was partially removed (between the two outer support columns) leaving a gallery all round the building. Most of the roof had to be considerably altered with the removal of both of the centre columns to provide the necessary space for locomotives.

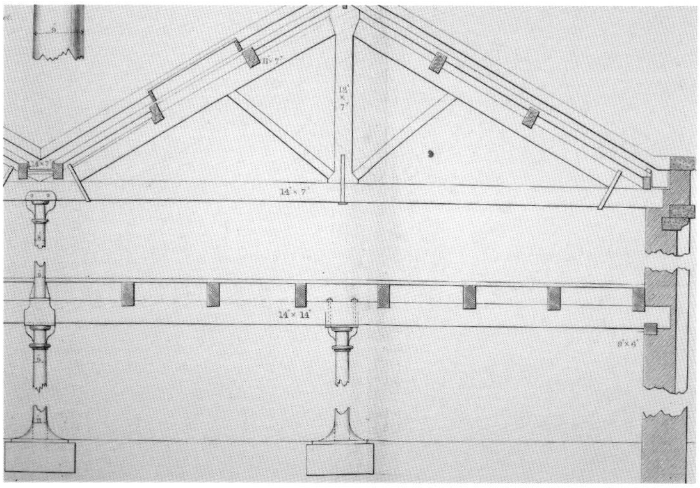

A split cross section of the original roofing over the Carriage and Wagon Shops. The cast-iron support columns being nine inches in diameter (the upper tapering off to eight inches at the top). All of the cross members were of heavy wood, the upper floor timbers being 14-inches square. As described previously the roof section was altered somewhat, except for the 40 foot wide section at the southern end which was used for carriages and also a saddlery.

Right: A drawing of the Carriage and Wagon Shop showing the main wooden cross members and support column locations.
National Railway Museum

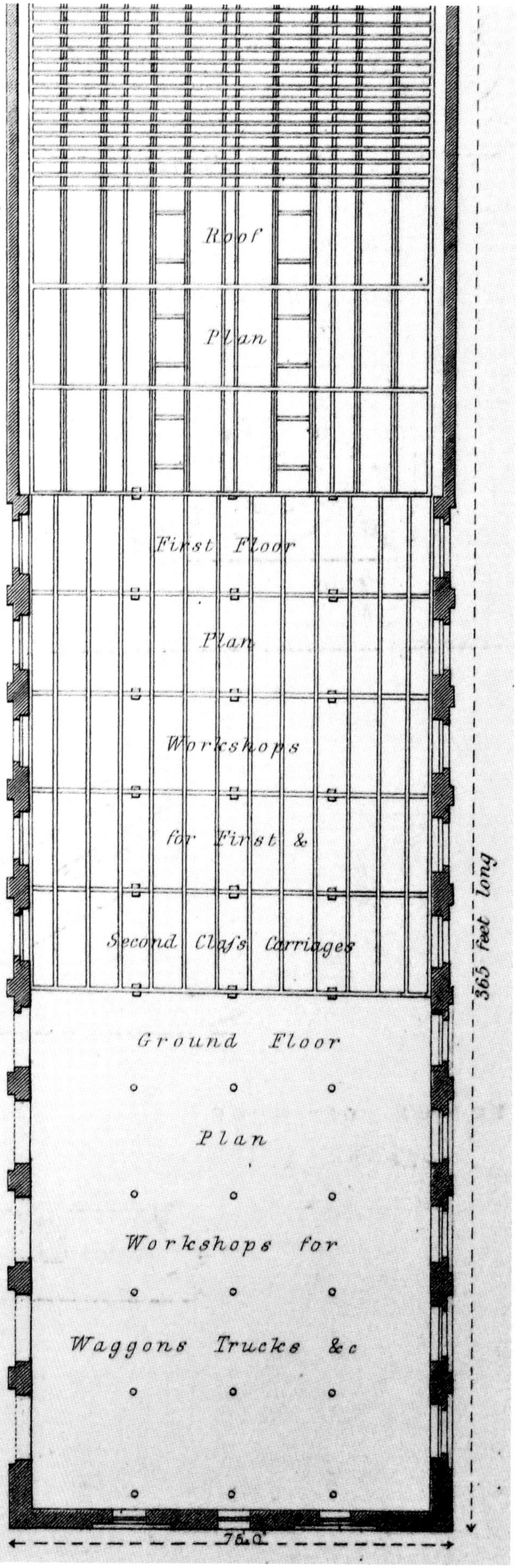

continued from page 13

revolving crane, going full circle around the building, one end of the crane beams resting on rollers at the main central column on a collar and the other end running on rails built into the walls of the building. The crane carriage running along the beams. There is doubt that this was eventually fitted as there is no photographic evidence of any rail supports on the circular wall, though there is a collar shaped fixture on the centre column that could have supported the central runners. The roof of the building was of wrought iron, glazed for lighting and louvres installed for ventilation.

A furnace for lighting up the loco fires was situated directly under the clock tower with a flue inside the tower rising through to the top of the clock tower roof, see drawing page 15.

Erecting Shop

The erecting shop, see plan page 14, was the largest of the four shops in this section of the complex and was 180 feet long by 60 feet wide, and was transverse to the three other shops.

The erecting shop had nine roads feeding into the shop via the traverser. The shop had provision for eighteen locomotives positioned in two bays, each bay had a crane travelling longitudinally with their cross beams running on rails mounted at one end on rails supported at one end on the wall and the other end positioned centrally on columns down the shop and capable of lifting a locomotive.

A section of the erecting shop at the southern end had two smaller shops approximately 30 feet wide integrated into the shop, these being a copper shop and the other designated on the architects drawing as a 'model room', no doubt in modern parlance this would be the 'pattern shop'.

Carriage and Wagon Shop
Looking east onto the west wall at the north end.
The Roundhouse clock tower, glazed roof of the Roundhouse and engine/boiler room chimney in view behind the Carriage & Wagon Shop
The bottom floor housed the single-acting worm-screw drive machinery for raising and lowering the passenger carriages to the upper floor.
Immediately in front of and bordering this building would have been Green Lane, leading to Green Lane level crossing.
Green Lane was most probably rerouted somewhat to make way for the construction of the shops. Green Lane was later to become Wellington Street, later renamed Widnes Street.

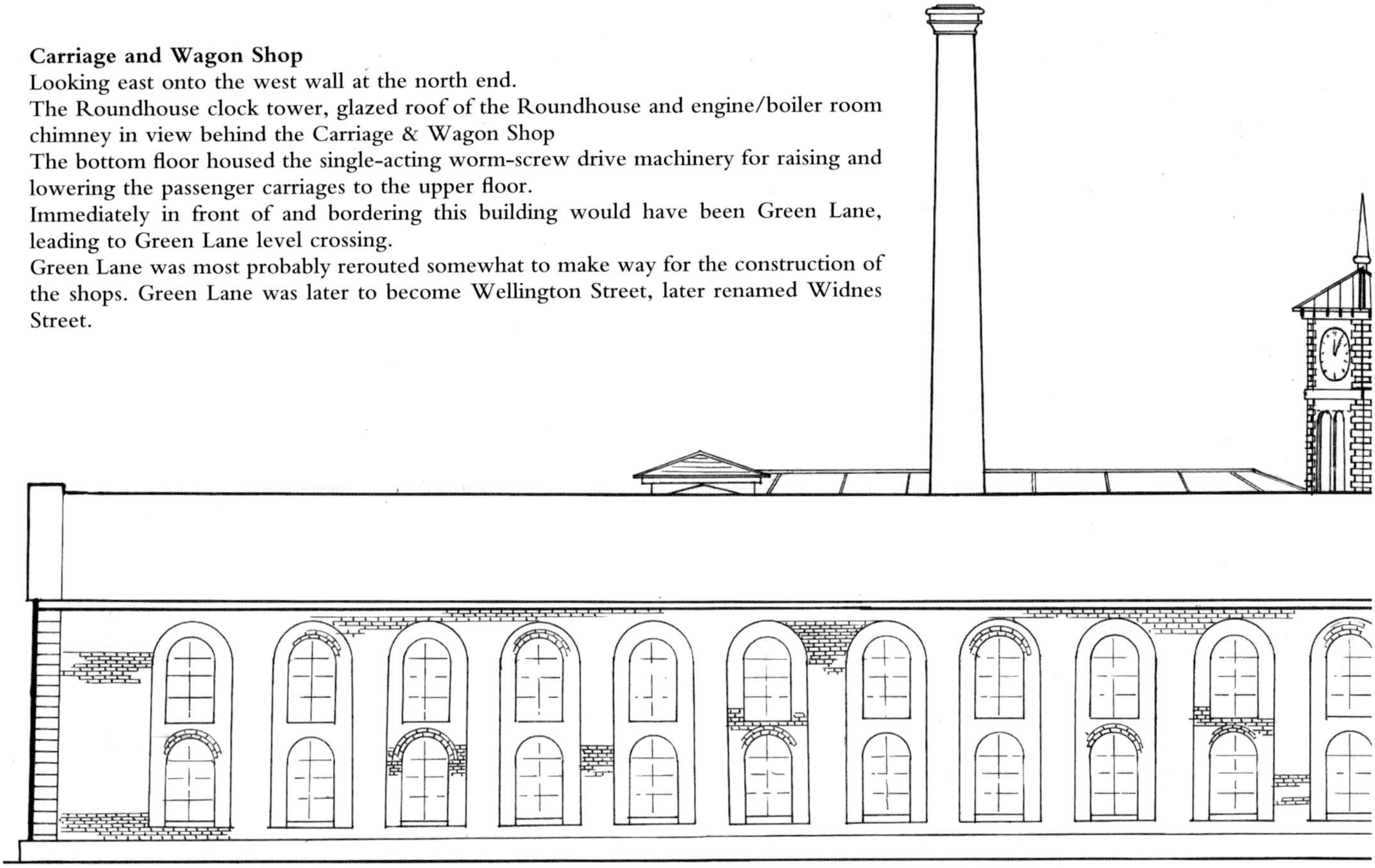

The works looking west – at the south end
Dominating the view of southern end of the Complex and looking west are :
The Carriage & Wagon Shop.
The single storey building to the left in front of the Carriage & Wagon Shop is the Paint Shop and stock holding shop
Further to the right and partially in view is the two story Office building and store.
The Roundhouse portal is viewed directly behind the offices.
The four gated sections are the access lines from the main line into the works.

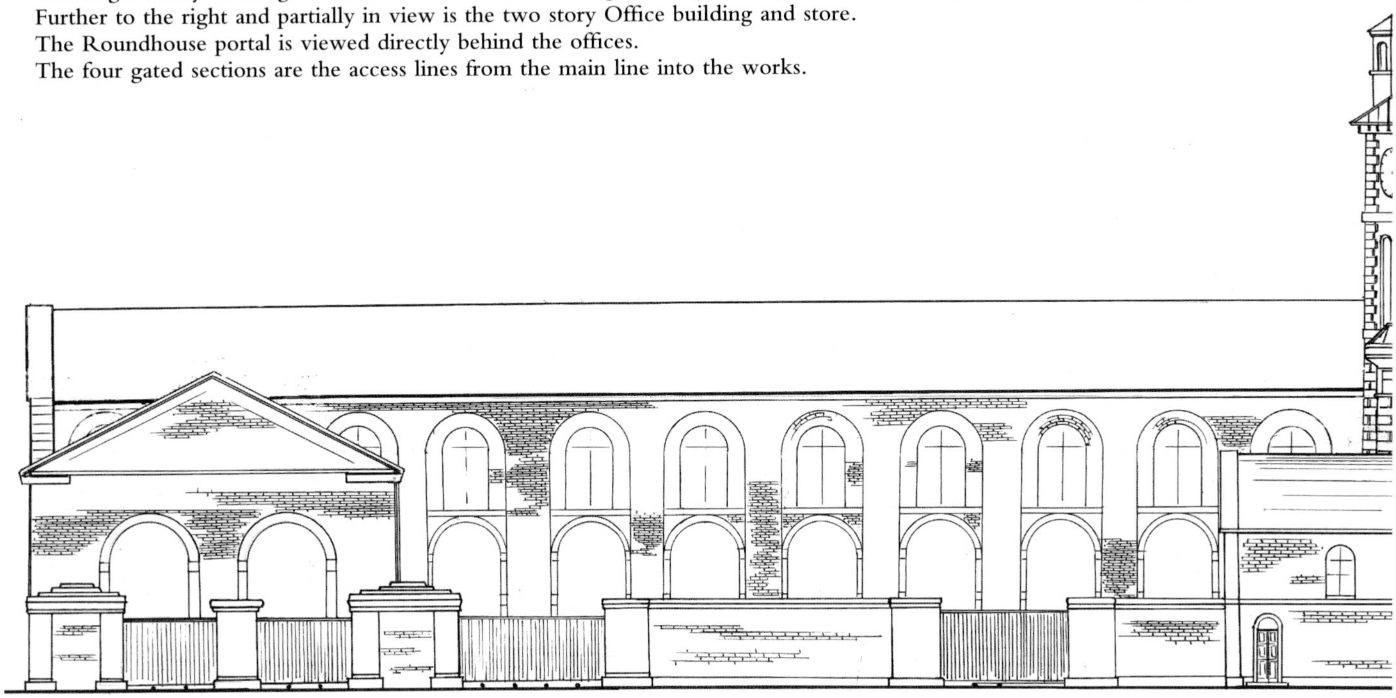

As mentioned, the carriage and wagon shop, was a two storey building and was by far the largest building and faced north to south. The south end of the shop was adjacent to the main railway line. The building was 380 feet total in length and 70 feet wide, this comprised a 40 foot wide 70 feet long saddlery and trimming shop at the south end. The ground floor could accommodate up to a total of 50 wagons, and the upper floor 38 passenger carriages. The carriages were lifted to the upper floor by means of a single acting worm hoist situated under the saddlery and trimming room, powered from the shop steam engine. A traverser, the full length of the building on the east side of the shop fed 19 roads at ground level into the carriage and wagon shop and it also fed two roads into the shop under the saddlery and also nine roads into the erecting shop on the other side of the traverser along with two roads into the paint shop. The traverser table was 20 feet long and 12 feet wide and ran on three rails. This was of ample length for carriages and wagons and locomotive wheel bases of the day. The traverser travelled between the carriage and wagon and other shops in a space 36 feet wide, offering eight feet of open space between buildings on either side of the table. The area behind the first three windows to the right on the ground floor was the 'saddlery' shop. Later on in its life this section of the shop became the machine shop millwrights shop.

In view are:
In the foreground is the two storey office block with the single storey store/ spares area to the right.
Immediately behind the office block is the Roundhouse with clock tower and portal.
Further behind the Roundhouse can be seen the Carriage & Wagon Shop with the power house chimney in between.
The gable end of the boiler/boiler smiths shop is to the right.
The roof line between the Boiler Shop and the Carriage & Wagon Shop roof is the Erecting Shop.

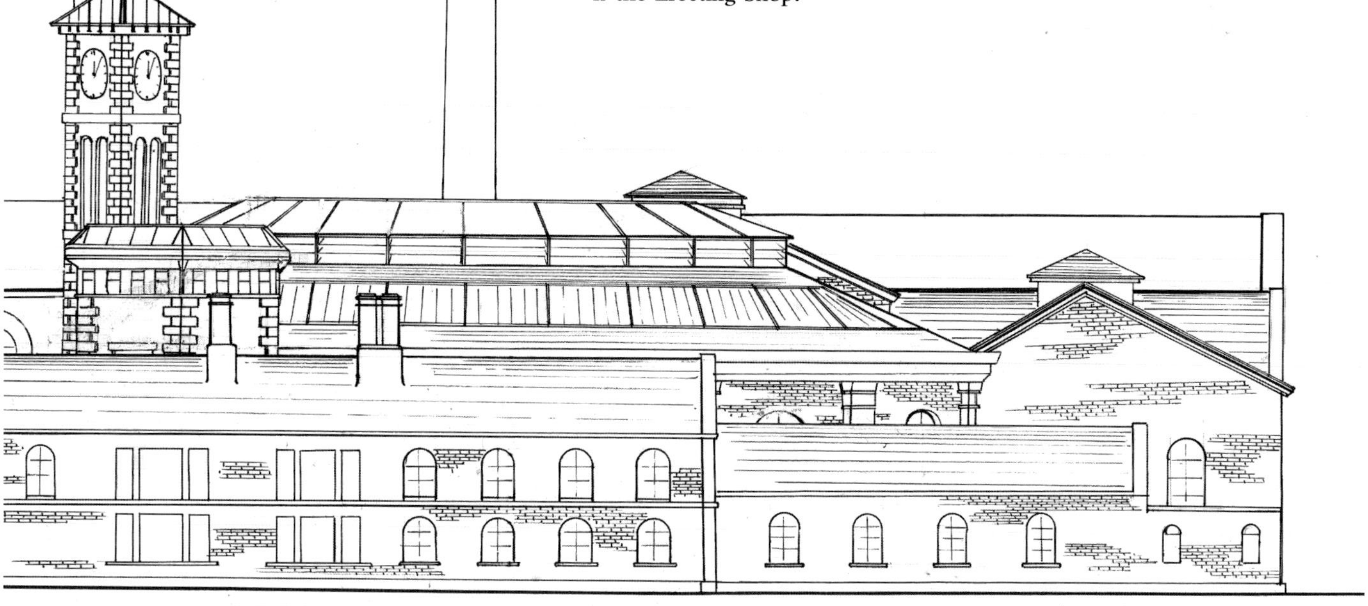

author's drawings

Main Offices/Stores

The last buildings of any note were the main offices. These offices comprised of a two storey building covering approximately 130 feet in length by 30 feet wide. This included the employees entrance and booking on and off offices. Attached to the offices was a store area for general spares and equipment.

Paint Shop & Rolling Stock Shop

The paint shop was 60 feet long by 40 feet wide and consisted of two roads fed via the traverser.

The rolling stock shed was joined to the paint shop forming one building. This section of the building was 165 feet long and 40 feet wide and was used for storing stock that was available for traffic. The shop having two roads. These shops were on the south side of the complex near to the main railway line on the opposite side of the traverser to the carriage and wagon Shops. Outside the rolling stock shop to the east was the coking shed this was 100 feet long by 40 feet wide covering two roads with a platform in between. The shed consisted of two roads, one for wagons containing coke supplies and the other for locomotives being fuelled. Fuel was off loaded in baskets and transferred to the locomotives on the other side of the platform. This shed was approximately 150 feet to the East of the stock/paint shop on the roads that lead into the stock/paint shop. Coke was the predominant fuel at this early period of railway development, coal was very soon to follow and was being used experimentally at this period in time.

Principal Locomotive Maintenance Buildings

This area of the works complex was a series of buildings all joined together to form a central maintenance area and consisted of four main shops, three of which were 120 feet by 60 feet wide and one 180 feet long by 60 feet wide.

Fitting Shop

This shop was 120 feet long and 60 feet wide. Machine tools and equipment in this shop consisted of fitting benches at the inner end of the building, lathes, drilling machines and other powered machinery was placed down each side wall of the shop, Planing machines were installed centrally down the middle of the shop. All machinery in this shop was driven by the main engine in the engine and boiler house. The line shafting from the engine room travelled down each of the fitting shop walls. One of the shafts continued out of the building and over above the traverser to drive machinery in the carriage and wagon shop and the lifting hoist at the south end. The worm hoist consisted of the driving worm wheel geared to the driven worm wheel.

Smithy Forge Shop

This shop was next to the fitting shop and was 120 feet long by 60 feet wide. The shop consisted of a blower/fan and sixteen blacksmiths fires, eight down each of the shop walls.

Boiler Shop

This shop was next to the smithy and was 120 feet long x 60 feet wide.

The equipment in the boiler shop consisted of eight Smiths' fires situated along the wall nearest to the Smiths' shop. On the opposite wall was four fires for heating boiler plating. Punching and shearing machines were located down the centre of the shop. All equipment including fire draught fans in this shop was driven by line shafting driven from the main engine house crossing the ends of all these shops.

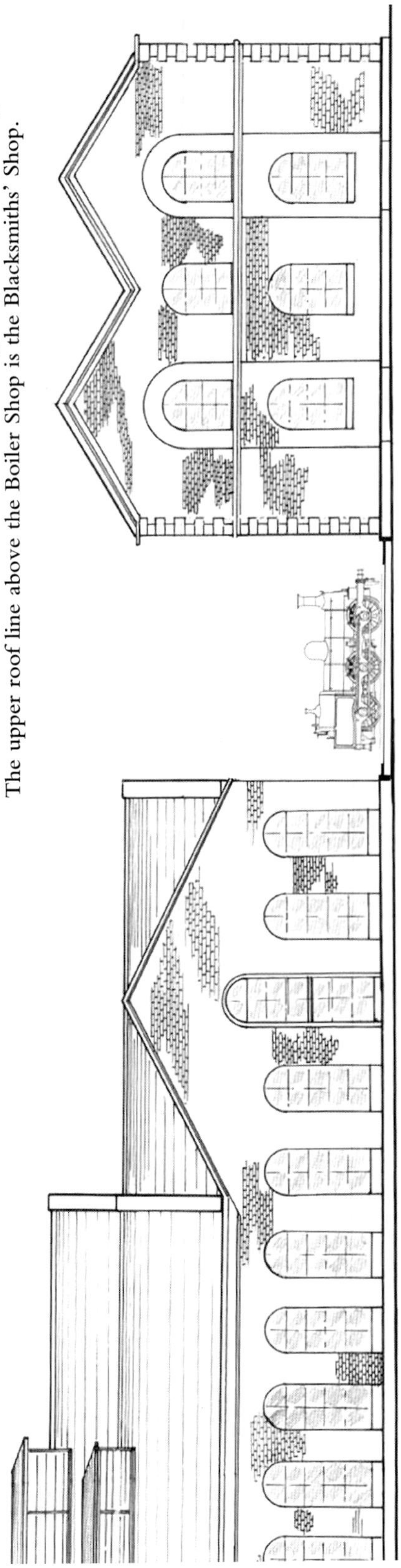

The works looking south, at the west end.
In view are:
Towards the right, is the two storey Carriage & Wagon Shop.
The gable end building in view is the two bay Erecting Shop.
The space between the next buildings is the area taken up by the 20 foot traverser, (with locomotive added to give location clarity).
The lower roof line to the left of the Erecting Shop is the Boiler Shop.
The upper roof line above the Boiler Shop is the Blacksmiths' Shop.

The works looking south from the east end.
In this view are:
Main two storey offices and stores to the left..
Roundhouse with portal and clock tower.
The first building to the right is the rolling stock holding shop and Paint Shop.
In front of the rolling stock shop is the boiler room/engine room.
Just peeping into view on the far right is the boiler and boiler smiths' shop.

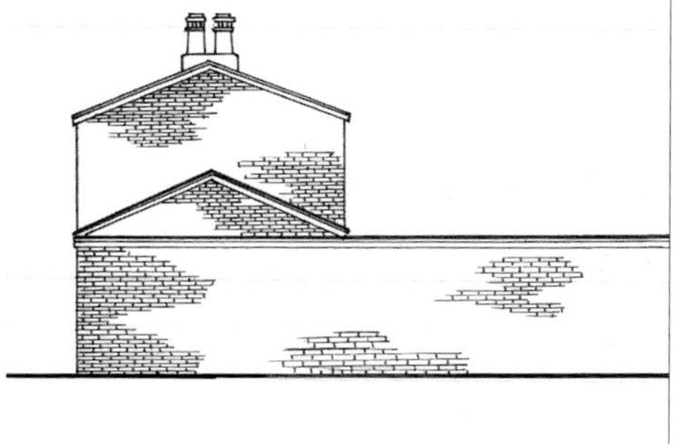

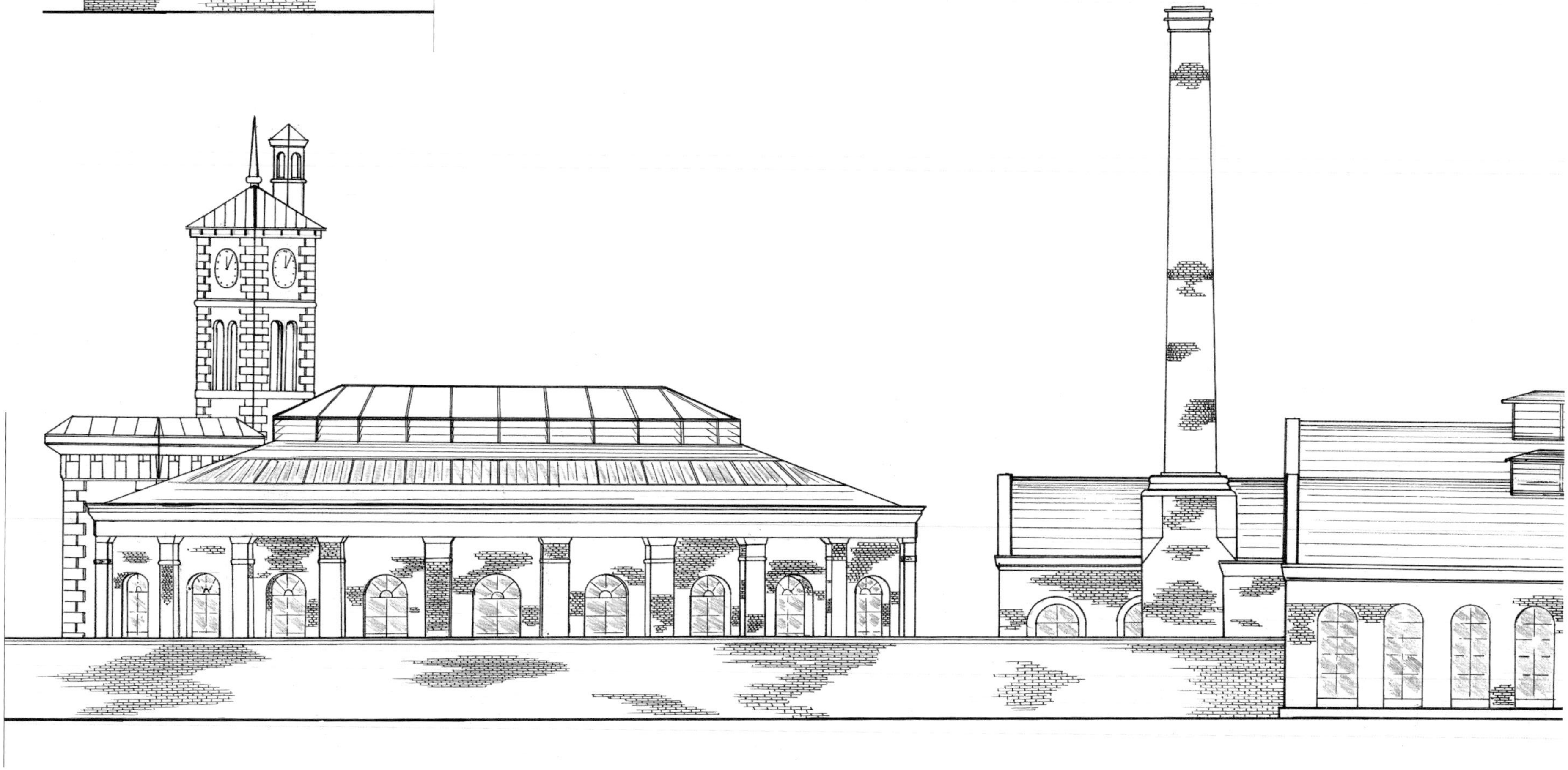

The Canal Depot

Construction of the Ashton Canal had commenced in the early 1790s and was completed in 1796. The Stockport branch was opened in 1797.

The junction of the Ashton Canal and the Stockport canal was known as Stockport Junction. The tow path spanned the junction via a stone bridge. From here the Stockport Canal ran south and under Ashton Lane (Ashton Old Road), then over the bridge which at that time was called Pack Horse Bridge. This bridge being at a point where goods were transferred from road to canal and canal to road. Very close by was the 'Pack Horse' public house, no doubt a resting place for weary road wagon and horse handlers and bargees alike and their faithful horses. The bridge on Ashton Old Road was later to be known as Openshaw Bridge. The Pack Horse public house is sadly no longer with us. Openshaw Bridge still stands to this day though the canal under the bridge has long since been filled in and is now a cycle and pathway leading into Gorton and on to Reddish. The Stockport Canal continued its southwards journey and went under Crabcroft Bridge, which carried Dunkerleys Lane from the tiny hamlet of Crabcroft to Ashton Road, passing a very small farm (Dunkerleys Farm), Dunkerleys Lane later became Ogden Lane. From this under bridge the canal continued south across the aqueduct over the main line. It then continued through Gorton, under the Hyde Road Bridge, through Reddish and into the Stockport Canal basin; a distance of just under five miles from its start at Stockport Junction in Clayton.

The Gorton Works canal site was located just to the south of Crabcroft Bridge, (Ogden Lane Bridge) and on it were built the houses for the works employees and their families. The works' reservoir was fed from the canal via three settling ponds with a sluice gate controlling the water admission.

In 1855 a school was set up for the education of the MS&LR employees children and infants on the canal depot site. It was extended in 1889 into two separate areas, one for infants and girls, the other for boys. The school staff included a 'live-in matron'. The schools attendance was just under 1,200 pupils. Five years later, the education of the children was taken over by the Manchester School Board. The school was extended in 1889 and carried on for another five years until it closed down in 1894 and education was carried on by the Manchester School Board. It is quite likely that after the school closed the pupils started to attend Varna Street School, which was located very close by on the other side of the canal and was built in 1896. Years later, one of the school buildings, the boys school, became the works canteen and kitchen (at the side of Ogden Lane). The other building which faced onto Cornwall Street was later to become the barracks for the locomotive footplate men.

The employees cottages were removed sometime in the early 1860s and the land was taken over for the construction in the canal depot. The depot had an arm on it coming off from the canal and a dry dock added for the maintenance of the companies narrow boats. One particular boat, a maintenance boat was called *Maria* which was built by Jinks Boatyard in 1853 and was used mainly for transporting ballast for the MS&LR up until 1897. On the formation of the GCR she was used as a canal maintenance boat. *Maria* carried on in this role throughout L&NER days and on into the BR era. The boat was abandoned in 1961 at the Portland Basin in Ashton-under-Lyne. She was later restored by the Peak Forest Canal Society. *Maria* is still in use to this day on the Peak Forest Canal as a horse drawn narrowboat. She is the oldest operating narrowboat in existence and is used as a heritage horse drawn passenger boat and sometimes used for its intended purpose i.e. as a working boat. It is quite probable that *Maria* was replaced with a new boat of the same name very early in the 1900s.

Until just before 1900 *The Daily Mail* newspaper had been printed in London. From 1899 Alfred Harmsworth – later Lord Northcliffe – sent his newspaper north from Marylebone via the newly opened Great Central's London Extension Line. Prior to the opening the *Mail's* Deansgate presses a stop gap printing operation was installed at Gorton. Using the former MS&LR school adjacent to Gorton Tank. The 'temporary' operation lasted almost three years. The machines used for the newspaper production were (then) state-of-the-art quadruple Hoe presses. Later transferring to Deansgate, the *Mail* newspaper carried on production in Manchester for eighty-five years.

During later BR days the British Railways Staff Association (BRSA) took over the part of the buildings, namely the library section, for their social club. Fishing became an active part of activities on the depot reservoirs.

The gas works with its gasholder was later added to the canal depot. The gasholder on the west side of the original carriage and wagon works was later removed to make way for the new wheel shop that was built in 1905.

The canal depot in more recent times (as a way of keeping this review in its chronological format) is continued further on in the pages of this book.

One of the Great Central Railway's canal barges that would have been repaired in the canal depot. *Pope/Parkhouse Archive*

CHAPTER TWO
1854-1899 MS&LR TO GCR

Very early in 1854 Richard Peacock left the employ of the MS&LR and, in partnership with Charles Beyer formed the beginning of a new locomotive construction works, 'Beyer, Peacock and Company Ltd' (known locally as Gorton Foundry). Beyer, Peacock's new factory was built on land on the opposite side of the MS&LR main line directly opposite Gorton Depot. In 1854 Gorton Foundry was being formed and before long construction started in open fields.

Richard Peacock was greatly admired and highly respected not just by the MS&LR hierarchy but by everybody who had worked under him and with him. Gorton locomotive works in particular was losing a great young man. This was reflected in the farewell gifts he received and by the MS&LR. He was presented with a magnificent candelabra and a silver plate to the value of £400. A very large sum of money for the 1840s almost subscribed entirely by the staff, about a third of whom worked at Gorton.

William Grindley Craig

Richard Peacock's vacant position as Locomotive Superintendent was taken over by the appointment of William Grindley Craig (circa 1818–24 Jan 1886) as Chief Mechanical Engineer on a salary of £500 per annum, a position he held from 1854 to 1859.

During Peacock's tenure at Gorton Depot all locomotives owned by the MS&LR had been built by outside contractors, all repairs and overhauls and conversions to locomotives and rolling stock being carried out in Gorton locomotive works. In those early years Gorton Works was too busy to carry out any new construction.

Early on in Craig's time at Gorton the works started to produce gas for the works with enough capacity to be able to supply gas also to Beyer, Peacock's 'Gorton Foundry' on the other side of the main line. Gorton Works also started to make its own axle grease at around that time.

In 1857 the decision was made for Gorton works to start to turn out new locomotives. Two locomotives were built, these to replace older worn out ones. The new locomotives were 0-6-0 double-framed goods engines, these were designated as Class '5'. Craig was influenced by locomotives that were being produced by Beyer, Peacock Ltd (over the road) for the Madras Railway at that time and the Gorton locomotives turned out were of a similar design. The two locomotives were named *Archimedes* built in March 1858 and *Phlegon* the following month (numbers 6 & 7 consecutively).

Two more 0-6-0 locomotives were built to the same class in 1859, (numbers 36 & 53). In the same year Craig became the victim of his own cost saving plans. His contract with the MS&LR was not renewed, although he was retained in a consulting position.

Charles Reboul Sacré

Craig's vacant position was filled by Charles Reboul Sacré. Sacré's official position was 'Chief Engineer and Locomotive Engineer' and he commenced in this role on the 1st April 1859. Sacré was born on the 4th September 1831. In 1846 he was apprenticed to Archibald Sturrock at the Great Northern Railway locomotive works at Boston in Lincolnshire. On completion of his apprenticeship he was appointed as Assistant Locomotive Superintendent at Peterborough (which at the time was an outstation of the GNR main locomotive workshops) before his move to the MS&LR.

Charles Reboul Sacré
4th September 1831 - 3rd August 1889
Amourness

With Sacré at the helm, Gorton works started to turn out large numbers of very successful double-framed 0-6-0 goods engines, solidly built and so thoroughly reliable that a number lasted into L&NER days along with some of his 4-4-0 classes of locomotives. He was also responsible for producing the fast Class '14' 2-2-2 type passenger locomotives with a seven-foot diameter driving wheel.

On the 1st April 1859 under Sacré's tenure Samuel Waite Johnson succeeded to the post of works manager. Hailing from Leeds, Johnson began his career as an apprentice at E.B. Wilson's Railway Foundry in that city. This was at the time when Wilson's were building large numbers of the famed 'Jenny Lind' locomotive design. Prior to his move to Gorton, Johnson was engaged as works manager at Doncaster on the Great Northern Railway under Archibald Sturrock. Johnson remained at Gorton for five years. From Gorton, Johnson became Locomotive, Carriage & Wagon Superintendent at the Edinburgh & Glasgow Railway.

After two years in Scotland Johnson moved south to become Locomotive, Carriage & Wagon Superintendent of the Great Eastern Railway at Stratford. From here he moved to Derby to take up the position of Locomotive Superintendent of the

Midland Railway, the post he held until his retirement in 1903. Johnson was described by the Midland Railway locomotive expert Jack Braithwaite as the 'supreme artist engineer', during Johnson's reign at Derby he produced a range of extremely elegant and aesthetically pleasing designs that have never been surpassed for their elegance and beauty. Even a casual glance at Johnson's designs reveals more than a nod to Sacré's influence.

Sacré had a very long career at Gorton, during his time he designed a series of very successful classes of locomotives.

In 1863 a new rolling mill was installed by the MS&LR on the spare land between what was later to become Cornwall Street and the works original main offices for Gorton to manufacture its own steel crossings and points. The trend was now to move from iron and use steel rails throughout the system and as a consequence two Bessemer converters were installed at the Rolling Mill towards the end of 1871 to manufacture steel rail. The converters and mill were closed down in 1886 after giving satisfactory service. The falling price of steel was the sole reason for the decision to be made for rail to be purchased from outside contractors and thus make the mill and converters redundant. It is believed that some of the rolling mill equipment ended up for further use as far away as New Zealand.

An artists impression depicting a typical rolling mill, similar to that which would have been installed at Gorton in the mid 1860s for the production of railway track *author's collection*

A detailed development of the MS&LR works 1880s

By the late 1880s, the locomotive and carriage & wagon works had taken a massive expansion. The area taken up by Gorton locomotive works had reached its maximum limits. Its borders stretched from Cornwall Street in the east to Bessemer Street in the west and the MS&LR main line in the south to Whitworth Street in the north. Openshaw was now rapidly becoming an engineering powerhouse with numerous factories dotting the skyline and scores of rows of terraced houses crammed in between to house the factory employees and their families.

Under Parker, the MSL&R Carriage and Wagon Superintendent at that time, a new large carriage and wagon works was built in 1879 at the far north of the works outside the original perimeter butting onto Whitworth Street. In addition new carriage and wagon shops were built on the other side of Wellington Street (Widnes Street) butting up to Whitworth Street and Bessemer Street in 1881. These shops comprised two buildings with a traverser between the two. A new ten-road locomotive shed was built between Wellington Street (Widnes Street) and the new carriage and wagon shops in 1879, this shed was extended before completion into a twenty-road shed capable of accommodating 120 locomotives. (The running shed was initially built as a ten-road shed, but a further ten-road shed built immediately afterwards joining in on its west side to make a twenty-road shed.) A four road paint shop adjoined the running sheds on its western side. A new coaling plant was built in the running shed yard with lines on either side to enable two locomotives to be loaded with coal simultaneously. A turntable was installed close to the coaling plant. Access to the running sheds from the main line was made at Priory Junction in February 1879.

With the new carriage and wagon shops being built, the original carriage & wagon shop of 1847 during this period (1879/80), was converted for the overhaul and repairs to existing locomotives on the ground floor of the building, To accomplish this the upper floor (ex carriage shop) was taken down but a gallery around the walls was left which was then utilised as a machine shop for smaller machine tools (lathes etc.). The roof was raised and converted from a two apex roof to a three apex roof, this to do away with the centre columns that would have otherwise impeded into this new erecting shop. The traverser between this building and the original erecting shop was still in use.

For new locomotive construction, new erecting shops were built to the north of the original paint and stock holding shed. Two bays constructed for this purpose and one bay for tenders, this in effect giving the works two erecting shops with the boiler shop adjoining the new locomotive build erecting shop on the north side. Access to the running sheds and carriage & wagon works was made from the main MS&LR line at Priory Junction to the west of the works boundary. When the new running shed was put into use, the roundhouse was converted into a smithy, steam hammers being installed in 1879.

The old original erecting shop was converted to a wheel shop once the larger erecting shop was built and put into use.

In addition to the major buildings that had been built, a smaller row of adjoining workshops was constructed between the old roundhouse and the new carriage & wagon works to the north, some attached to the old office block. Amongst these shops were several small fitting shops, moulding shops, an iron yard area, brass shop, pattern stores, joiners' shops, a small smithy and a copper shop. Two larger separate shops were also built a little closer to these new carriage and wagon shops, one being a wagon shop and the other a wagon sheet shop.

On the Canal Depot site the employees cottages were replaced by a long building that comprised several workshops that housed the boat dry dock. These shops included, a mortar mill, a smithy, engine house, saw mill, stables, blacksmiths' shop, gas house, carpenters shop, waste shop, lime house and a gas house (gas house for the gas holder that was also on the site). A travelling gantry crane was added along the east side of the shops and to the canal arm.

Charles Reboul Sacré retired in 1886 following a successful twenty-seven years with the MS&LR. On his retirement Thomas Parker took the reins and became the MS&LR's new Locomotive Superintendent.

In this new role he had a new large erecting shop built in 1890 to the west of Widnes Street, a reservoir had to be drained and filled in before the shop could be built. The existing erecting shop of 1879/80 was converted into a machine shop on the ground floor; the gallery was retained.

Now that the new large erecting shop was in use, the shop that was built for the construction of new locomotives was given up and made way for a boiler shop complex.

With this new erecting shop being built on the west of Widnes Street the pedestrian walkway from Widnes St to Railway Street was provided with a long foot bridge that spanned the new erecting shop to make a safe thoroughfare for the public to use for access to Railway Street over the other side of the main line in Gorton. This was built in 1890. This bridge is further detailed later on in this book as it forms an integral part of the locomotive works.

Development of the Works 1847-1905

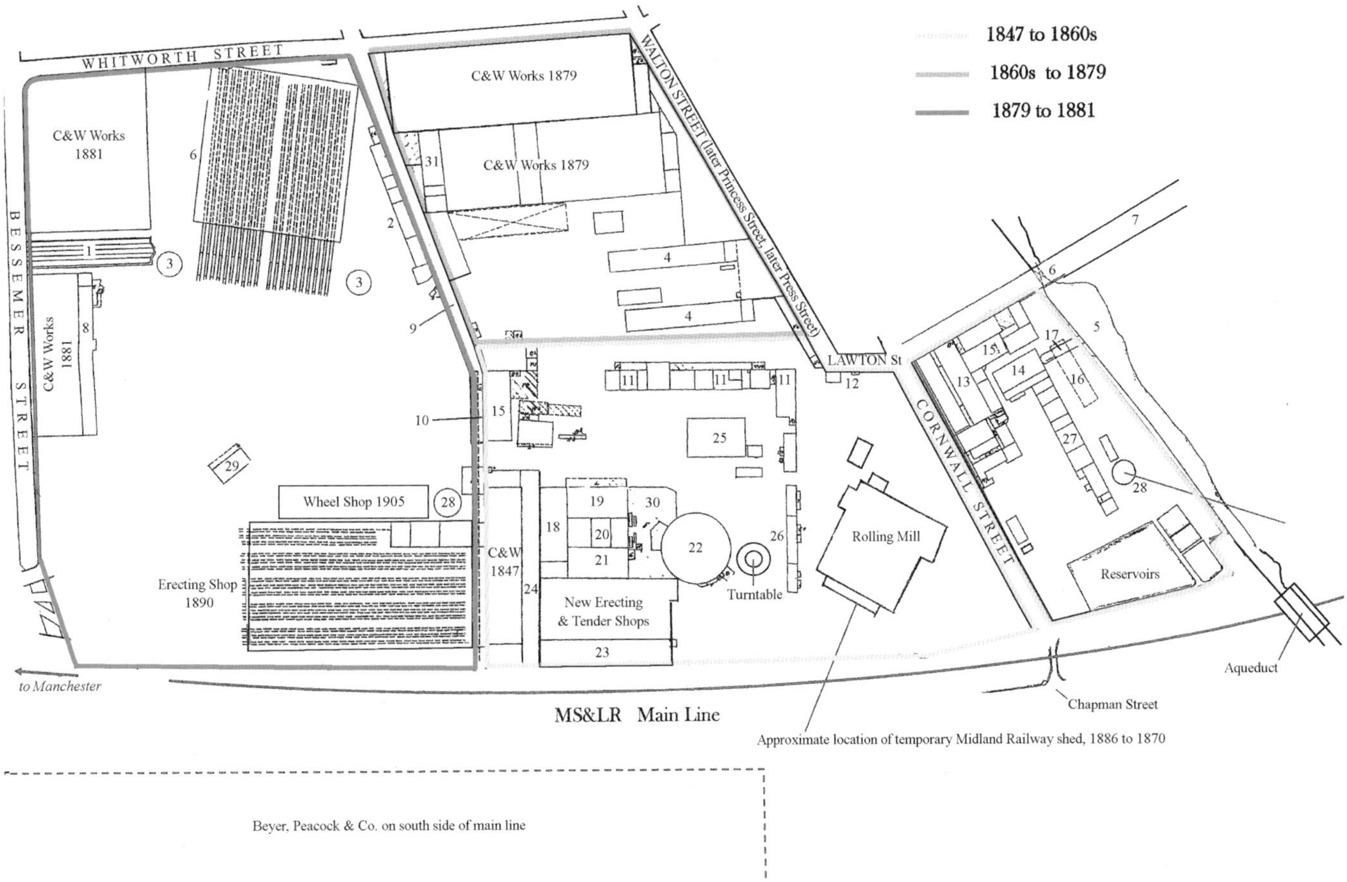

1. 1881 Carriage & Wagon Traverser.
2. Running sheds administration.
3. Running sheds turntables.
4. Wagon sheet sheds.
5. Stockport Branch of the Ashton Canal.
6. Running Sheds.
7. Dunkerlys Lane, later Ogden Lane,
8/ Saw mill.
9. Wellington Street, later Widnes Street (originally Green Lane going south before the works was built.
10. The Birdcage
11. A row of workshops comprising: small brass foundry, copper shop, PW smithy, fitting shop, Turning shop, screwing shop, grease house, spike room, stores and offices.
12. Works main entrance (Lawton Street .
13. Girls school, playgrounds, library and matron's quarters.
14. Canal depot dry dock.
15. Moulding shop/brass foundry.
16. Overhead travelling gantry crane,
17. Canal arm leading into the depot from canal.
18. 1847 Erecting shop, still in use until 1879.
19. Old boiler shop.
20. Old Smithy.
21. Fitting shop.
22. Roundhouse (became smithy in 1879).
23. Old paint and stock holding shed, later white metal shop, paint shop, file cutters and fitters,
24. Traverser.
25. Iron yard.
26. Main offices.
27. Canal depot workshops comprising: Mortar mill, Engine and boiler house, Smithy, black-smiths, carpenters shop, waste shop, gas house, purifying house and lime house.
28. Gas holders.
29. Coaling plant.
30. Main forge-hammer shop.
31. Carriage and wagon smithy, engine and boiler.
32. Boys school.

MS&LR Locomotive Review

It is unfortunate that the SAuL&MR and the MS&LR in those early days did not realise that in future times there may have been a great deal of interest in what their locomotives and rolling stock looked like. As a result very few images exist of the earliest locomotives that ran the first trains in early 1840s.

No enclosed cabs were fitted to locomotives then, just a plate to the front of the cab supposedly to act as some sort of windshield for bad weather protection. Conditions for the footplate crew must have been horrendous giving practically no protection from the rain and extreme cold that they would have endured especially in the winter time going over Woodhead. The smoke and ashes that spewed out of the chimney as they passed through one of the single bores of the Woodhead tunnels must have been an absolute nightmare also.

As mentioned previously, the intended review of locomotive photographs in this book is primarily to illustrate locomotives built at Gorton or designed at Gorton. However, to give a good insight into the types of locomotives running and receiving attention by the MS&LR and later GCR at Gorton during this time, it is fitting to add some photographs of the types of locomotives built by many of the outside contractors for the MS&LR and its constituent companies. All these locomotives from outside contractors would no doubt go through Gorton's shops during their life span for overhauls, repairs and rebuilds and are therefore worth an inclusion. The following pages give a general example of early locomotive designs that ran over not just the MS&LR and later the GCR but other railways in Great Britain. Some of the relatively high numbers of rebuilds that took place to locomotives in their later days are added to this review to show their transformation. Unfortunately space dictates the large numbers of classes built and rebuilt here, but the reader will gain a good insight to the majority of the types in use in those early days. It will become obvious that the 0-6-0, 0-4-2, and 2-4-0 types with double frames (preferred by Sacré) dominate this early period in locomotive design.

0-6-0 'Sphynx' Class built by Sharps was running on the SAuL&MR and MS&LR as early as 1846.
Coupled wheels: 5ft 0in.
Cylinders: 17in. diameter x 24in. stroke.
Boiler: diameter 3ft 4in.
Barrel: length 10ft 0in.
Firebox: copper.

author's collection.

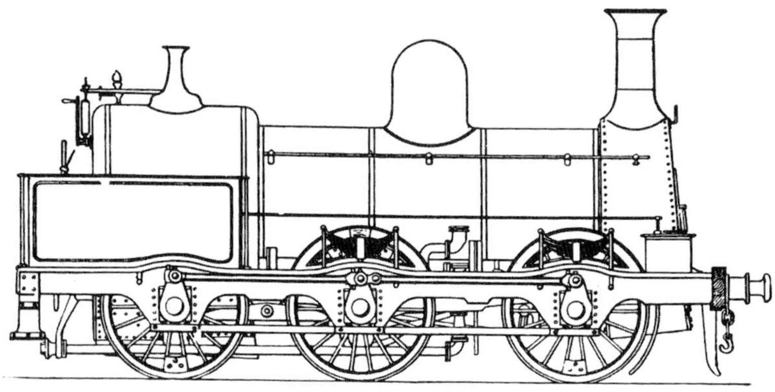

0-6-0 type built by Stephenson,1852.

Drawing courtesy E. M. Johnson

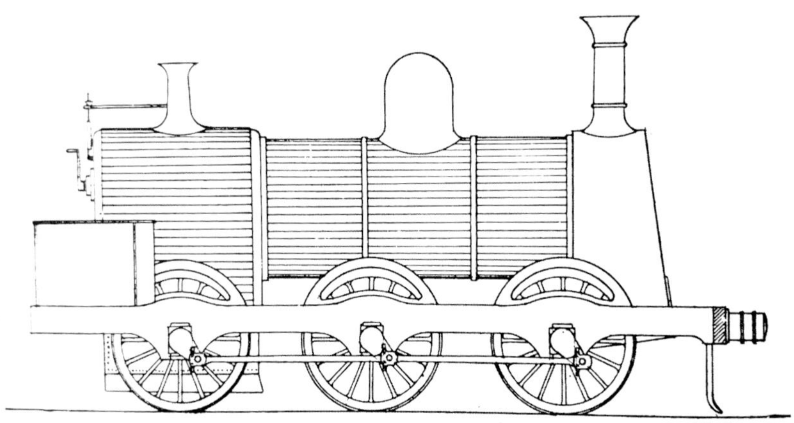

0-6-0 No. 118 and named *Pollux* was built by Sharp, Stewart in December 1853. This locomotive was later hired out to the Oxford, Worcester & Wolverhampton Railway.
Coupled wheels: 5ft 0in.
Cylinders: diameter 18in. x 24in. stroke
Boiler Pressure: 120 psi.

V.R. Webster collection, courtesy E. M. Johnson

2-2-2 type locomotive No. 70 built by Fairbairn in 1849 and named *Grisi.*
Driving wheel: 5ft 6in.
Cylinders: 15in. diameter x 21in. stroke
Boiler: diameter 3ft 9in.
Barrel: length 10ft 3in.
Firebox: copper.
Cost £2,150.

Dow, Great Central, Part One

2-2-2 Type : No. 60 Class *Jenny Lind*. Built by E. B. Wilson & Company of Leeds in 1848. Designed originally for the London Brighton and South Coast Railway. They proved so successful that Wilsons adopted the design as a standard type for use on a number of other railway companies including the MS&LR.
Driving wheels: 6ft 3in.
Cylinders: 15ins x 24in.

Dow, Great Central, Part One

Built by Sharp Brothers and delivered on the 22nd July 1850 was 2-2-2 Type No. 73 named *Venus*.
Coupled wheels: 5ft 6in.
Cylinders: diameter 15in. x 20in. stroke
Boiler: diameter 3ft 7½in.
Barrel: length 10ft 3in.
Firebox: copper.
Cost £1,900.

V.R. Webster, collection, courtesy E.M. Johnson

Sharp, Stewart 0-6-0 was named *Orestes* and delivered in 1853.
Coupled wheels: 5ft 0in.
Cylinders: diameter 18in. x 24in. stroke
Boiler: diameter 4ft 1in.
Barrel: length 11ft 9in.
Firebox: copper.
Cost £2,500.

Dow, Great Central, Part One

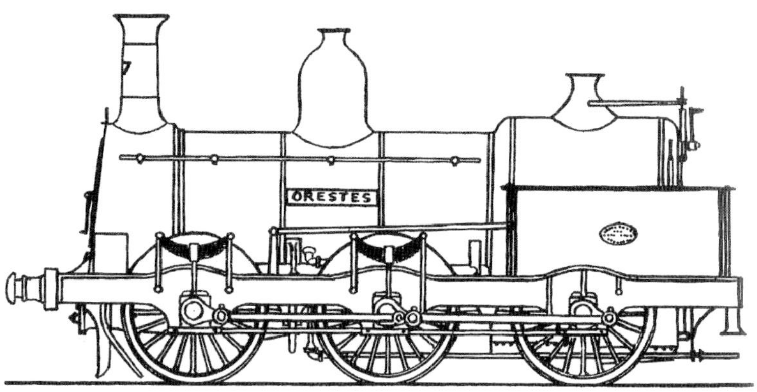

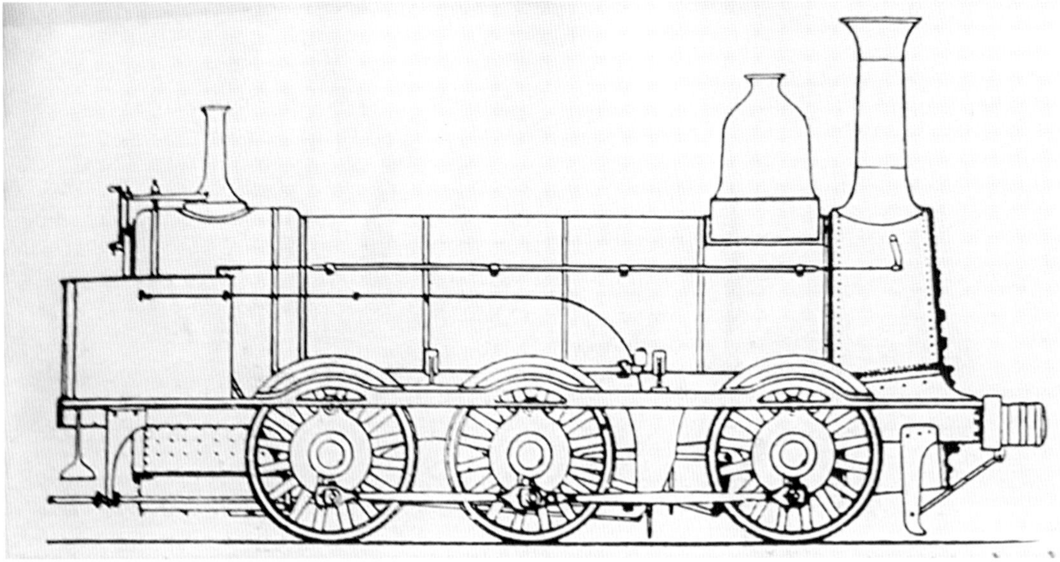

Drawing of Sharp 0-6-0 'Atlas' Class locomotive as built in the 1840s for the SAuL&MR. (Subject of the photograph below)
Drawing: E.M. Johnson

0-6-0 No. 3. of the MS&LR. This locomotive is a 1864 rebuild of a Sharp 'Atlas' Class 0-6-0 of 1846 vintage. Built originally for the Sheffield, Ashton-Under-Lyne & Manchester Railway (SAuL&M). Coupled wheels 4ft 6ins, cylinders: diameter 16in. x 24in. stroke.
MLS collection

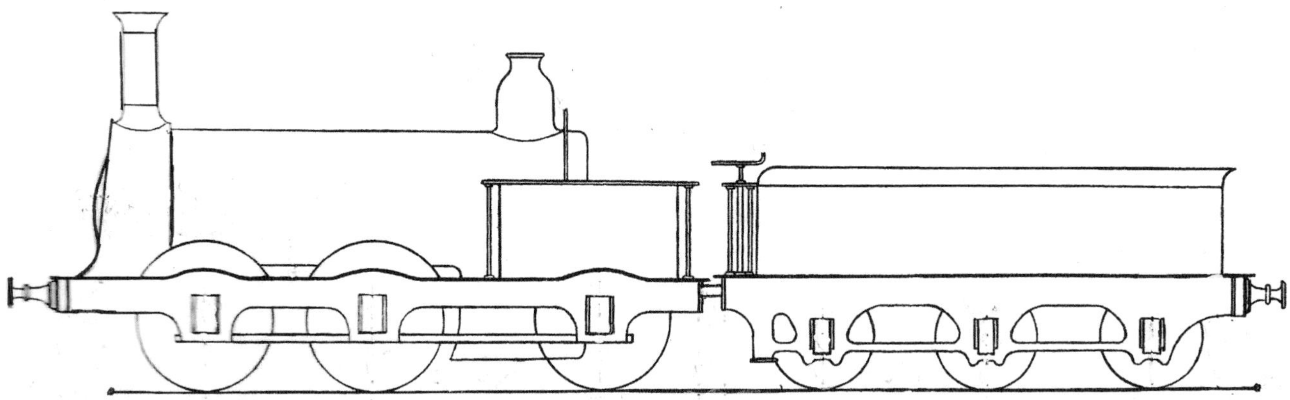

Gorton's first new build locomotives – March 1858. Class '5' 0-6-0 tender goods engine designed by William Grindley Craig.
Drawing based on a drawing in G. Dow's Great Central part one and a sketch by V.R. Webster

In April 1857, ten years after Gorton Works was completed, Craig was granted permission to build two new locomotives. The locomotives were of a simple design and built to replace two old worn-out locomotives. The first was completed in March 1858 and the second in the following month. As mentioned previously they were numbered and named. No. 6 *Archimedes* and No. 7 *Phlegon* respectively. They was designated Class '5'. Each locomotive was fitted with double frames and the dome placed centrally over the firebox. They were tender engines of 0-6-0 wheel arrangement designed as 'goods' engines with 5ft 0in. coupled wheels and having cylinders with a diameter of 17in. x 24 in. stroke, with their coupled wheel base being 14ft. 7in. (the workshops traverser length at Gorton was twenty feet long – thus giving a good indication that the tender would have to be separated from the locomotive to travel on it). One other 0-6-0 locomotive of the same design, Class '5', was turned out at Gorton in 1859. These two being Craig's last engines before he left the MS&LR, these being No's 36 and 53.

Charles Reboul Sacré - Locomotive development

With Sacré being in charge at Gorton for 27 years he, though still influenced by the designs of classes from outside contractors building locomotives for the MS&LR, started to put his own mark on his engines as they were built and also his rebuilds. From this, it is worth a few notes on the developments that took place under him that would eventually pass through to Parker and Pollitt and from there to John G. Robinson as a matter of evolution.

As already mentioned, in 1859 Sacré took over from William Craig to become the MS&LRs Locomotive Superintendent. When he assumed this office the stock of locomotives numbered 1 - 122 all bore names. This was discontinued and after 1860 the names were gradually removed, most probably as they passed through the shops. Most of the locomotives between 1859 to 1873 at the time had plain round domes and brass safety valve columns placed over the firebox casings. From 1873 onwards Ramsbottom valves on polished brass mountings were substituted for the lock up and lever type valves and the columns were abandoned. A new type of chimney with a cast iron cap took the place of the previous bell topped type. Until 1869 all firebox casings were raised above the boiler barrels but from this date all firebox casings to the barrels of goods locomotives were flush with the boilers. Of the passenger locomotives from 1873 the 311 (2-4-0) and 423 (4-4-0) classes had flush firebox casings, nearly all the others had raised casings until the end of 1885 (The *Locomotive Railway Centenary Supplement* of 1925 stated that only these two classes had flush firebox casings, but, No's 71, 409 and 410 built at Sheffield had flush fireboxes.).

During Sacré's time the locomotives were painted dark green, lined out with black bands and white and red lines. The underframes were brown similarly lined out. The brass number plates were painted with dark blue backgrounds, wheel rims left bright, buffer beams vermilion with brown buffers. The cab interiors were light yellow.

Double frames were used exclusively until the end of 1868, when, Sacré adopted single frames for a period of time up until 1873/74. However, it was found that the inside frames at that time did not fair too well with locomotives working hard on severe gradients and the engines were spending more time in the shops receiving attention. Sandwich pattern double frames were afterwards employed. The 1865 batch of Class '23' 0-6-0 locomotives turned out by Neilsons had double frames with 3½inch timber planks between 2 x 1 inch frame plates. After 1865, plated frames were used on an additional fifty goods engines built 1876/67.

Sacré's first – Class '1', the first of two 2-4-0WT locomotives Nos. 23 & 24, built in 1860. These locomotives were the 5th and 6th built new at Gorton following Grindley's four Class '5', 0-6-0s. As was normal practice at this period, it had double frames. Slide valves were fitted and actuated by link motion. Both of the locomotives were allocated to the MSJ&A line for most of their career. Several more Class '1's were built over a few years. From the photograph it is noted that there was a small splasher over the leading wheels. The reversing lever was situated alongside the firebox. Only the rear coupled wheel had a brake, operated by hand. The brass number plate had the companies initials and the build date. Spring gear provided a compensating lever between the coupled wheels. The first two locomotives had sandwich frames, subsequent engines of the class had more robust and a deeper frame. Nos. 23 & 24 were replaced in 1880 by two new engines. The remaining locomotives of this class were rebuilt with side tanks and became Class '1A' and were given a full cab and the coupled wheels springs underhung. A total of ten Class '1' locomotives were built in very small batches up to 1866. *Dow, Great Central, Part One*

This view is of particular interest as it was taken in Gorton works yard at a very early period and, though the image is faded, the original works buildings can be seen in the background and is probably one of the earliest photographs ever taken at Gorton. The locomotive is named *Pegasus*. Its history is a little blurred: it was built in 1847 by Tulk & Ley, Manchester, as Class 'A', No. 35, a 2-2-2 Crampton-type locomotive for the SAuL&MR. In its original form it had a driving wheel 6ft 0ins in diameter and cylinders 16in. in diameter x 20in. stroke. As a 2-2-2 it was not very successful and was rebuilt by Sacré as a 2-4-0 in October 1876 and renumbered 35B, as in the photograph here. Studying the photograph, the original works two storey offices can be seen directly to the side of the locomotive's smoke box. Directly behind the footplate crew is the portal of the Roundhouse while just to the left of the same crew is the clock tower. Rising at an angle upwards from the gents head on the wagon is the slope of the Roundhouse. Behind this is the tall chimney of the engine/boiler house. Far left is the gable end of what was the Fitting Shop. This would therefore place the locomotive close to the coke (fuelling) shed.

Sacré Class '24' 2-4-0 No. 180 stands outside Gorton's fabled roundhouse. The locomotive was built at Gorton in 1865. Looking at the pristine condition of the engine it is more than likely that it is new, if so, this dates the photograph at 1865. The spare stock/paint shop is just visible behind the locomotive's boiler. Coupled wheels 6ft 0ins. Cylinders diameter 16in. x 22in. stroke. *MLS collection*

Sacré Class '24' 2-4-0 No. 153. The locomotive is decorated in honour of Prince Edward and Alexandra's (then Prince and Princess of Wales) visit to Sheffield in 1875. The plate around the top of smoke box reads 'Welcome Prince and Princess of Wales'. *MLS collection*

From 1869 to 1874 a switch was made to simple framed goods locomotives, this probably with a view to their main use being on the flatter lines east of Sheffield but in 1883 a reversion was made that made double frames become the standard up until 1888. It was claimed the greater bearing surface areas gave a considerable saving due to less occurrence of breakage. Better springs could be provided and the greater width between spring centres greater stability.

Sacre's fourth design. Class '13' 0-6-0. Only four locomotives in the class built between 1862 and 1864. Apart from the first engine the locomotives had telescopic boilers i.e the middle boiler ring of the three rings had a larger diameter than the outer two. Coupled wheels 5ft 0ins. Cylinder diameter 16in. x 24in. stroke
Drawing by V.R. Webster. E.M. Johnson collection

Class '15' 2-4-0. No. 215. The last of a class of only four locomotives built in November 1865 at Beyer, Peacock & Co. Coupled wheels 5ft 6in. Cylinders diameter 16in. x 30in. stroke. *MLS collection*

A Sacré rebuild, Class '19' 2-4-0 No. 82. From a small number of locomotives supplied by Hawthorn & Co. dating back to 1849/50. No. 82, along with No's 81 and 83, were rebuilt into Class '19' as above, the rebuilding taking place at Sheffield. No. 82 was scrapped in May 1901. Coupled wheels 5ft 6in. Cylinders diameter 16in. x 20in. stroke. *MLS collection*

Class '2' 0-6-0 No. 270 seen at Manchester London Road Station. Built by Kitson's in 1860. Purchased from the Mid Wales Railway in July 1866. Coupled wheels 4ft 6in. Cylinders diameter 16in. x 26in. stroke. *MLS collection*

Beautifully turned out double framed Class '24' 2-4-0 No. 57 stands on a centre road in the train hall at Manchester Central Station. Built at Gorton in September 1867 the class with 6ft 0in. diameter coupled wheels was intended for fast running between Manchester and Retford. No. 57 was scrapped in November 1904.

Sacré designed Class '23' 0-6-0 No. 124, built by Kitson & Hewitson in 1860. A large class of locomotives built between 1859 and 1867 by a number of companies including: Beyer, Peacock; Neilsons; Kitson & Hewitson; Sharp, Stewart; as well as in Gorton's own workshops. With so many builders there was a number of variations within the class over the years. Built as goods engines the variation put them into two categories, medium goods and heavy goods due to their varying power outputs. No. 124 was fitted with a steam tender as were a number of others in the class, it was found though that maintenance costs outweighed the benefits of having the additional power and was not economical, furthermore the boiler was unable adequately to supply steam to two sets of cylinders and so the tender was soon altered to the ordinary type. The locomotives that had been fitted with steam tenders could be recognised by their unequal wheel base. This engine was rebuilt in 1870 and scrapped in November 1902. *E.M. Johnson collection*

Sacré Class '23' No. 176 goods locomotive, one of several constructed by Beyer, Peacock & Co. in February 1864. Coupled wheels 5ft 3in. Cylinder diameter 16in x 24in. Stroke. This particular engine originated on the South Yorkshire Railway where it carried the number 25. *MLS collection*

A Neilson-built locomotive to Sacré's Design, Class '23' 0-6-0 No. 199 was built in 1865 for goods haulage, this was Sacre's third design dating back to 1859. This particular locomotive was built in 1865 (three years after the first of the class built at Gorton) *MLS collection*

Class '8' 2-4-0 No. 68. The locomotive was a Sacré rebuild in 1872 of a 2-2-2 that was built by Sharp Brothers in October 1840 and originally named *Cadmus*. Coupled wheels 5ft 6in. Cylinder diameter 15in x 20in. stroke. *MLS collection*

Another Sacré rebuild. Class '16' 2-4-0 No. 101. Rebuilt in November 1865 from a Fairbairn (later Sharp, Stewart & Co.) 2-2-2 of 1850. The locomotives became the 'Tempest' Class in 1865. Coupled wheels 5ft 6in. Cylinder diameter. 16in. x 21in. stroke. *MLS collection*

Built at Gorton, Sacré single-framed Class '10' 2-4-0 No. 95 turned out in October 1869. This class of locomotive was used in the Barnsley district and used on the Leeds route via Wakefield round about 1886. Engine scrapped in 1893. *E.M. Johnson collection*

Goods tender locomotive Class ‘18’ 0-6-0 No. 22 the first of the class built at Gorton in 1869 for goods haulage. This handsome locomotive and some of others of the class were subsequently converted to saddle tanks and reclassified as Class ‘18con’. Coupled wheels diameter 5ft 0in. Cylinder diameter 17in. x 24in stroke. *MLS collection*

Sacré Class ‘18’ 0-6-0 single-framed Goods locomotive No. 308 built at Gorton in February 1873. This was one of the later batch built with a flush firebox. The engine enjoyed a relatively long life of 36 years and was scrapped in November 1909. *E. M. Johnson collection*

Another photo of a Class ‘18’ 0-6-0 No. 61, built in 1871 at Gorton, is standing outside the magnificent train hall of Manchester Central Station. This locomotive was later converted to a saddle tank and assumed the classification Class ‘18con’ completely altering its appearance. *MLS collection*

Saddle Tank Class '18T' 0-6-0 No. 370 built in 1875. There were a large number in the class that were built over a number of years from 1871 to 1881 in several batches, all at Gorton. Coupled wheels 4ft 9in. Cylinder diameter 17in. x 24in. stroke. *courtesy E.M. Johnson*

Class '6A' 0-6-0 No. 391 built in October 1876 at Gorton. Coupled wheels 5ft 3in. Cylinder diameter 17in x 26in. stroke. The locomotive was rebuilt in 1889 as class 14B. *MLS collection*

Sacré Class '6B' 4-4-0 No. 433. Built in December 1877 as one of a class of twenty-four locomotives built from 1877 to 1879 for passenger work. No. 433 was the eleventh of the class to be built. Coupled wheels 6ft 3in. Cylinder diameter. 17in. x 26in. stroke. *MLS collection*

Sacré Class '11' 0-4-2 single-framed tender locomotive No. 406, built in June 1877 at Gorton works. A class of seven locomotives, No. 406 was the last of the class, the first being built in April 1874. A possible rebuild from earlier engines No's 37 to 43 from Garforth's and Sharp Brothers. Coupled wheels 5ft 3in. Cylinder diameter 16in x 22in. stroke. *MLS collection*

Sacré Class '7' 0-6-0T No. 530 (later renumbered 15) was the last built from a class of six locomotives. All were built at Gorton Works in 1885. Coupled wheels 3ft 9in. Cylinder diameter. 15in x 29in. stroke. *MLS collection*

'Single' No. 399, the first of the class of 1882. Renumbered 104 in 1893. No. 99 was fitted with plain frames without cutaways at the front and rear of the frames. Note the frame difference between the two photographs. Manchester Central Station. *MLS collection*

Standing at Liverpool's Brunswick sheds is Sacré single No. 501. Built in June 1883 the locomotive has been turned out in the usual immaculate condition typical of the MS&LR. This locomotive was the third of the class to be built. The engine was scrapped in March 1905. *E.M. Johnson collection*

Another superb photograph of one of Charles Sacré's Class '14' 2-2-2 passenger locomotive No. 508, built in October 1883. The locomotive is pictured outside Gorton sheds on No. 8 road. At the side of the engine are the two story offices of the shed foremen. This was situated between No. 10 and 11 roads. The first of twelve locomotives in the class, No. 399 was built in 1882, the remaining eleven were built in 1883 (numbered 501 to 510). Coupled wheels 7ft. 6in. Cylinder diameter 17.5in. x 26in. stroke. *MLS collection*

Kitson built Parker Class '2' 4-4-2 No. 561 inside framed locomotive stands at Manchester London Road Station. A class of thirty-one locomotives. No. 561 was exhibited at the Manchester exhibition in 1887 as a joint exhibit between Kitson's and the MS&LR. For this no builders plate was fitted, it carried a modified chimney which became the standard. After 561, the next eighteen were built at Gorton, the remainder by Kitson's. Coupled wheels 6ft 9in. Cylinders were diameter 18in. x 26in. stroke. *V.R. Webster/courtesy E.M. Johnson*

Parker Class '6D' 2-4-0 No. 17 built in October 1887. Only three were built in the class, these being No's 10, 17 & 79 (later renumbered 506, 507 & 509) Coupled wheels 6ft 9in. Cylinder diameter 18in. x 26in. stroke. Manchester London Road station. *MLS collection*

Parker designed Class '6DB' 4-4-0 No. 400 (was No. 511) built in October 1888 as part of a small class of just three engines. Coupled wheels 6ft 9in. Cylinders were diameter 18in. x 26in. stroke. These locomotives were built to replace the three Class '6D' 2-4-0s that were unsteady on express passenger trains. Manchester London Road station. *MLS collection*

Standing outside Gorton's erecting shop is double-framed Class 'D' 2-4-0 No. 509. The locomotive was the third and last of the class and was turned out in November 1887. Originally the engine was given the number 79 and it became No. 509B in 1909 on the engine duplicate list. The coupled wheels were double framed with the leading being of the single inside type. Coupled wheels 6ft 9in. Cylinder diameter 18in. x 26in. stroke. *E.M. Johnson*

Parker designed Class '3' 2-4-2T No. 610 built in July 1890. One of twenty-seven built by Neilson's with the first twelve built at Gorton. The majority of the class were built between June 1889 and July 1892. Three more locomotives emerged from Gorton in 1893. Coupled wheels 5ft. 7in. Cylinder diameter18in. x 24in. stroke. Twelve of the class built by Neilsons had bunkers extended by six inches and were classified as Class '3A'. Gorton running shed yard with the Carriage & Wagon Works in view behind the locomotive. *MLS collection*

Gorton's Second Erecting Shop

This was built in the 1860s and joined the northern side of (what was then) the stock holding shed (which later itself became the boiler mounting shop). This second shop was built for the erection of new locomotives and tenders giving relief to the overcrowded existing erecting shop. To have an idea of how this erecting shop must have looked like, refer to the photographs on pages 248 and 249 (the shops just before demolition after the works closed). After the last erecting shop was built in 1890 on the west side of Wellington Street, these shops became boiler shops.

On completion of the new C&W shops being built at the north end of the works in 1879 the existing two storey C&W building was altered to turn the building into an erecting shop and light machine shop. This was achieved by altering the roof from a two apex design to a three apex design to eliminate the centre roof support columns. The upper floor (carriage floor) was partially removed leaving just a gallery around the sides of the building. Extra pillars were used to support the gallery floor which was required to hold the weight of the machine tools. The galleries are well illustrated on later pages to give an example of their layout (in GCR days).

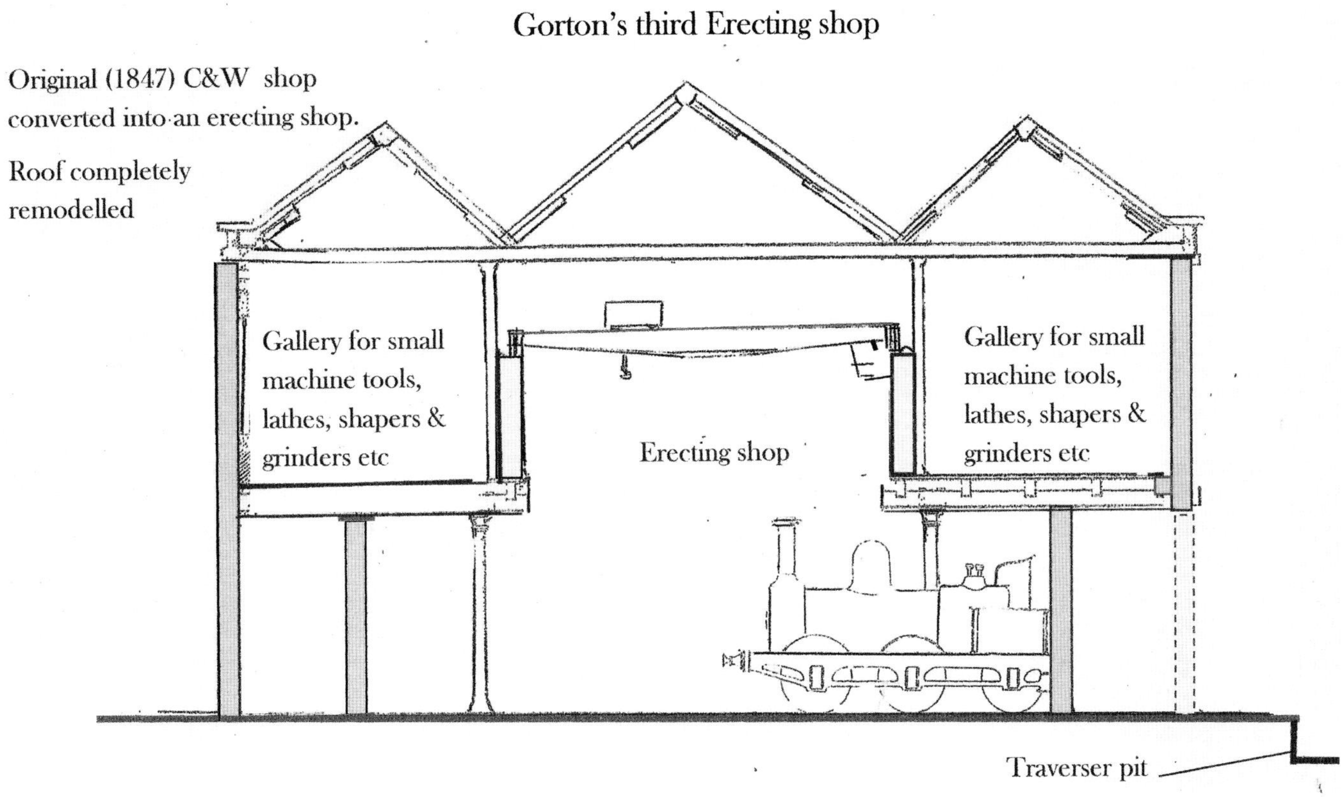

The above drawing gives an idea of how the original carriage and wagon shops of 1847/8 were after conversion into an erecting shop for the overhaul and repair of locomotives in 1879. *Author's drawing*

Looking west through the Boiler Mounting Shop in GCR days. The shop was part of the original 'Peacock' buildings and were then the Paint Shop and stock holding shed. Behind the far wall is what was at that time the Heavy Machine Shop (Danube) gauge room in later BR days. The 'Danube' was, until it was converted, the traverser that fed the locomotive shops and carriage and wagon works. The boiler in the far centre of the photograph appears to be complete with all fittings and could have been in the process of being 'hot' tested or about to be. From here the boiler will be conveyed into the next Bboiler Shop bay for moving through the machine shops and into the Erecting Shop. *National Archives*

CHAPTER THREE
GREAT CENTRAL RAILWAY

On August 1st 1897 the MS&LR had a name change. The MS&LR was building its new railway line from Manchester to London. The line ran from Manchester London Road station to London's Marylebone station via Sheffield, Leicester and Nottingham. This was the last main line to run into London. The stretch of line became known as the London Extension. The name change came about because the MS&LR now needed something more befitting for a major railway company running a main line into London. As large as it was, the MS&LR was in all effects a cross-country railway by name. On July 25th 1898 the newly named Great Central Railway commenced running goods trains over the route to settle the earthworks involved with the track laying. The first passenger trains ran on the 15th March 1899 with Harry Pollitt seeing off the first train from Marylebone station. In June 1900 Harry Pollitt resigned from the GCR and his position was taken over by the appointment of John George Robinson to the position of Chief Mechanical Engineer. Robinson, prior to this, was the Locomotive Superintendent of the Waterford & Limerick Railway in Ireland, having previously been an engineering apprentice with the Great Western Railway. With trains running longer distances on the new main line to London, Robinson was given the job of building classes of locomotives that would be up to the task. 'John G.' took no time in putting his mark on the new types of locomotives that Gorton Works was to start turning out. He was lucky enough to have inherited a works that was well equipped but very little room left for any perceived expansion. Pollitt's last design, the Class 'X4' 4-2-2 singles were still being built when Robinson took over and he cut the order from ten to six due to the increase in traffic sizes demanding exclusively coupled wheeled engines. Two 'X4's had already been completed when Robinson assumed the CME's job. Pollitt's 4-4-2 engines though influenced him to go down that track initially.

John George Robinson 1856-1943
Chief Mechanical Engineer, Great Central Railway.
Author's collection

Robinson's first design came early in his reign in the shape of a new 0-6-0 locomotive, This became Class 9J. Building commenced in 1901. A very successful class that had a very long life span that lasted for over forty years when it was still going strong and became the L&NER standard goods engine. The locomotive became known as 'Pom Poms', this no doubt coming from the loud 'barking' noise from the engines exhaust that sounded similar to the quick firing guns that were used during the Boer War. Robinson recommended continuing with the construction of the Class '9H' Pollitt locomotives that were still being built at Gorton in line with the '9J's. The Robinson locomotives will be reviewed in a later chapter.

A general view of the locomotive works as viewed from the GCR main line looking north. The two-storey buildings on the left are the drawing offices for both the locomotive and carriage & wagon departments, works managers offices, chain testing shop, copper stay shop, stores, blueprint printing room with a platform outside to facilitate daylight printing and a Halden's continuous printing machine. The next building quite clearly visible is the smithy (ex roundhouse) complete with clock tower and portico. To the right of the smithy is the iron foundry and plate foundry (the four cupola stacks just being visible). To the right of the foundry is the two-storey pattern making and carpenters shop. The main offices are at the extreme right of the photograph. The chimney behind the smithy clock tower is the original engine house boiler room chimney of 1847/8. *Author's collection*

The main offices at Gorton which had a postal address on Cornwall Street. In Great Central days the nearest offices to the camera were occupied by the Chief Mechanical Engineer, John G. Robinson. After the takeover by the L&NER the CME was located in headquarters at London and Doncaster and the Gorton the works manager took over the office here. The remainder of the block was home to senior engineers, both of the locomotive and carriage and wagon departments. The offices in far distance (with just the chimney in view) were those of the Chief Accountant. *Author's collection*

East end of the shop seen on page 46, again looking west with the boiler mounting section at the far end. Steel plating is lying in wait for rolling into boiler barrel sections. Boiler firebox face plates already pressed into shape are stacked on the left. The arches to the other two bays can be clearly seen to the right, which were windows prior to other additional bays being built. The windows on the left looked out onto the GCR main line. *National Archives*

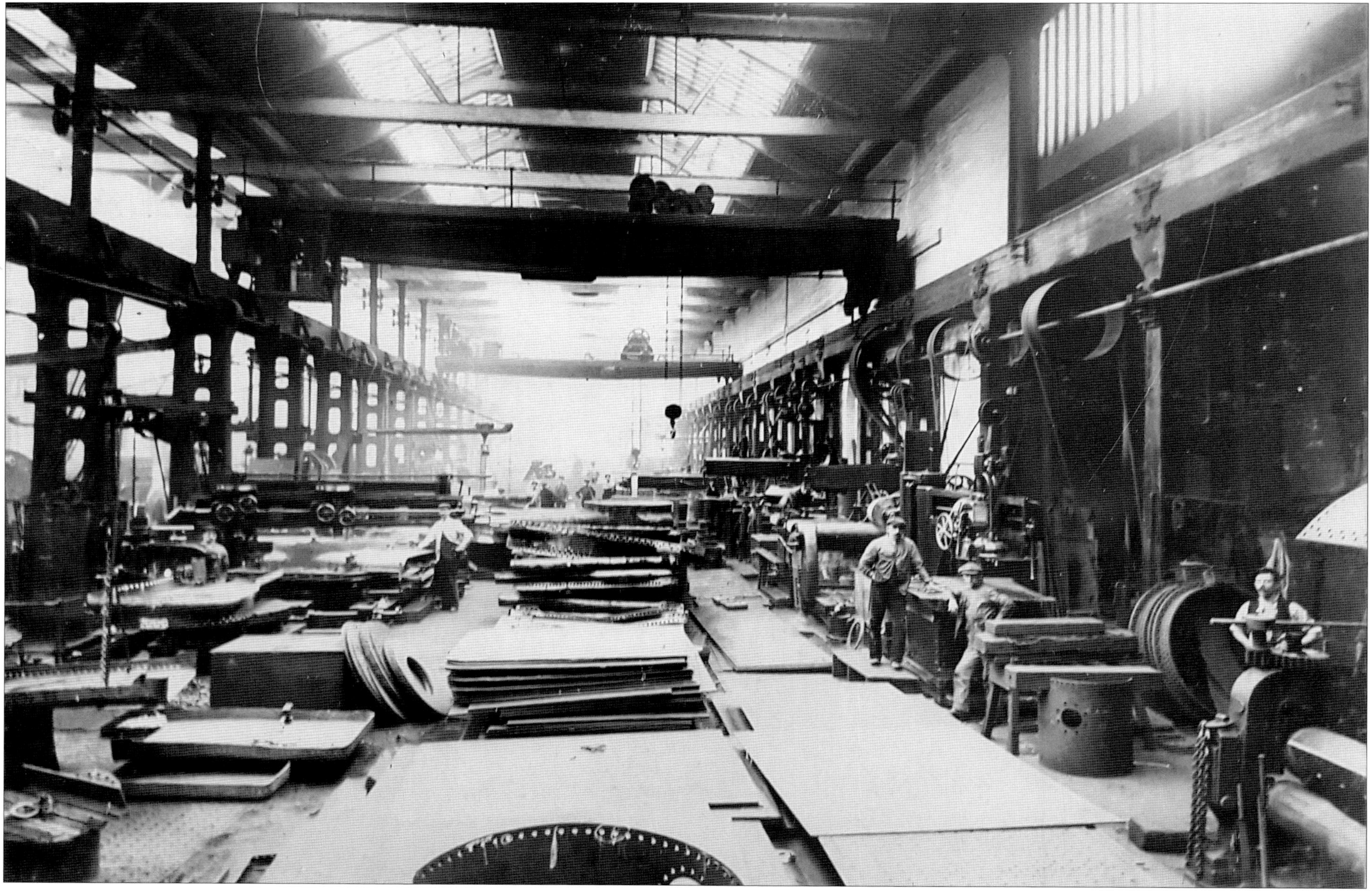

BOILER SHOPS. In total three bays were built between the Boiler Mounting Shop and the original fitting shop of 1848 (see plan, page xx). The overhead cranes (two per bay) are clearly seen and were rope driven at this period, the rope 'runs' for moving the cranes along the bays are high up on the left-hand side roof support columns. The cranes were later converted to electric power. Line shafting for belt-driven machine tools is evident under and bolted to the crane rail supports. Machinery for bending boiler plating into shape also can be observed. As stated earlier, in MS&LR days, prior to being used as boiler shops one bay was the Tender Shop and two bays were solely for constructing new locomotives – the Tender Shop moving later on to the shops at the northern end of the works northern building complex the 'New Locomotive Shops' as they were known at the time. *National Archives*

No. 2 Bay of the main boiler shop complex. The place looks like it is bursting at the seams with the amount of boilers being repaired. It looks though as everybody from all the bays have congregated and stopped (momentarily) for the cameraman. The horrendous noise normally associated to the boiler shop would probably have stopped during the time making things a little easier for the photographer, who, looking from the angle of the photograph is no doubt perched on top of a boiler. *National Archives*

Opposite, top: Bay No. 2 of the Locomotive Stripping Shop. Locomotives entering the works for overhauls and repairs first entered this shop where they were stripped down of all their components. After removal the boilers, dependent on their condition were either conveyed to the main Boiler Shop for repairs or to the Boiler Machine Shop in Bays 6 & 7 should they require only minor repairs. All other parts went to the various shops for attention after going through the bosh (cleaning plant), the frames obviously to the Erecting Shop, locomotive tenders or tank engine tanks were moved to the main Tender Shop in Bay No. 3. No 4 Bay also formed part of the Tender Shop also though a section of this bay included a machine shop which included two wheel lathes. Each bay of the Locomotive Stripping Shop was equipped with a 12-ton 'Royce' overhead electric crane. The photograph shows locomotives in an advanced stage of stripping down, to the fore are various side tanks from tank locomotives, these would go to the Tender Shop for attention. Looking across to the right of the photo is No. 1 Bay with other locomotives in the process of being stripped down. The photograph also shows the narrow gauge tracks used for conveying parts to and from on railed trucks. *Railway Magazine, 1914*

Opposite, lower: **BOILER MACHINE SHOP.** This was situated in Bays 6 & 7 of the 'Northern Building Complex' (this area of the works was known as the 'New Locomotive Shops' in GCR days) built during the massive works expansion programme of 1879. Following locomotive stripping-down in No. 1 Bay in the Locomotive Stripping Shop, boilers would either go to the main boiler shops for major repairs, or, if only light repairs were necessary the boilers would be sent here via the traverser (situated outside this complex of buildings). The traverser was electrically powered and movement on and off the table was by means of capstan haulage. Boilers were moved around the works on old tender frames adapted for the purpose (a practice that continued up until works closure). This shop also had a boiler mounting section. No. 6 Bay was strictly a tender plating and boiler machine shop and was equipped with a 12-ton electrically operated overhead 'Vaughan' crane with all the machinery necessary for boiler work being installed in this bay. No. 7 bay was the bay that dealt with the light repairs to boilers. This whole building was originally built for carriage and wagon purposes at the northern end of the works bordering onto Whitworth Street East. When the newer (at that time) carriage & wagon shop was built in 1881 on the far north western end of the complex (adjacent to Wellington Street – later Widnes Street), the rolling stock was transferred there and these shops were converted for locomotive repairs. *Railway Magazine, 1914*

Tender Shop

The Tender Repair Shop was situated in No. 3 & 4 bays of the same northern building complex, unfortunately the Tender Shop is not illustrated in this review. No. 3 Bay was equipped with two 12-ton 'Broadbent' overhead cranes utilised for all tender repairs. No. 4 Bay also carried out tender repairs and had a machine shop section which included two wheel lathes This bay had two 15-ton 'Craven Bros' overhead cranes.

BRASS SHOP. The Brass Shop consisted of lines of machine power tools down each wall, with centrally positioned rows of fitters' (and brass finishers') benches. The machine tools in this two-bay shop were belt-driven from line shafting along each wall and up in the roof structures, however, electricity was starting to make a presence in powering some machines throughout the engineering industry. Notice the clutter of brass components on the floor, no doubt all will be assembled correctly after receiving attention on completion of machining and inspection. Notice also the older type of cumbersome bench vices on the left hand side of the bench, very common in all the workshops in those days but gradually replaced when worn out with the more user-friendly type. No doubt the foreman in the shop gave his men a little 'time off' to pose for the cameraman but would soon have them back at work. *National Archives*

Right upper: The other bay in the Brass Shop. Notice here that the lathes are powered by electricity as against the opposite bay. The gent in the suit and bowler hat further down the bay no is doubt a foreman. *National Archives*

Right lower: A little further along the same bay. The foreman is still posing along with his workforce. Notice the large grinding machine with no safety guard fitted over the wheel, the blur of its drive belts indicating that the wheel is spinning unattended, quite acceptable in that period of time. The power take-off drive motor for the line shafting is clearly visible mounted high up on the wall at the far end of the building. Brass fittings clutter the benches and floor, a trip hazard, no such thing as Health & Safety in those days! *National Archives*

PATTERN SHOP, Ground Floor. Three views of the Pattern Shop which was situated between the main offices (Cornwall Street Offices) and the iron foundry, the pattern makers' shop was a two-storey building. The shops catered for all the patterns used in the manufacture of the mouldings for castings manufactured at Gorton, this included the manufacture of the moulds for the large casting of cylinder blocks and superheater headers in the Iron Foundry. The shops also carried out general carpentry work for repairs around the works workshops and running sheds including locomotive footplate flooring. *all National Archives*

Seen posing outside Gorton's Pattern shop are some of their carpenters and patternmakers. Amongst them standing on back row sixth from the left (neatly groomed) is Mr. Richard Hardwick. *E.M. Johnson collection*

Richard Hardwick

Richard Hardwick was born in Openshaw on the 22nd May 1883. On leaving school around 1889 he took an apprenticeship at the Crossley Brothers works on Ashton Old Road. In his early twenties however, on learning that better pay was to be had at Gorton Works, he forsook his work at Crossley's and metaphorically 'jumped ship'.

Richard's trade was a patten maker. He may well have inherited his manual dexterity from his grandfather, Joseph Constantine, who was a stonemason working at Gorton. Richard rose from apprenticeship level to that of chargehand. When the question was raised as to why he never became a foreman, his daughter replied, '*No, he wouldn't take that job as the foreman's job is reserved for Freemasons*'. In Richard Hardwick's time at Gorton the pattern shop foreman was Mr W. H. Bedford who retired in January 1921 with a smoking concert held to mark the occasion. His place was taken over by Louis Rimmington.

Richard was a very skilled and much appreciated man. Legend has it that when a problem arose that seemed impossible to solve, the cry would go up 'Send for Dick Hardwick!' His daughter, Gertrude France, related to a little nugget: it was when Mr Gresley was designing his A4 Class locomotives. He visited the works and spoke to my Father who made a suggestion about something to do with the inside cylinder. '*That's a good idea Mr. Harwich, make a note of that Mr. Thom*' said Gresley. Gorton had an excellent reputation for both patternmaking and casting, so I think we can verify Gertrude's story.

Come Richard's 65th birthday in May 1948 he was due to retire, a cursory note from Management would have simply have sent him on his way. However, it seems that Richard's skills were too good to lose, so his retirement was rescinded and he stayed on in his post as chargehand patternmaker for a little longer, retiring eventually on February 17th the following year. Doubtless he was glad to do so as railway pensions in those days were derisory.

Richard's grandson, John France, recalls with pride granddad's craftsmanship. Richard made two small chairs, no nails, no screws or glue. They were made with such close precision that they could be disassembled and made into a money box.

Richard Hardwick died on April 26th 1954, just a few weeks before his 73rd birthday.

MAIN IRON FOUNDRY. Divided into two sections, the Iron Foundry and Plate (chair) Foundry. The main foundry dealt with all major castings, i.e. locomotive cylinders, superheater headers etc., whilst the Plate Foundry dealt with track chairs, brake blocks, fire bars etc, supplying these parts to the whole of the GCR system. There was also an iron fettling section for 'dressing' up the finished castings, this was situated in a shelter adjacent to the foundry buildings. Judging by the size of the mould in the foreground, it appears that it is for a cylinder block. Once this is set up and the cupolas had filled the ladles with molten iron it would be a non-stop process to cast the block without any delay. A single mistake here and things could go horribly wrong. The foundry foreman would have ensured that all the personnel were completely aware of the precision timing that is required before the 'pour' starts. The sizeable cranes installed, one a ten-ton capacity and the second at six-tons capacity, gives indications of the heavy weights that were lifted in the foundry shops. The work carried out was no doubt very hot, dusty, hard and unpleasant. *National Archives*

Apologies for the poor images but well worth an inclusion so as to illustrate what the scene was like whilst a 'pour' was taking place into a mould, particularly a large exercise like a cylinder block being cast. No health and safety in sight! Note the rudimentary stands including a wheelbarrow that the iron founders are standing on and the total lack of protective clothing. All in all quite a dangerous environment. Note also the gent on the left turning the handle to tilt the ladle in the top photograph, no doubt a foreman foundryman. The products that came out of Gorton Tank's foundry were recognised within the railway industry to be of a the highest standards available and the envy of all the railway workshops on Britain's railways. *National Archives*

The Plate Foundry section of the iron foundry. It was here that all plates were manufactured. This process would be endless, day after day satisfying the thirst for the permanent way department. Literally thousands of the castings would be produced in a week. Once released from their moulds, the castings would be sent to the fettling shed outside the foundry to be 'dressed' up. Note: plates are a base plate that was fitted between the rails and the sleepers and used to secure the rail to the sleepers. The plates were bolted to the sleeper and the rails were fastened to the plates. *National Archives*

Axle box moulds are in the foreground. The weights on top of them are to hold the moulds in place when the molten iron is poured. Other moulds appear to be for permanent way plates and chairs. The foundry complex was a very busy place, even more so the main foundry in later days when Nigel Gresley put it on Gorton to manufacture the three cylinder mono-block castings. Rolling stock brake blocks were also cast here. The plate and chair foundry overall dimensions were 135 feet long by 105 feet wide. *National Archives*

The main iron foundry had two bays, the other bay to the left of this photograph had one crane, this at 10-tons capacity and was nearest to the four cupolas. At the northern side of the foundry was the core making shop with a 1½-ton capacity crane, next the core shop was the drying oven shop and the stores. The eastern side of the building housed the sand house and dressing shop which had a six ton capacity crane installed. Overall dimensions of the building were 165 feet long by 127 feet wide. The cupola bay was 105 feet long by approximately 30 feet wide. *National Archives*

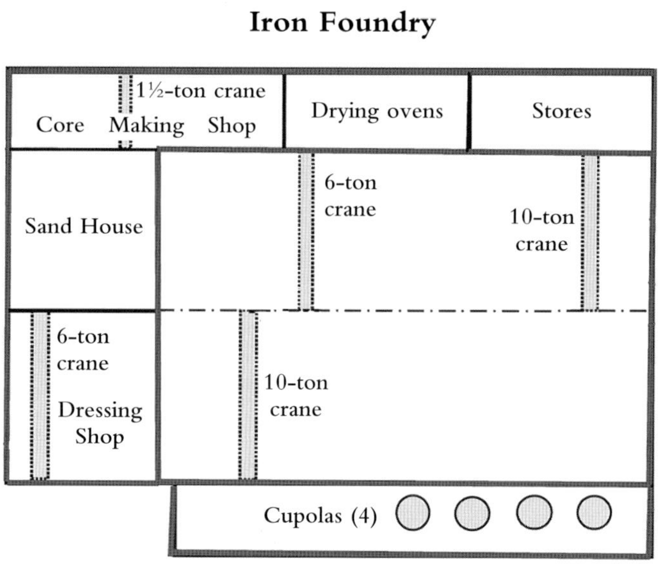

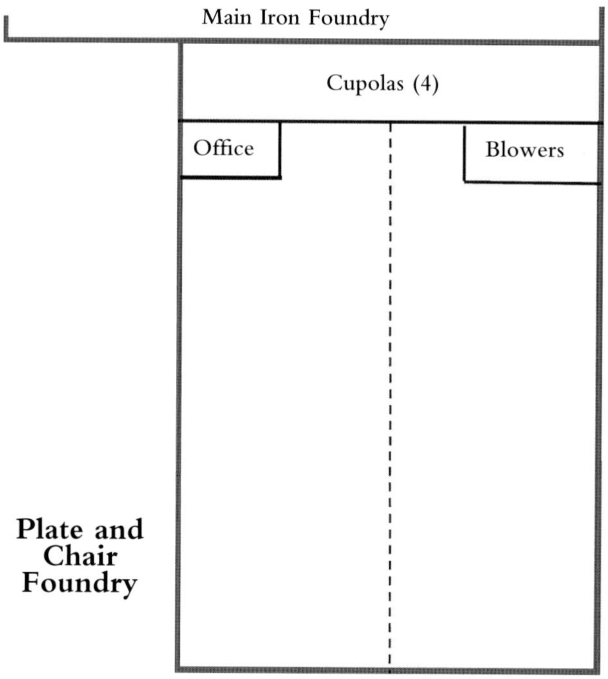

Millwrights' Machine Shop. There were a number of millwright shops scattered around the works. This millwright shop forming part of the Danube appears to be concentrating on the maintenance to the overhead layshafts and mechanisms used for driving machine tools via the pulleys to the belt driven machine tools that were in abundance at this period of time. The extensive use of layshafts no doubt created full time work to keep them maintained, especially the numerous amount of plummer blocks along the shafts length. This shop is the old 'Model' (pattern) Shop. Looking west and through the arch was the Danube bay of the machine shop, the Danube being the original traverser pit which was built over to convert it into an enclosed shop about 1900 (see page 13, lower plan 'G') with new heavy machine tools being installed on completion. Later on, this Millwrights Shop was again changed to become the White Metal Shop where they carried out the process of lining all plain bearings and sundries, axle boxes being the main components that went into the shop for re-metalling.
National Archives

Brass Foundry. This was situated to the north of the iron foundry, it was at this time quite a cavernous building. The brass foundry also occupied another building next door (brass mould shop). Judging by the semi circular components in front of the wheel barrows/foundry door, the moulds in the photograph could possibly be for manufacturing axle box linings. Numerous parts were fitted to locomotives and rolling stock that were manufactured from brass and bronze, and no doubt each individual item was manufactured in large quantities to satisfy the demands from the stores departments. Considering the lack of lifting equipment the work carried out here appears to be manhandled, heavy work indeed. Note the layshafts mounted on the wall with pulley wheels probably for driving fettling and grinding tools. *National Archives*

Drop Hammer Shop - showing one of the large hammers. This hammer and all other types of hammers whether drop stamp hammers, steam hammers and forge hammers would more than likely have been a product of B&S Massey. This company had works situated just a short distance away in Openshaw on the Ashton Old Road opposite to Cornwall Street. The forge shops also included the chain smithy. The following pages show the array different types of Massey, Rigby hammers, note the photos showing the 'roundhouse' general smithy (originally the 17 road locomotive roundhouse). Note also the large swing arm cranes in the photos which depicts the size and weight of the forgings that has to be formed into the final shape. A very skilled operation, no room for any errors. Also to be seen in the following photos are the assortment of hand tools that were the norm for any forge/smithy i.e. tongs, anvils, forming tools, quenching tanks and the traditional 7 and 14lb hammers. The smiths furnaces being in abundance close to the hammers. *National Archives*

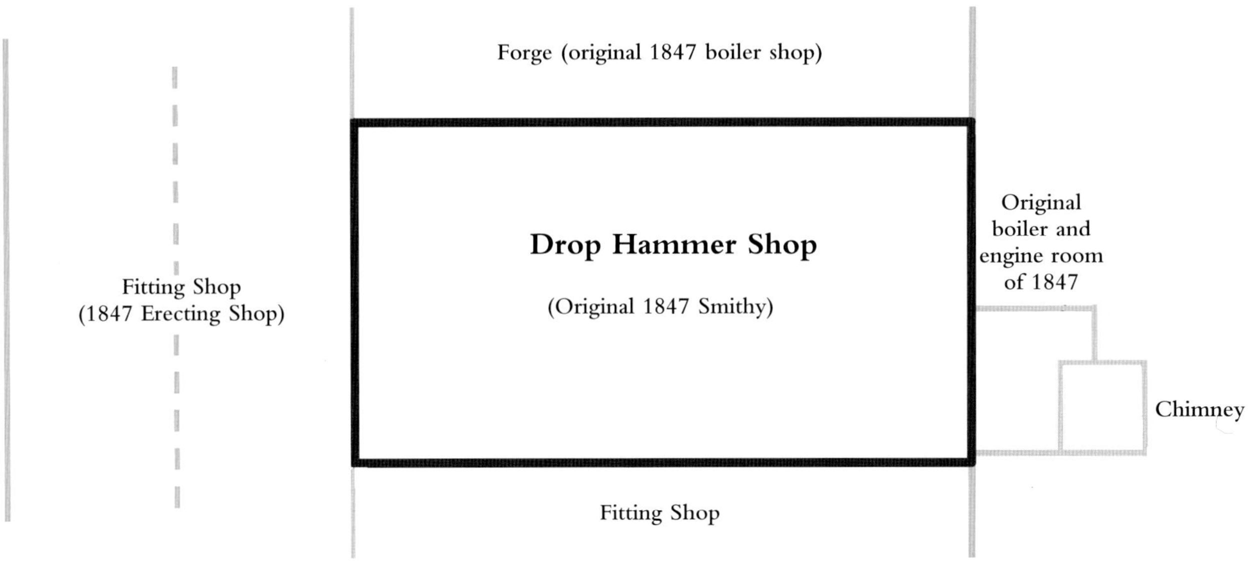

Drop Hammer Shop. Another view of the inside of the drop hammer shop. Note the massive swing arm crane used to lift the heavy ingots onto the hammer anvils. *National Archives*

The Main Forge. The usual assortment of Smiths tools are scattered around the shop floor. Protective workwear was not an obligatory requirement. The only 'extras' to normal everyday working clothes being leather aprons, knotted handkerchiefs or caps and gloves being quite common. Note the foreman surrounded by the smiths posing for the cameraman. *National Archives*

The Smithy. Formally the seventeen road roundhouse of 1847. The roundhouse was converted in 1879 for this purpose when the new running sheds were built on the other side of Widnes Street (previously Wellington Street). The Smiths' hearths were located around the wall of the building with the steam hammers closer in towards the centre with the main roof column still in position holding up the roof.
E.M. Johnson collection

The roundhouse smithy.
National Archives

Press Shop. A section of the shop showing one of the heavy presses used primarily for forming boiler firebox throat and backplates into shape. The size of the large swing-arm crane required to lift the large plating giving indications of the weights involved. The press is a product of Henry Berry & Co. of Hunslet, Leeds, manufacturers of heavy machinery for the engineering industry. *National Archives*

Location of the Press Shop

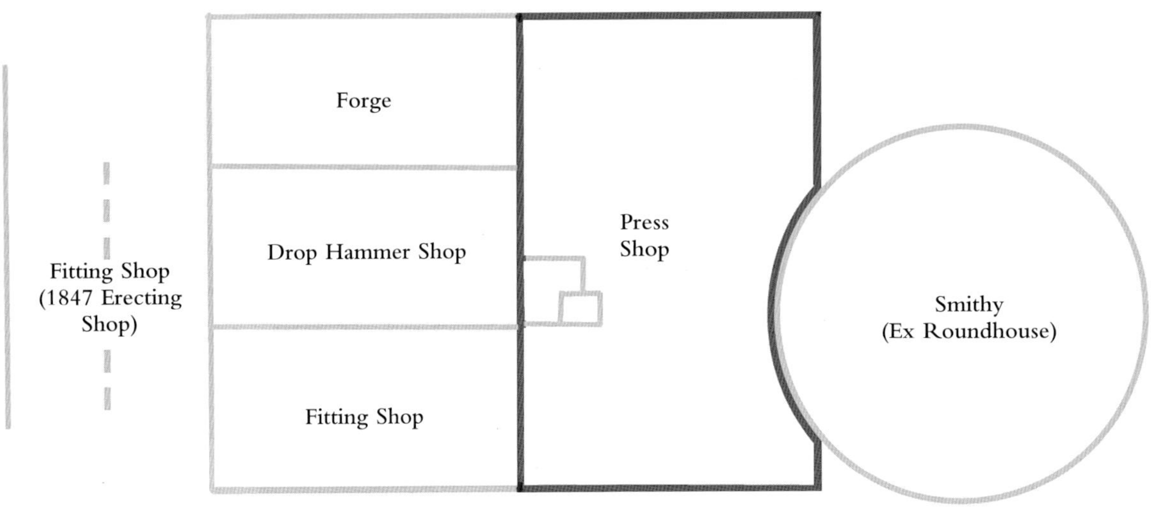

Plate Shop. The large 'guillotines' (belt driven of course) being able to cut thick steel plating to the required shapes. The work being carried here appears to be small section plate sizes. The radial arm drill in the background no doubt drilling bolt or rivet holes in the plating. The swing cranes over the guillotine are evidence to the weight of the plating that has to be dealt with. One wonders if the cranes ever came into contact with the drive belts. The belt pulleys, bearings and layshafts themselves bolted to the massive roofing timbers. The stack of plating in the foreground appear to be off-cuts, but would probably be put to good use for smaller jobs.

National Archives

The Copper Shop. This was built into the north-east end of No.5 Bay of the erecting shop. In view are the furnaces for heating the pipework prior to quenching in water troughs and thus making it possible to easily form and bend copper items, in particular pipes, copper pipes being used extensively on locomotives and rolling stock. Towards the front of the photo is a narrow gauge rail track. Gorton had no narrow gauge railway locomotives within the workshops. The narrow gauge track in the photo was used for wheeling small trucks around the various shops to carry parts and items to their required location, pushed by hand. Later on, petrol powered 'Lister Auto trucks' would become the norm for this purpose due to their manoeuvrability, and the narrow track system became redundant. The gas lighting mantles hanging from the roof gives an indication of the type of lighting employed at this period in time. The erecting shop was to the left of this photograph. *National Archives*

Main Machine Shops

During the expansion of the workshops of the late 1870s the area around the original works changed dramatically. The building structures basically remained the same though their purposes changed. The Carriage & Wagon Shops of 1848 (see page 13, lower diagram item 'C' were converted to the Machine Shop in 1900, earlier though, between 1879 and 1900 it became an Erecting Shop when the 1848 shop became too small for its use – see page xxx).

In order for the building to take on this new role the roof was raised, the upper floor was partially removed leaving a gallery around the walls. To accommodate the gallery, the roof was changed from a double apex design to a triple apex for the purpose of adding extra support columns for the gallery. The gallery was fitted out with smaller and lighter machine tools leaving the main ground floor level to accommodate the larger machine tools, planning, shaping and large boring machines etc.

With these major changes the traverser that fed the 1851 shops was no longer required and the whole of the traverser area was covered in and roofed. This became another machine shop bay. Large machine tools were installed in this bay, a large section of this bay was dedicated to work involved on locomotive cylinders and thus became known for a time as the cylinder shop. This bay became more widely known in later times as the 'Danube'.

The following machine shop photographs show the large amount of belt driven machinery used in the machine shop at this period. Electric lighting appears to have been installed, health and safety was at a minimum. The large amount of belts and exposed pulley wheels driving the machinery must have made the area very hazardous especially when every inch of space was being used for the machine tools. The photographs taken from the gallery show the large quantity of smaller machine tools employed in the shop, namely lathes, shaping and grinding machines.

Note the large quantity of support columns for both the gallery, overhead crane and roofing in the following photographs. The images from the gallery level show how the 'cutting speeds' of the machine tools were arranged, this by moving the belts onto the different size pulley wheels and therefore changing the speed of the machine tools.

Pages 77 and 78 clearly show the Danube Bay. This was the ex-1848/51 traverser area and it can be clearly seen how the traverser fed the carriage and wagon works and erecting shops during those early years before remodelling began.

Looking north from the gallery at the south end. A general view of the whole of the machine shop. The window arches just in view above the crane rails on the right hand side of the of the photograph were the windows of the carriage works (upper floor). No doubt the coach builders in those early days would have been able to look down through the windows and see locomotives, carriages and wagons being moved along on the traverser table to their designated locations. The rails travelling across the shop just behind the man near the front of the view were for moving boilers across from the boiler shop on the right to the erecting shop. After the boiler shop and smithy, this must have been a very noisy shop with all the machinery and drive pulleys and belts all running all day long. *National Archives*

The Main Machine Shop. Looking north from the shop floor level. Once the original two-storey carriage and wagon works of 1847 the roof for the upper floor has been removed. This was removed in MS&LR days when the shop was converted to (at that period) an Erecting Shop for overhauls, repairs and conversion/rebuilds. When the floor was removed, a gallery was left in place and used as a machine shop for light machine tools. The traverser in the adjoining shop was filled and enclosed to form the Danube Machine Shop. The massive columns are being used to not only hold up the roof and overhead crane but also the gallery. Some of the machine tools in this shop were still in operation at the time of the works closure, a large double-head 'Plano milling machine being an example which was used mainly for boring out both ends of connecting rods simultaneously. *National Archives*

Opposite top: Viewed looking north along the west side gallery, the ground floor displaying its rows of heavy machine tools. As usual all machinery is belt driven from the long line shafting. Light machine tools and fitting benches adorn the gallery floor. Behind that west wall is the main Erecting Shop of 1890. The famous 'Birdcage' foot bridge runs along the upper reaches of the outside the wall connecting Wellington Street (later Widnes Street) to the north and the GCR Manchester to Sheffield line on the south end of the shop. *National Archives*

Opposite lower: Looking a little bit further down the bay beyond the connecting rods, eccentrics and machine tools were the stairs up to the gallery. Past the stairs was the inspection bay. Here was a large cleaning tank for components that came from the erecting shop (The Bosh). The bosh was a large cleaning tank where components were submerged in hot caustic soda, after removal they were then inspected for condition before being distributed to their relevant sections for repairs in the Machine Shop fitting sections. This bay of the Machine Shop was an extension built later on. The extension had an additional entrance at the rear of the bosh, where the parts that were transported from the Erecting Shop were placed into the bosh dip tanks at the erecting shop end and removed from the tanks at the machine shop side. The inspection bay ran at right angles and ran across the main Machine Shop and into the Danube Machine Shop with a separate overhead crane. *National Archives*

This photograph shows a view under the west side gallery. Look at the large counterweights and chains used to assist moving the tool post heads of the machine tools into position for machining, no electric motors to move the heads. Once all is set up by the skilled machine tool operators, only then will the machining operation take place. The Erecting Shop is behind the windows. *National Archives*

A view under the east side of the gallery. There appears to be a stack of inside cylinder connecting rod large ends in the middle distance, with one set up in the lathe to the right. Floor boards seem to have been removed from the gallery roof further down the bay! Probably to lower equipment or components to the shop floor. The large openings to the left were once where goods wagons came into and out of the shop from the traverser. Now, those archways lead into the Danube Machine Shop. *National Archives*

Looking through the many columns that hold up the gallery and the weight of equipment on it, the scene shows the large amount of machine tools in the shop surrounded by fitters' benches and masses of locomotive parts scattered around the shop, a very cramped area indeed. *National Archives*

A view from the west side gallery floor looking north, rows of belt driven small machine tools and stacked up work benches. *National Archives*

West side gallery, looking south. Through the archway at the south end was the original saddlery room. This section of the building was altered differently and the complete upper floor was removed leaving a large work shop which became the Machine Phop millwrights' department dedicated to repairs and maintenance to the shops machine tools. *National Archives*

A view from almost the same position as the photograph above' although probably taken at a different date. It is very doubtful that the Health and Safety Executive in force nowadays would accept the use of the large open grinding machine that is in the photograph or the unguarded machine tool drive belts. *National Archives*

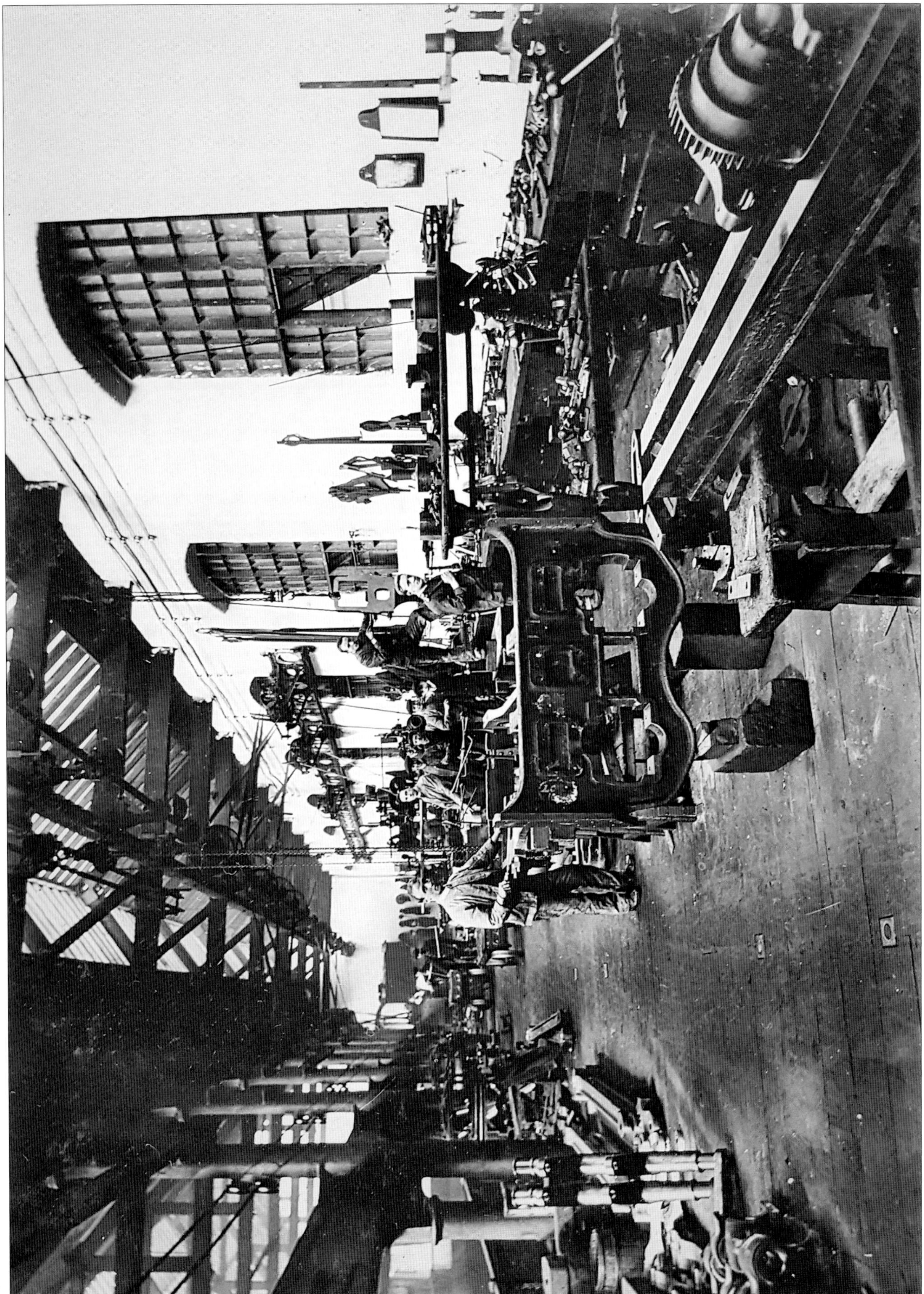

Looking north on the west side of the gallery. Connecting rods and an inside motion bracket dominate the front of the photograph on this section of the gallery floor. *National Archives*

The Danube Machine Shop, looking south. Again the original buildings features can be identified. The two arches on the left-hand side of the photograph were the entrances to the building described as the 'Paint and Stock Holding Shop, these being accessed via the traverser of the day. This later to became offices and later still the machine shop gauge room. The gable end wall was built when the shop became enclosed. Beyond the windows was the GCR main line. To the right but just out of view was the entrances to the carriage and wagon shops, all fed by the traverser, now the main machine shop. At this time the photo shows what appears to be trestles presumably for laying out steel plating for what will be no doubt become locomotive bogie frames. The row of stands to the left of the trestles probably for standing the plating in a vertical position, the bogie frame far left in front of the left hand window in the photograph bears witness to this. Immediately behind the photographer was a railway line that was used to convey boilers on a truck (old tender base) to and from the boiler shop on the left of the Danube to the erecting shop on the other side of the main machine shop. In later days, the Danube had some of the largest machine tools installed. *National Archives*

The Danube. The cameraman now swings his camera 180 degrees to the previous image to be looking north. This view of the Danube gives a better perspective of how the traverser was utilised before being transformed into a machine shop. The traverser table was 20 feet long with eight feet either side. In the 1850s, the traverser fed carriages and wagons through the arches on the left and the erecting shop and paint shop on the right. This shop in GCR days, apart from its name 'Danube' was known as the cylinder shop. Immediately to the front of the image appears to be a cylinder block with other cylinder and piston parts in view, The machinist on the right appears to be dealing with pistons or piston valve rings. A few sand boxes are in the photograph to add into the mix. In later days large planing machines were installed in the Danube in addition to of the larger types of milling machines. *National Archives*

GCR era machine tools – Gorton

John Robinson inherited at Gorton a locomotive works that was well equipped with some modern machine tools of the day. The following is just a very small selection of the different types of tools in use to give the reader an idea of the tooling that was in use and was probably used throughout the heavy engineering industry in general, though obviously some were quite specialised for the railway industry. Apologies for the relatively poor quality of the images. Most of the machine tools were belt driven at that time at Gorton, as was the norm everywhere. Electric power was slowly starting to take precedence over belt drives at Gorton but it would quite a number of years before belt driven machines would become a thing of the past. In fact the Machine Shop at Gorton still had a small number of belt driven machine tools in use at the time the works shut down. Where practicable belt driven machinery was converted to electrical power. As its name implies, the machine shops were the obvious place where the machine tools were employed, especially the large machines. Another place where large tools were to be found was in the wheel shop and also at the carriage and wagon workshops.

An automatic turret lathe powered by an electric motor. Manufactured by Craven Brothers of Manchester. The lathe was used for general bar work of all types including square and hexagonal section in addition to round bars. The smaller machines of this size would have been placed in the machine shop gallery.

High speed planing machine. Manufactured by Craven Brothers of Manchester. The machine seen here was machining six locomotive axle boxes in one simultaneous operation.

all images on this page Railway Gazette *1919*

Another turret lathe by the same manufacturer. This type of machine would have been in abundance throughout the works.

Craven high speed screw cutting machine with Craven patent headstock.

Left: Manufactured by Kendall & Gent, Manchester, this high speed radial arm drilling, studding and tapping machine had two spindles as against the normal single one. The second spindle was for tapping out holes and automatically stopped when it reached the desired depth. The tap was withdrawn at a much greater speed to extract the tap.

Below: Manufactured by William Muir & Co., Manchester, this of hole punching and slotting machine. This particular machine has a working stroke of eight inches. The ma-chine was driven via an electric motor.

both images Railway Gazette *1919*

A high speed planing machine manufactured by Alfred Herbert Ltd of Coventry. It was equipped with two tool posts and gave a rough cut on the forward stroke and a finishing cut on the return. Since installation the machine was recorded as giving excellent service.

Railway Gazette *1919*

Double-headed drilling and boring machine which was friction driven with four spindles and manufactured by J. Holroyd & Co., Milnrow, Rochdale. It was still in use until Gorton closed down, its primary function in latter years was for boring both ends of connecting rods simultaneously.

Horizontal milling machine manufactured by Craven Brothers of Manchester. This large machine had a working area of 10ft long by 4ft 6ins wide on its bed and was capable of a working height of 4ft 6ins. *both* Railway Gazette *1919*

The Danube, again looking north showing the original arches that the traverser would have fed carriages and wagons into to their designated bays. To the right at the far end of the photo but not visible was the original erecting shop. A locomotive bogie appears to be under construction in the foreground, more or less fully fabricated. The square-topped door opening on the left was an opening into the original carriage and wagon shops, this and another entrance just out of view lead into the saddlery section of the carriage and wagon shop. In BR days this led into the machine shop millwrights and maintenance electricians' shop and to the machine shop supervisor's office. *E.M. Johnson collection*

The GCR Erecting Shop, built in 1890. This is No. 1 bay looking east with a mixture of Robinson GCR locomotives receiving attention. Photographed from the frame of a Class '8A' 0-8-0 'Tiny' (precursor to the '8K' Class 2-8-0) the cameraman has captured a pure GCR scene for generations to admire. The locomotive on centre stage is one of Robinson's celebrated 'Jersey Lily' 4-4-2 Atlantic engines Class '8B' No. 1088 turned out from the North British Locomotive Company in October 1905. The wheels to the left of the 0-8-0 frame are quite probably from that locomotive.

E.M. Johnson collection

No. 6 road in No. 2 Bay is the scene for the construction of GCR Class '9P' 4-6-0 No. 1164 *Earl Beatty*. Turned out into traffic in June 1920. The locomotive is the second of the class following No. 1169 *Lord Faringdon* which was built three years earlier.

E.M. Johnson collection

No. 1 Bay. No. 1 road. A Class '9Q' 4-6-0 under construction. The locomotive is surrounded by what is most likely to be the frames from other 4-6-0 types, perhaps other '9Q's under construction? *E.M. Johnson collection*

Again, No. 1 Bay, looking west. The photograph is taken from the 'stage' (note the stair handrails leading down onto the erecting shop floor). A boiler slung in the air, more than likely delivered from the boiler shop and on its way to be mounted on its frame somewhere within the shops. Note the size of chains used during that period, no wire slings in sight.
National Railway Museum

Erecting Shop, No. 1 bay. An unidentified '8K' 2-8-0 (L&NER 'O4') about to be lowered onto its wheels. Note the size of the chains involved with the slinging of the locomotive. Further down the bay is a tender and a boiler on the cross rails is being transported between the bays, either it is on the way to the boiler shop or has been returned. An inverted cab lays on a truck along with a sheet of firebox cladding on No. 1 road. Are these to go the engine that is under construction on No. 3 road? Note the safety valves on the locomotive on No. 3 road. *Courtesy: S. Mills*

The same locomotive with wheels and coupling rods now fitted. Very little has changed around the engine. The boiler cladding and cab are still in the same place on the bogie, the boiler halfway down the shop is still positioned between the bays. The crane drivers jacket is still hanging on the cranes cross bridge hand rail. The crane in the next bay has not moved. All in all it appears that the photographer has left his camera on its tripod between shoots knowing that the fitting of coupling rods and wheels were going to be assembled in a very quick operation and thus have a before and after photograph. *Courtesy. S. Mills*

One could be forgiven for thinking this is the Boiler Shop, it is, however, a bay in the Erecting Shop. A large selection of boilers receiving attention, note the riveters' furnace at the side of the boiler on the right. On the left are two round-topped firebox boilers, pre-Robinson designs. Why there is such a large array of boilers in the shop is not known. Perhaps the boiler shops were inundated with boilers at that period in time, or there was some form of workshops reorganisation. Surprisingly, the boilers are facing different directions. It was usually Gorton's practice to have all their locomotives face eastwards (towards the machine shop at the end of the bays). Notice the gentleman peeking through the firebox door on the boiler to the left. Where fitted, all the boilers are carrying Robinson pattern chimneys. *National Archives*

A bay full of locomotives in the erecting shop. Not a soul to be seen, perhaps it is lunch time or a weekend. What looks like a Class '1A' tank of MS&LR origin stands on the centre road minus its cab while the frames and coal bunker of another tank locomotive stands alongside. Further down the bay, a row of GCR types are standing waiting for the erecting shop personnel to return to work and continue their work on them. *E.M. Johnson collection*

John G. Robinson's last tank locomotive design. GCR Class '9N', 4-6-2T (L&NER Class 'A5'). They were designed to haul suburban passenger services out of Marylebone station, a duty they performed admirably for over thirty years. Initially fitted with Schmidt Superheaters these were replaced over time with Robinson's own superheater. The locomotives were built over a number of years in batches as required, the last being built in L&NER days. The L&NER also had some built but by outside contractors, these to work in the North Eastern area. The locomotives ran well into Nationalisation (British Railways). *Courtesy S. Mills*

Left: Fitting a smokebox seal in the erecting shop. Note the left hand steam pipe, the superheater, superheater elements and the chimney petty coat inside the smokebox. On entering the shops for attention the work in the smokebox must have been one of the dirtiest and dustiest tasks that had to be undertaken. Working underneath locomotives was hardly much cleaner. *National Archives*

Below: A new build, 'Jersey Lily' 4-4-2 Atlantic is slung in the air during construction. Lifting is courtesy of two Craven Brothers 40-ton cranes. In the bottom right-hand corner of the photograph an erecting shop workman takes a glance at the cameraman who has his camera perched on the stage at the east end of the shop.
E.M. Johnson collection

Erecting Shop. A very young man heating up rivets in an open hearth. *National Archives*

Coppersmiths' Shop. The smiths in the far centre probably forming inner firebox plating. Note their large soft hammers for 'working' the copper plating. An old locomotive boiler serves as a steam supply for the shop. *National Archives*

Machine Shop. A machinist using a vertical boring mill to machine the outside of a locomotive piston valve liner, here checking the diameter of his work with the use of outside callipers. *National Archives*

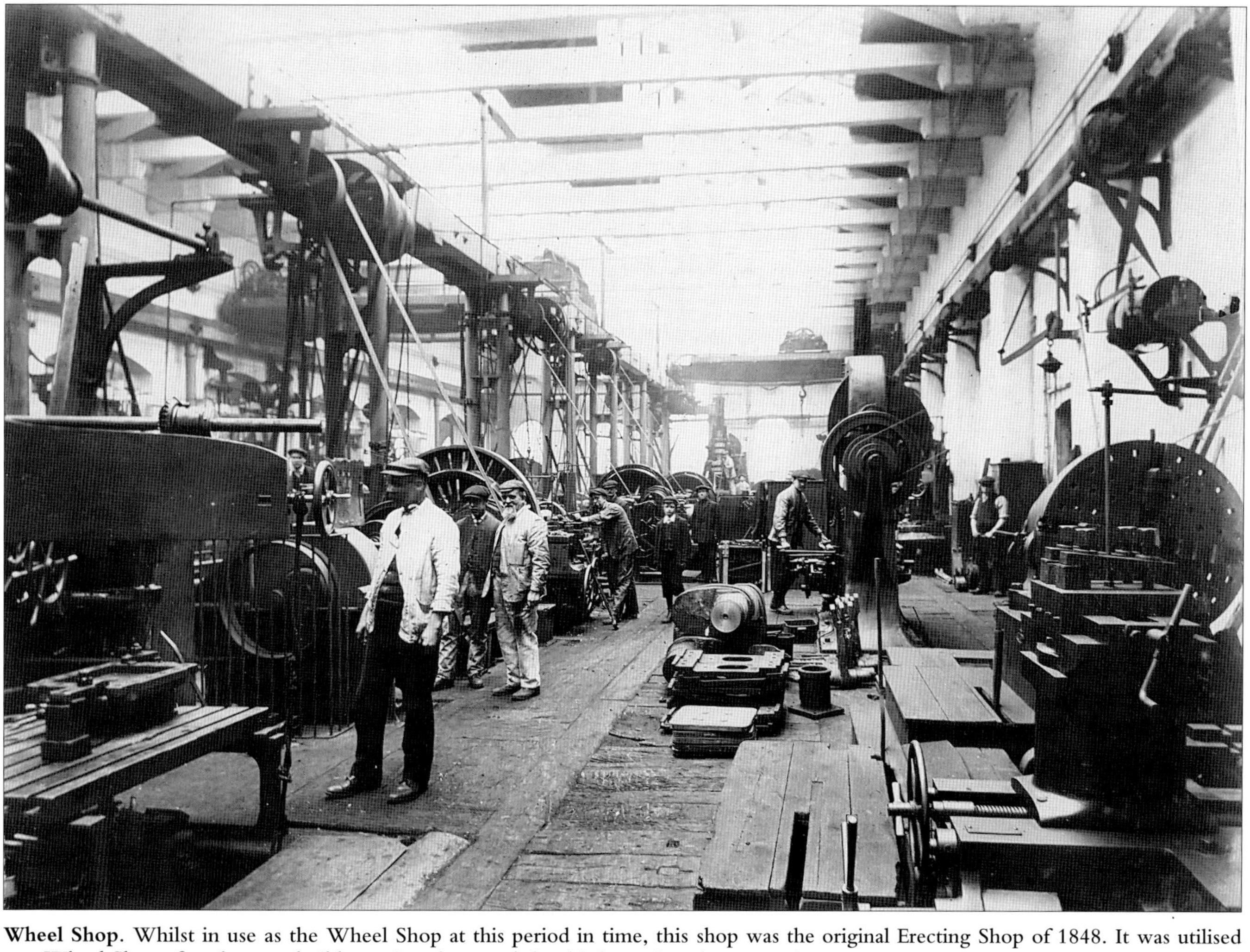

Wheel Shop. Whilst in use as the Wheel Shop at this period in time, this shop was the original Erecting Shop of 1848. It was utilised as a Wheel Shop after the new build erecting shop, and the third erecting shop came into use. *National Archives*

Machinist operating a screw cutting machine.
National Archives

Riveting stays in a locomotive firebox. Note no eye or ear protection – the noise would have been unbearable. *National Archives*

All work has stopped whilst this splendid scene is captured for future generations to admire. From No. 2 Bay at the crossover rails in the erecting shop, the camera has captured a rare view looking across to No. 5 Bay and the Wheel Shop beyond. On section seven is a GCR Class '9J' 0-6-0 No. 978, built by Neilson, Reid & Co. in September 1901 at a cost of £3,445. On section twelve in Bay 3 is what appears to be a Class '9L' or '9K' 4-4-2T. On the cross road near to No. 4 Bay is a boiler on its truck (usually converted tender bases). Note the narrow gauge tracks in the 'four foot' of the rails. The youth in front of the '9J' barely looks fourteen years old, the young man leaning on the belt driven drilling machine looks similar age. Note also the gent standing on the overhead crane rails leaning on the crane trying to get in on the act. Is that a vertical boiler far left in No. 5 Bay? Perhaps off a breakdown crane?

National Archives

Gorton's train crews barracks

Converted from the then closed girls' and infants' schools on the canal depot site, the barracks must have been a welcome facility made available for the crews, who up until then would have been accommodated in lodgings nominated by the GCR. The barracks faced onto Cornwall Street immediately opposite the works main offices. The main entrance to the barracks was on Ogden Lane. Later in BR days after the barracks became disused, the building was used for storage. The area through the main entrance became the car park for the BRSA social club. The disused boys' school was later converted into the works canteen. The barracks facilities included a dining room/mess sitting room, a live-in matron, gardens and benches, shower and bath facilities. All no doubt giving the crews as much relaxation as possible and, with the hope of keeping some of the more thirsty away from the numerous public houses that appeared to be on every street corner of the rows of terraced houses in Openshaw and Gorton, and along Ashton Old Road in particular. The BRSA club joined onto the barracks and comprised of the old GCR/L&NER reading rooms and library, see page 192.

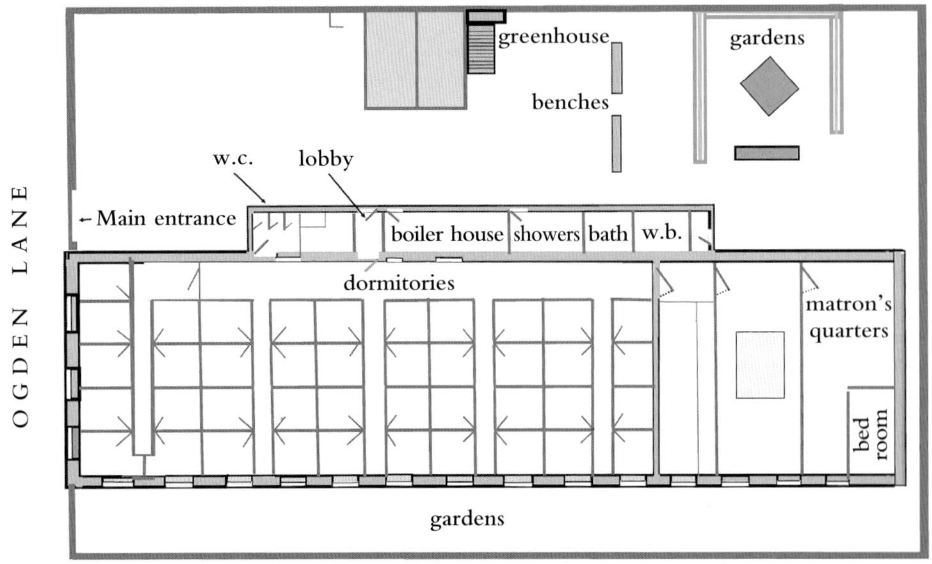

Hostilities 1914-1918 Gorton's war effort

During World War One, Gorton, like all large engineering facilities became involved with the war effort in supplying armaments. Whilst Dukinfield Carriage & Wagon Works constructed ambulance/hospital coaches, Gorton concentrated on armaments. In this photograph, taken in No. 1 Bay of the Erecting Shop, is a completed 8-inch howitzer, whilst around it are other gun carriages for more howitzers under construction. In the background are a mixture of GCR locomotives including a Robinson Class '1B' 2-6-4 Tank engine probably a new build and a '9J' 0-6-0 in the next bay. Further down that bay is what appears to be an ex MS&LR locomotive. *National Archives*

The Wheel Shop was used for the machining of gun turning racks for gun mountings. Notice the weights and chains controlling the cutter. Locomotive tyres are also amongst the mix in the photograph. *National Archives*

In The Danube 14-inch solid shells were being machined, with what looks like wheels in the middle distance for the 8-inch howitzer guns that were being built in the Erecting Shop. The view is looking south. The wall on the right-hand side being the original carriage and wagon shops with the arches that the rolling stock went through via the now filled in traverser, but now these arches lead into the main Machine Shop. Immediately to the left at the side of the cameraman were arches that led into the old erecting shop, this shop later became the Wheel Shop until the later wheel shop was built in 1905, then it became fitting shops and toolrooms. *National Archives*

Robinson Superheater

John G. Robinson's innovative mind apart from being a great locomotive engineer gave him the gift to being an inventor of several innovations that not only benefitted the railway industry but also into the marine and stationary boiler engineering world. The superheating of steam locomotive boilers, though not entirely new at the time of Robinson's appointment with the GCR, was not fully implemented and was still in its infancy. Superheating was becoming recognised as the means of making locomotives more efficient when it came to fuel economy. The cost of superheating a locomotive and its maintenance was relatively high as compared to a 'saturated' locomotive but the economies gained far outweighed the initial conversion or build and running costs. One drawback with superheaters at the time was the necessity of having to carry out repairs to the superheater elements should one or several develop a problem, in that the superheater elements had to be removed from the header to effect a repair. Robinson's patented superheater header eliminated this problem by giving each individual element easy access for removal and thus avoid a long process of having to remove several elements to just access one, thus maybe causing the disturbed elements to give problems themselves. Robinson's superheater header had their tubes expanded into the header instead of being clamped into place. Removable covers on the header gave easy access for the elements to be expanded into position and gave a 100% press tight seal. Robinson patented his superheater header and formed his own company, The Locomotive Superheater Corporation, Ltd. From there, the superheater gained widespread success in its application. It was adopted as the GCR standard and overtook the 'Schmidt' type superheater that was generally in use in its preference for use by other railway companies, not just by the GCR and later L&NER but by other railway companies both within Britain's Railways but also worldwide. The marine engineering world followed suit and also adopted the Robinson form of superheater and it was also used in stationary boiler applications.

Robinson's patented superheater on display inside a GCR boiler smokebox at the Latin-British Exhibition held at Shepherds Bush, London in 1912. On each side of the boiler are sectioned superheater headers showing the means of construction and ease of how tubes can be removed and replaced. A brilliant piece of advertising showing an equally brilliant piece of engineering machinery.

E.M. Johnson collection

Opposite: Close-ups of the sections of Robinson's superheater heaters as seen above. *E.M. Johnson collection*

THE "ROBINSON" SUPERHEATER.
ANY SUPERHEATER PIPE CAN BE REMOVED WITHOUT REMOVAL OF ANY OTHER.

IMMINGHAM
THE ROBINSON SUPERHEATER.
WITH REMOVABLE FRONT COVER AND DRAUGHT RETARDER.

With what looks like a job that could have been be carried out in the Erecting Shop a lot more easily, one of Robinson's early 4-6-0 locomotives is undergoing what looks like several items of repairs going on at the same time. All the axles have been removed and it is packed up on small trucks under the cab and at the front. The pistons may have been removed, cladding and insulation has been taken off the firebox and the dome outer cover removed. Perhaps it has failed in traffic after being turned out of the works and some of the Erecting Shop crew have been sent down to 'fix' it. All in all a lot of work for the shed crew to tackle in the sheds.

E.M. Johnson collection

Opposite: **The Paint Shop**. Positioned in what can only be described as one of the most inhospitable places in the whole of the locomotive works for painting, the shop was situated directly next door to the running sheds, where all the soot, ash and dust from the sheds would have been no doubt air borne for periods of time making the painting of locomotives a difficult process. However, looking at the paint finish on the graceful Robinson locomotives it is a tribute to the paint shop staff for them to turn out those magnificent machines in all their glory. On leaving this shop and after trial running - in turns the locomotives would show off their beautiful lined our GCR green and claret colours along with their 'Forward' crests over the wheel splashers and on the tenders for all to admire. The Paint Shop was a four road shop in GCR days. Heated throughout to keep the shop warm and eliminate moisture, it would no doubt be one of the better places to work in the works complex during winter time. The paint shop was later converted to just two roads, giving up the space for conversion to a canteen to cater for the running shed and carriage and wagon personnel. *National Archives*

Great Central Locomotive Review

The following is quite a comprehensive review though not every class (space prohibits this) or rebuild is illustrated. It does though indicate the amount of significant progress made in locomotive design during the GCR reign under John Robinson at Gorton.

The Pollitt Class 'X4' 4-2-2 Singles, with a driving wheel 7ft 9in. in diameter, a cylinder diameter 19½in. x 26in. stroke, and a 200psi boiler pressure, were being built at Gorton at the time of John Robinson's take over as the 'Chief'. A class of ten were on order but Robinson realised, as did his counterparts on other railways that coupled-wheeled machines were now needed to haul heavier and faster trains – the days of the 'Singles' had come to an end – and he reduced the order to six locomotives. Here Class 'X4' (GCR Class '13') No. 967, which was built at Gorton in January 1900, is seen at Manchester Central Station behind the 'B' signal cabin. This was the first of the 'Single' express passenger locomotives, primarily built for the London Extension although they had a relatively short time on the London expresses and were transferred to the Cheshire Line Committee (CLC) section of the system. Weight in working order 92tons 17cwt. Tractive effort at 85% boiler pressure 14,457lbs. *MLS collection*

Robinson rebuilt No. 969 with a five feet diameter boiler in 1911 as a trial, still at 160psi but it was reverted back to four feet three inches in 1915 after showing no marked improvement in performance. Note the boiler mounting differences from the photograph above and Robinson's style of cab and chimney. Manchester Central station. *MLS collection*

Sacré designed Class '12AT' 2-4-0 No.450B was built for the MS&LR in March 1881 at Gorton. Seen here in the GCR era, the 'B' after the number denotes it is on the duplicate numbering list. The locomotive was 'Motor Fitted' in April 1911 and reclassified 12AM. Coupled wheels 5ft. 0in. Cylinders diameter 16in. x 24in. stroke.

E.M. Johnson collection

Now in GCR days is Sacré 'Single' Class '14' No. 108. Originally No. 503 and renumbered in later MS&LR days. The locomotive was scrapped in January 1905. Trafford Park. *MLS collection*

Standing outside the erecting shop, No. 5 Bay, on a sunny day is Class '5' 0-6-0ST No. 890. '*Boiler in No. 5 Bay 10/7/23*' is daubed with chalk on the coal bunker and '*wanted*' on the chimney, No. 890 was one of the first locomotives to be built for the new GCR in July 1897. Quite possibly the locomotive is entering the shop for a new boiler! In front of No. 890 is Robinson GCR Class '8' 4-6-0 No. 1071 built by Neilson's in 1902.

E.M. Johnson collection

Above: Sacré Class '6A1' 0-6-0 No. 552 looking a little grimy in GCR days. The third built in November 1887 out of a class of eleven locomotives. Coupled wheels 5ft 3in. Cylinders diameter 18in x 26in. stroke. *MLS collection*

Right: MS&LR No. 20 rebuilt as Class '1A' (1892) from a well tank to a side tank and displaying its new GCR identity. *MLS collection*

Sacré designed Class '6B' 4-4-0 No. 426. Built at Gorton in July 1877. Captured here In GCR days. Coupled wheels 6ft 3in. Cylinders diameter 17in. x 26in. stroke. *MLS collection*

Above and below: Pollitt Class '5' 0-6-0ST No. 889. A class of twelve locomotives all built between January and December 1897 for dock shunting work. No. 885 was the last engine built for the MS&LR and No. 886 the first to be turned out for the GCR. No. 889 was converted to a crane tank in 1905 and became an 0-6-2 where, it assumed the name *Little Dick*. The crane was removed in 1919. The engine is parked behind a Robinson Class '1B' 2-6-4 No. 272 on Gorton running shed. *MLS collection*

Sacré single framed Class '18' 0-6-0 No. 309B turned out from Gorton in February 1873 stands outside Gorton's erecting shop in GCR days. The letter 'B' with its number denotes that it is on the GCR duplicate numbering list sharing the with a Class 9J locomotive which puts the year after 1907. Coupled wheels 5ft. 3in. Cylinders diameter 17in. x 24in. stroke. *MLS*

Another MS&LR rebuild, Class '18', now Class '18A' ('18ACon') No. 52. Completely transformed from its more elegant tender version the engine was rebuilt in 1902 retaining its same driving wheel and cylinder sizes. *MLS collection*

Sacré Class '6B' 0-6-0 No. 466 built at Gorton in November 1881. Now in the GCR period. Coupled wheels 4ft 9in. Cylinders diameter 17½in. x 26in. stroke.
MLS collection

Sacré Class '6A' 0-6-0 No. 394, built in November 1876 at Gorton and pictured in GCR days. A small number were built at Sheffield with parts supplied from Gorton. *MLS collection*

Visually giving away its North American origins, Baldwin Class '17' 2-6-0 No. 956. A class of locomotive purchased from The Baldwin Locomotive Works. The engines were a stop gap to cater for a shortage of motive power on the GCR as UK manufacturers were unable to cope at the time with production demand. The locomotives had a short life, after a good start their condition deteriorated rapidly through failures to their bar frames. A total of twenty engines were delivered in 1900. Coupled wheels 5ft. 0in. Cylinders diameter 18in. x 24in stroke.
MLS collection

Great Central Locomotive Classes designed by John G. Robinson

Very shortly after the GCR was formed John G. Robinson came to the GCR and remained with the company until the end of its existence. It is therefore obvious that the greater percentage of locomotives built by the GCR were designed by him. Some were built at Gorton Tank and others by outside contractors to the great man's design. The following is a list of Robinson classes. This is just a general review. All classes of locomotives had variations, updates and modifications over the years and some converted for experimental use over the years and due to space may not be included in this review.

1901 Class '9J' (L&NER Class 'J11')

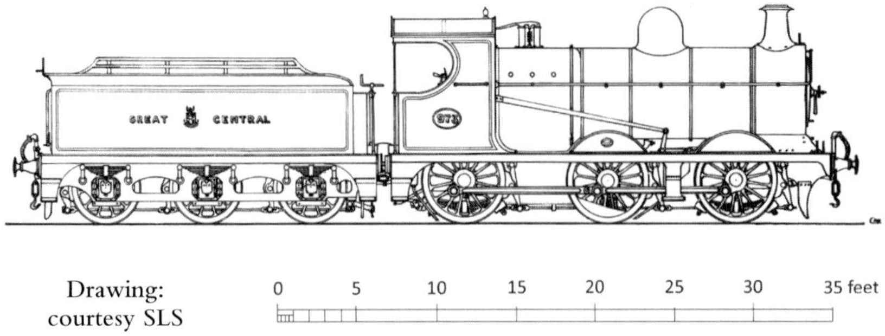

Drawing: courtesy SLS

Boiler pressure: 180psi
Coupled wheels: 5ft 1in.
Cylinders: diameter 18½in. x 26in. stroke
Weight: Engine 52 tons. Tender 44 tons 3cwt
Wheel arrangement: 0-6-0
Tractive effort: 21,959 lbs

Note: The '9J' 'Pom Pom' was regarded as the most successful 0-6-0 goods locomotive ever built for any railway in Great Britain. The whole locomotive class remained in service with modifications well into the BR era, a few survivors being sixty years old. Often used on passenger trains and sometimes pressed into express workings, they were certainly a very useful and versatile class of locomotive.

John G. Robinson's first design of locomotive for the Great Central Railway was his 'Pom Pom' (a development of Pollitt '9H' Class) in 1901. Robinson's Class '9J' (later L&NER 'J11') 0-6-0 No. 293 was built in 1907 at Gorton at a cost of £2,900.00. The locomotive depicted here is still in 'saturated' form as it was not superheated until well into L&NER days. *Mike Morant collection*

1901 Class '11B' (L&NER Class 'D9')

Boiler pressure: 180psi
Cylinders: dia. 18½in. x 26in. stroke
Wheel arrangement: 4-4-0
Coupled wheels: 6ft 9in.
Weight: Engine 55 tons 14cwt
Tender 44 tons 3cwt
Tractive effort: 17,385 lbs

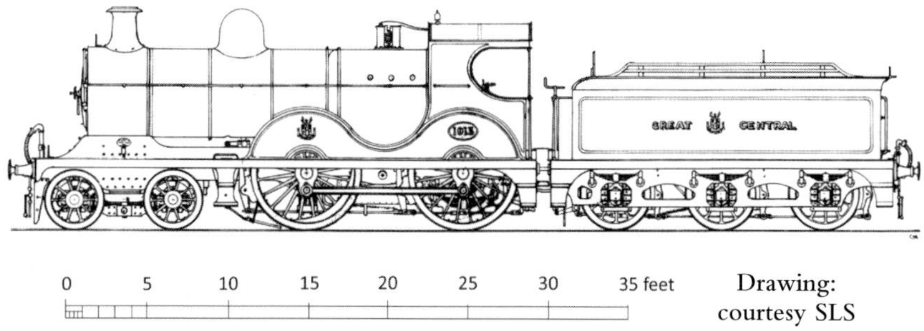

Drawing: courtesy SLS

Robinson Class '11B' 4-4-0 No. 1021 *Queen Mary*. Built by Sharp Stewart in February 1902 at a cost of £3,600. The locomotive's classic lines are followed on from the Pollitt/Parker era. *NRM*

1902 Class '8A' (L&NER Class 'Q4')

Boiler pressure: 180psi
Cylinders: dia. 19in. x 26in. stroke
Wheel arrangement: 0-8-0
Coupled wheels: 4ft 7in.
Weight: Engine 63 tons
Tender 44 tons 3cwt
Tractive effort: 26,441 lbs

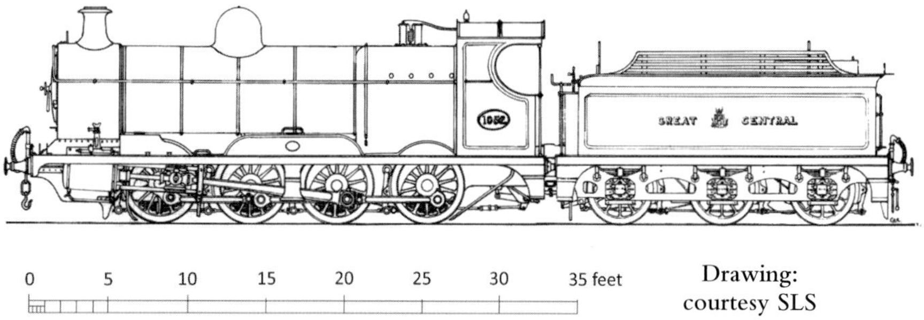

Drawing: courtesy SLS

Robinson GCR Class '8A' 0-8-0, ('TINIES') Number 86 was built by Kitsons of Leeds, Yorkshire in 1903. As is the norm for a mineral hauling locomotive, it was in a grimy condition when photographed at Guide Bridge. The class could be described as the precursor of the more famous '8K' Class. *E.M. Johnson*

1902, Class '8' (L&NER Class 'B5')

Boiler pressure: 180psi
Cylinders: dia. 19in. x 26in. stroke
Wheel arrangement: 4-6-0
Coupled wheels: 6ft
Weight: Engine 63 tons
Tender 48 tons 6cwt
Tractive effort: 19,672 lbs

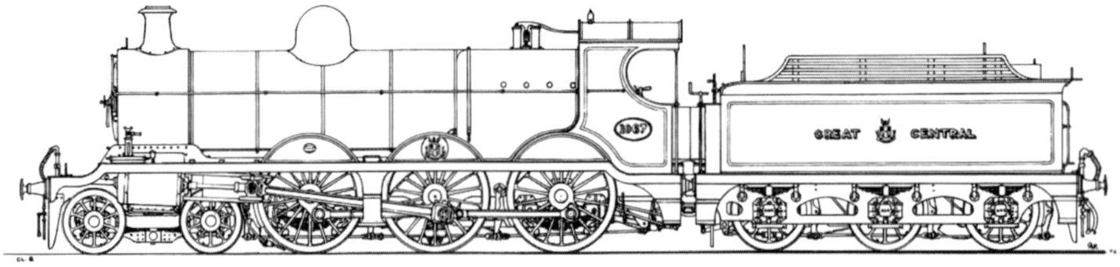

0 5 10 15 20 25 30 35 feet

Drawing: courtesy SLS

Robinson Class '8' 4-6-0 mixed traffic locomotive number 186, built by Beyer, Peacock in 1904. Photographed at Neasden Shed with a full tender of coal, it has been turned out in immaculate condition. Known as the 'Fish Engines' they were designed for express goods and passenger workings in addition to regularly working the fast fish trains from Grimsby to London Marylebone (as their nicknamed implied). *E. M. Johnson collection*

1903, Class '8B' (L&NER Class 'C4') 1906, Class 8D & E (L&NER Class 'C5')

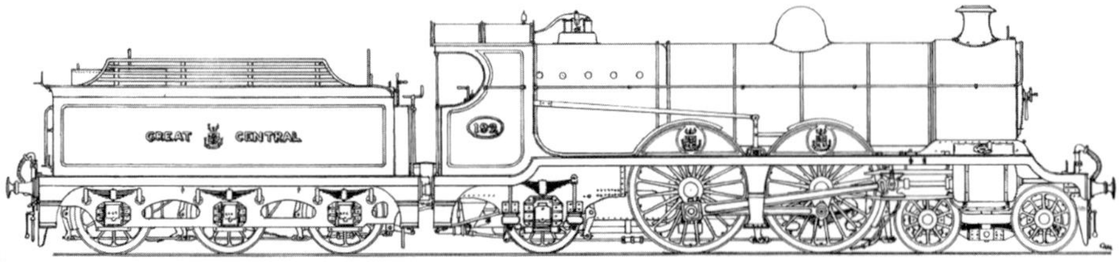

The Robinson 4-4-2 'Atlantic' type locomotives was split into two separate classes, Both were built on the same basic principal design. As the classes were designed that way and not a modification of the other, it is necessary therefore to give a thumbnail outline of each type without going into too much detail as this is not the intention of this book. The above drawing is from the first Atlantic No 192 built by Beyer, Peacock.

Simple example: 1903 Class '8B'
Boiler pressure 180 psi
Cylinders: diameter 19in. x 26in. stroke
Wheel arrangement: 4-4-2
Coupled wheel diameter: 6ft 9in
Weight: Engine 71 tons 18cwt. Tender 48 tons 6cwt

Compound example: 1906 Class '8D' & 'E'
Boiler pressure 180 psi.
Inside HP Cylinder diameter (1) 19in. x 26in. stroke
Wheel arrangement 4-4-2
Outside LP Cylinder diameter (2) 21in. x 26 in. stroke (HP: 66.67 % LP: 25%)
Coupled wheel diameter 6ft. 9in.
Weight: Engine 73 tons 6cwt. Tender weight 48 tons 6cwt.

Note: one of the simple two-cylinder locomotives was rebuilt as a three-cylinder simple for comparative tests against its compound counterparts and was fitted with Walschaerts valve gear to all cylinders with divided drive. The following photographs will show the detail differences of this locomotive. The locomotive concerned was built by the North British Locomotive Company locomotive in 1905, the conversion was carried out in 1908 and became Class '8J'. The locomotive was converted back to its original two cylinders in 1922 with Stephenson valve gear to bring it in line with the other simples.

A graceful Robinson Atlantic, 4-4-2 Class '8B' No. 1092 built in November 1905. The Atlantics soon received the nickname 'Jersey Lily', this no doubt as to the artistic and graceful outline of the machine as a reflection of Lily Langtry, the beautiful and famous Jersey-born actress of the day. 1092 is standing outside Manchester London Road station with St. Andrew's Church in Ancoats as a backdrop. Sadly both the locomotive and church are now long gone. *E.M. Johnson collection*

Class '8E' 'Jersey Lily' No. 259 *King Edward VII.* The three-cylinder compound stands at platform A at London Road station. No. 259 was built at Gorton in February 1906 and withdrawn in August 1947. With a full tender she will almost certainly be on a Marylebone express. *E.M. Johnson collection*

1903, Class '8C' (L&NER Class 'B1' later 'B18')

Boiler pressure: 180psi
Cylinders: dia. 19½in. x 26in. stroke
Wheel arrangement: 4-6-0
Coupled wheels: 6ft 9in.
Weight: Engine 67ton 15cwt
Tender 48ton 6cwt
Tractive effort: 17,729 lbs

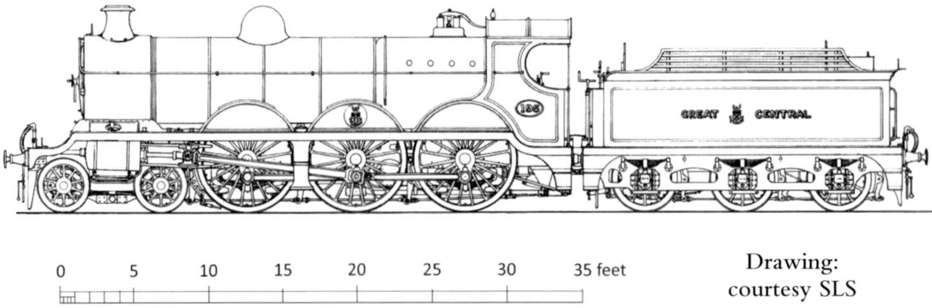

Drawing: courtesy SLS

Note: The '8C' Class was primarily built to give a comparison against the 'Jersey Lilies'. The preference at the time was to continue with the Atlantics. Only two of the class were built. Under the L&NER the class became 'B1', this was changed in 1943 to 'B18' so as to make way for Edward Thompson's new L&NER 4-6-0 class of locomotive which then became Class 'B1'.

Built in 1904 by Beyer, Peacock. No 196 was the second of the pair to be built. The first (No. 195) was built in the previous year. Both locomotives were withdrawn from service in 1947. No. 196 is seen alongside Gorton's old coaling stage. *E.M. Johnson collection*

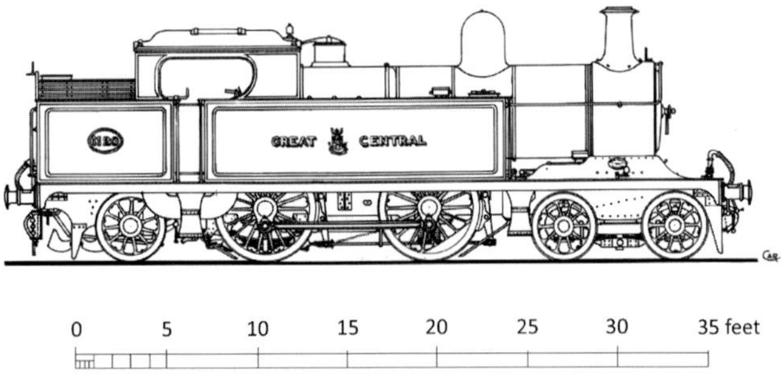

Drawing: courtesy SLS

1907, Class '9L' (L&NER Class 'C14')

Boiler pressure: 160psi
Cylinders: dia. 19½in. x 26in. stroke
Wheel arrangement: 4-4-2
Coupled wheels: 5ft 7in.
Weight: 70 tons 7cwt
Tractive effort: 17,100 lbs

4-4-2T Class '9L' No 1129 built by Beyer, Peacock in June 1907. Almost identical to the '9K' Class, a design going back to 1903. Note the jack mounted near the front of the running plate. This was used primarily for rerailing purposes. *National Railway Museum*

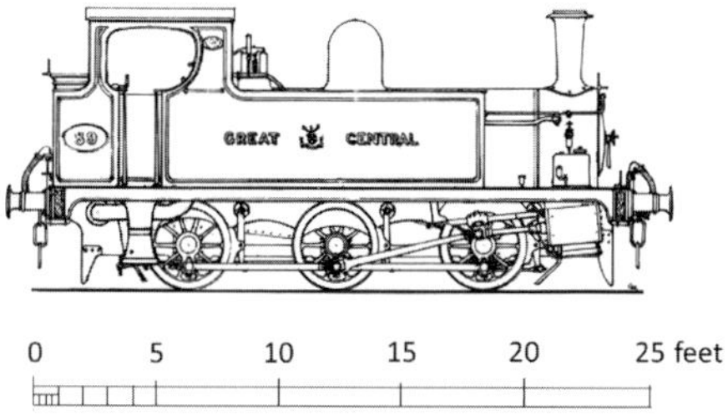

Drawing: courtesy SLS

1906, Class '5A' (L&NER Class 'J63')

Boiler pressure 150psi
Cylinders: dia. 13in. x 20in. stroke
Wheel arrangement 4-4-2
Coupled wheels 3ft 6in.
Weight: 37ton 9cwt
Tractive effort: 10,071 lbs

Class '5A' 0-6-0 No. 157, built in October 1906. The class was built for dockyard duties and were seen at various dockside locations including Immingham, Liverpool and Grimsby. A total of seven were built.
National Railway Museum

1906, Class '8F' (L&NER Class 'B4')

Boiler pressure: 180psi
Cylinders: dia. 19½in. x 26 in. stroke
Wheel arrangement: 4-6-0
Coupled wheels: 6ft 7in.
Weight: Tngine 70 tons 14cwt
Tender 48 tons 6cwt
Tractive effort 18,178 lbs

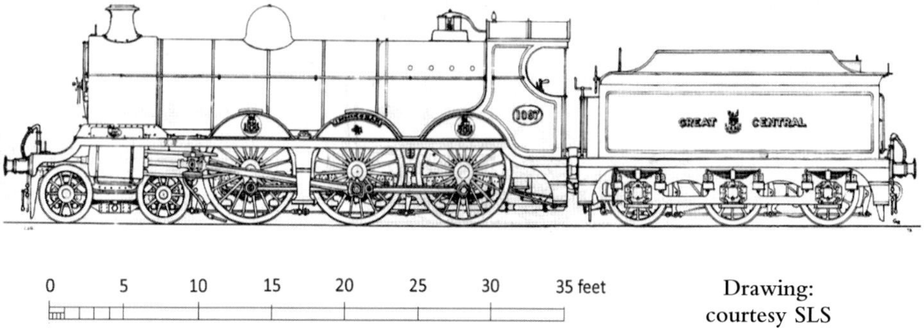

Drawing: courtesy SLS

Class '8F' 0-6-0 locomotive No. 1097, built by Beyer, Peacock in 1906. The class was built as a development of the '8C' Class, which also built to a Robinson design by Beyer, Peacock. *National Railway Museum*

1906, Class '8G'
(L&NER Class 'B9')

Boiler pressure 180psi
Cylinders: dia. 19.5in. x 26 in. stroke
Wheel arrangement: 4-6-0
Coupled wheels: 5ft 4in.
Weight: Engine 70 tons 14cwt
Tender 48 tons 6cwt
Tractive effort: 22,438 lbs

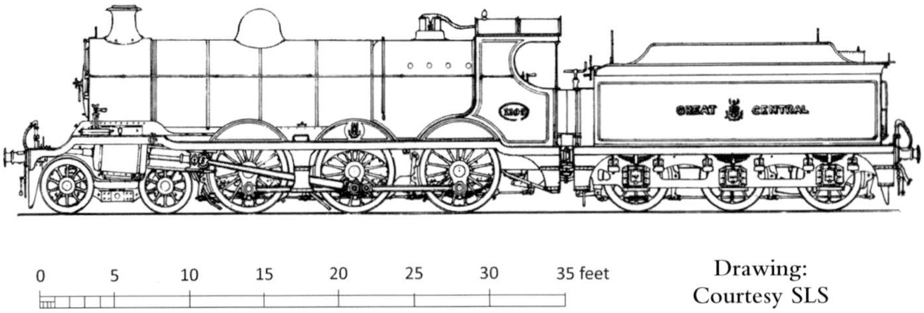

Drawing:
Courtesy SLS

Class '8G' 4-6-0 locomotive No. 1113, built by Beyer, Peacock in 1906 for mixed traffic purposes. A smaller wheeled version of the class 8F, there were ten engines built. *National Railway Museum*

1906, Class '8H'
(L&NER Class 'S1')

Boiler pressure: 200psi
Cylinders: dia. (3) 18in. x 26in. stroke
Wheel arrangement: 0-8-4
Coupled wheels: 4ft 8in.
Weight: Engine 99 tons
Tractive effort: 34,523 lbs

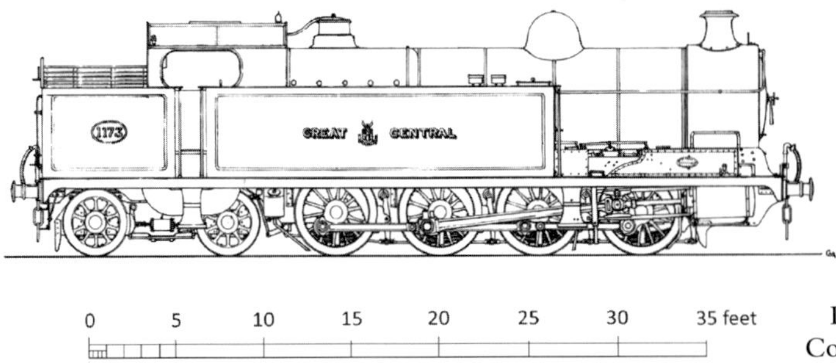

Drawing:
Courtesy SLS

Class '8H' No. 1171 0-8-4T Built by Beyer, Peacock in 1907. A very large tank engine design especially built for banking at the equally large Wath upon Dearne marshalling yard where marshalling was carried out on the 'Hump' system and the locomotives received the nick name 'Wath Daisies', a name that belied their huge bulk and high tractive effort. A class of four locomotives, two of the locomotives were built in 1907 and the other two in 1908. *National Railway Museum*

1911, Class '8K'
(L&NER Class 'O4')

Boiler pressure: 180psi
Cylinders: dia. 21in. x 26in. stroke
Wheel arrangement: 2-8-0
Coupled wheels: 4ft 8in.
Weight: Engine 66 tons 4cwt
Tender 48 tons 6cwt
Tractive effort: 31,325lbs

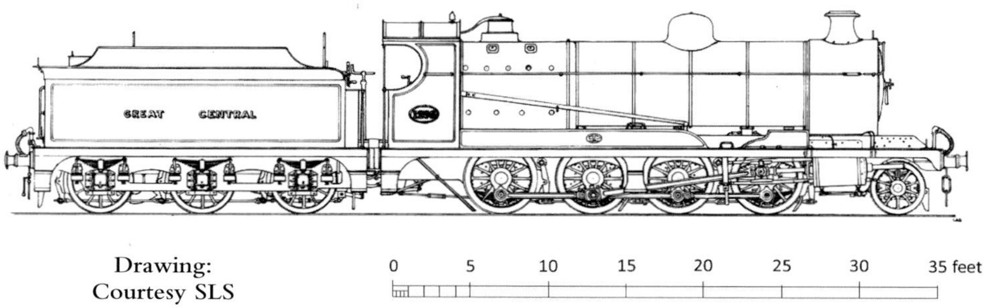

Drawing:
Courtesy SLS

Robinson Class '8K' 2-8-0 . Construction of these heavy freight/mineral locomotives started in 1911 and followed on into successive years ending as a huge class of engines totalling 666 including the (RODS). The example illustrated, No. 381, was built at Gorton in July 1913, but other members of the class were built by quite a number of builders. The locomotives, despite being freight engines, shared many of Robinson's artistic features. They were the most successful freight type of their day. It was a credit to them when engine men from other railway companies swore by them as against their own. In their early days they were used almost exclusively for hauling heavy coal trains over the Woodhead route into Lancashire as well as supplying coal to Immingham Docks for coal export. They were chosen as the preferred locomotives for the Railway Operating Department during the First World War and large numbers were sent overseas, especially to France, and a number never returned. Some travelled as far distant as Australia where there are still a number of survivors to this day. It is not the intention to detail these locomotives and their exploits here as it would take a book the size of an encyclopedia to describe them. Some of the class were modified extensively and others rebuilt, a number of un-rebuilt locomotives though lasted more or less as built into the early 1960s. Four locomotives of this class were used for experiments with alternative fuels, see following pages. One of the Gorton built locomotives has been preserved for all to admire, it is a Gorton built example, BR number 63601. *National Railway Museum*

1911, Class '9N' (L&NER Class 'A5')

Boiler pressure 180psi
Cylinder dia. 20in. x 26in. stroke
Wheel arrangement 4-6-0
Coupled wheels 5ft 7in.
Weight: Engine 85 tons 18cwt
Tractive effort: 23,743 lbs

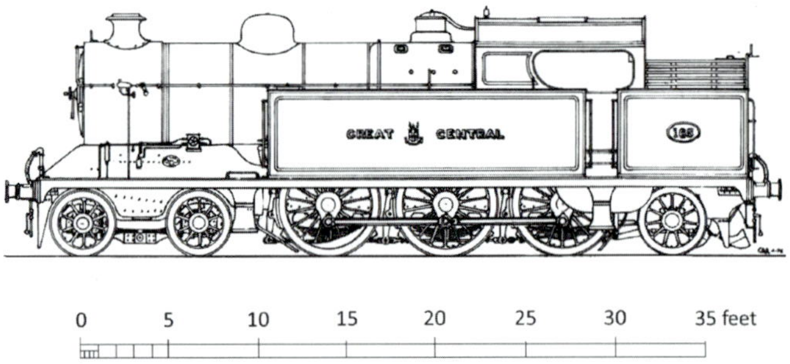

Drawing: Courtesy SLS

Class '9N' 4-6-2T No. 165, built in 1911, was the first of a class of 'Pacific' tanks which assumed the name 'Coronation' tanks as 1911 saw the Coronation of King George V and Queen Mary. Twenty-one were built between 1911 and 1917 in three batches at Gorton with a further batch built there in 1923 under the L&NER, followed by further locomotives built by Hawthorn, Leslie in 1925/6 giving a total of forty-four built. The class was built primarily for the heavy suburban passenger trains out of Marylebone, although the last batch were located in the north east.*National Railway Museum*

1912, Class '1' (L&NER Class 'B2', later 'B18'')

Boiler pressure: 180psi
Cylinders: dia. 21.5in. x 26in. stroke
Wheel arrangement: 4-6-0
Coupled wheels: 6ft 9in.
Weight: Engine 75 tons 4cwt
Tender 48 tons 6cwt
Tractive effort: 22,700 lbs

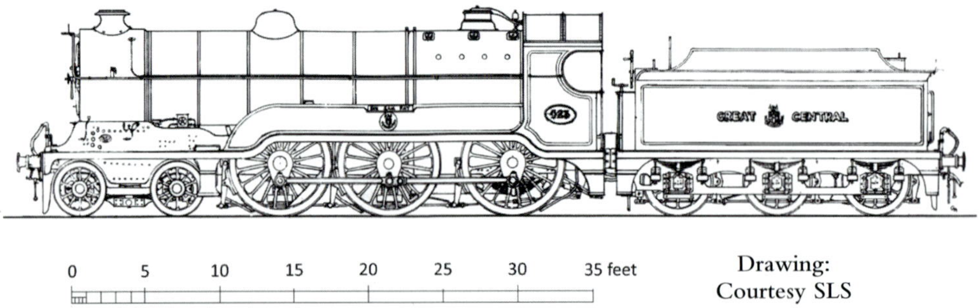

Drawing: Courtesy SLS

Class '1' (L&NER Class 'B2', reclassified 'B18' in August 1945). The first of this class of 4-6-0s was No. 423 *Sir Sam Fay*, built in December 1912 at Gorton a a cost of £3,364. History has recorded that the engines did not match their handsome lines when it came to performance and, as a result, were relegated to lesser duties when the 'D11' 4-4-0s entered service. Changes to boiler design were carried out with changes to boiler flue tubes and superheater tubes. The locomotives though regardless of reports of being of being less efficient than their later L&NER counterparts, soldiered on for slightly over 30 years, the last being withdrawn in November 1947. *E.M. Johnson collection*

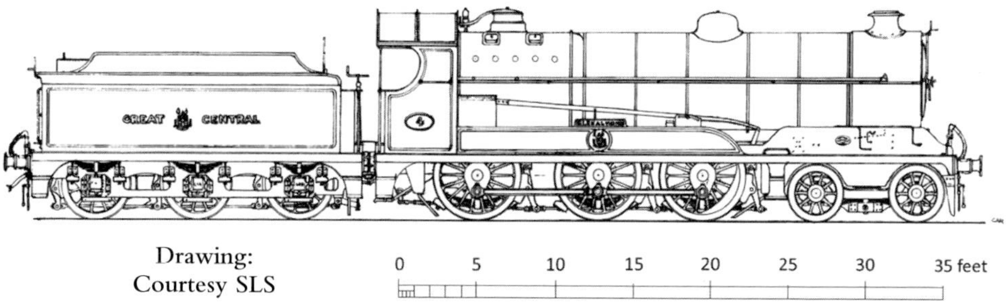

Drawing:
Courtesy SLS

1913, Class '1A'
(L&NER Class 'B8')

Boiler pressure 180psi
Cylinders: dia. 21½ x 26 ins stroke
Wheel arrangement: 4-6-0
Coupled wheels: 5ft 7ins
Weight: Engine 74 tons 7cwt
Tender 48 tons 6cwt
Tractive effort: 27,400 lbs

Class '1A' No. 4 *Glenalmond* was built at Gorton in June 1913. The locomotives were a smaller-wheeled version of the Class '1' predecessors and as a result they inherited some of the problems. With the smaller wheels, however, they were more suitable for fast goods traffic as against the Class '1's.
National Railway Museum

1913, Class '11E'
(L&NER Class 'D10')

Boiler pressure: 180psi
Cylinders: dia. 20in. x 26in. stroke
Wheel arrangement 4-6-0
Coupled wheels 6ft 9in.
Weight: Engine 61 tons Tender 48 tons 6cwt
Tractive effort: 19,645 lbs

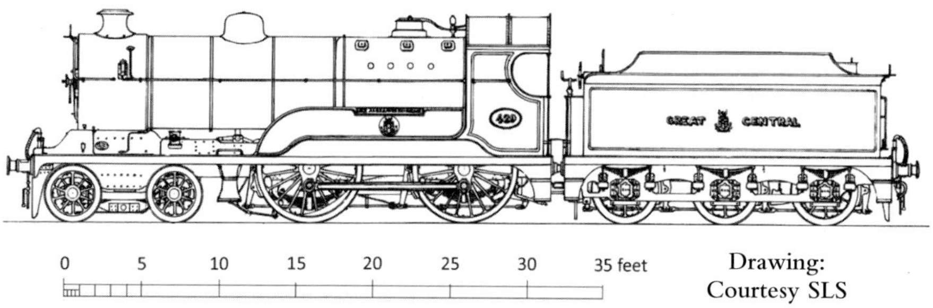

Drawing:
Courtesy SLS

The Class '11E' 4-4-0s, also known as the 'Director Class'. The class of ten locomotives were built in 1913 at Gorton with No. 430 *Purdon Viccars* seen here. The locomotives were an immediate success and proved worthy of mainline express passenger duties and soon took over from the Class '1's; the shorter boiler and larger grate area gave the locomotive better steam raising capabilities. *MLS*

1914, Class '1B' (L&NER Class 'L1')

Boiler pressure: 180psi
Cylinders: dia. 21in. x 26in. stroke
Wheel arrangement: 2-6-4
Coupled wheels: 5ft 1in.
Weight: Engine 97 ton 9cwt
Tractive effort: 28,759 lbs

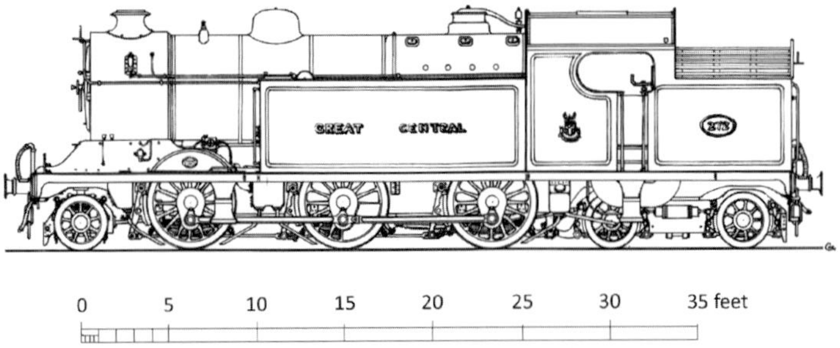

Drawing: courtesy SLS

Class '1B' 2-6-4T Tank No. 272 built in 1914 at Gorton. Robinson based the design on the Class 'M1' 0-6-4 of the Lancashire, Derbyshire & East Coast Railway (LD&ECR). Originally designed for taking coal trains to Immingham docks from Derbyshire and Nottinghamshire the locomotives were found to be inadequate for the purpose due to braking deficiencies and were soon allocated to other duties. In 1945 the L&NER Classification 'L1' was changed to 'L3' to make way for the Thompson new build 'L1's. *National Railway Museum*

1917, Class '9P' (L&NER Class B3)

Boiler pressure: 180psi
Cylinders: (4) dia. 16in. x 26in. stroke
Wheel arrangement: 4-6-0
Coupled wheels: 6ft. 9in.
Weight: Engine 79 ton
Tender 48 ton 6cwt
Tractive effort: 24,772 lbs

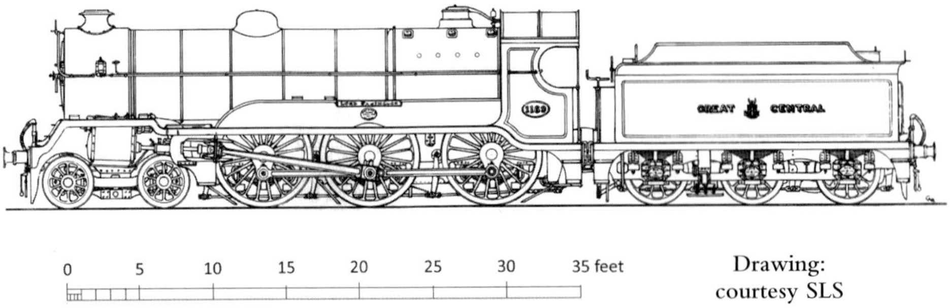

Drawing: courtesy SLS

Class '9P' 4-6-0 No. 1169 *Lord Faringdon* was part of a class of six locomotives and was built at Gorton in 1917. The locomotives were proven successful and capable when handled correctly. Two of the class were fitted with Caprotti valve gear which improved the fuel consumption, but the remainder of the class was not altered. In 1943 Thompson rebuilt No. 6166 in the style of his 'B1' Class. No. 6166 did not prove to be successful and no further rebuilds occurred. *E.M. Johnson collection*

1918, Class '8N' (L&NER Class 'B6')

Boiler pressure: 180psi
Cylinders: (2) dia. 21in. x 26 in.
Wheel arrangement: 4-6-0
Coupled wheels: 5ft 8in.
Weight: Engine 72t 8cwt
Tender 48t 6cwt
Tractive effort: 25,798 lbs

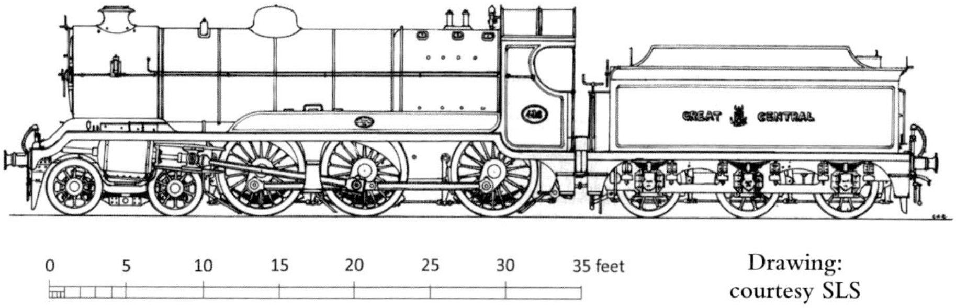

Drawing: courtesy SLS

Robinson Class '8N' 4-6-0 locomotive No. 52 was built in March 1921 at Gorton as the second of a class of only three locomotives. The first, No. 416 was built in July 1918. The third, No. 53 in April 1921. The second two built engines received side windows to the cab. 68% of the working parts on these engines were interchangeable with the Class '8M' 2-8-0 locomotives. *E.M. Johnson collection*

1919 Class 11F (L&NER Class 'D11')

Boiler pressure: 180psi
Cylinders: dia. 20in. x 26in. stroke
Wheel arrangement: 4-4-0
Coupled wheels: 6ft 9in.
Weight: Engine 61 tons 3cwt
Tender 48 tons 6cwt
Tractive effort: 19,645 lbs

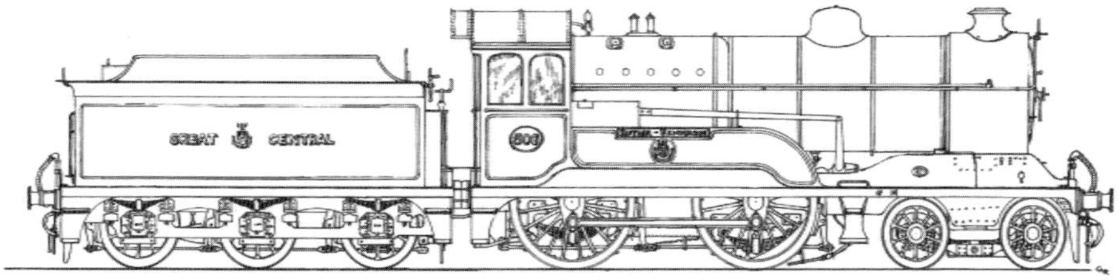

Drawing: courtesy SLS

Robinson Class '11F' 'Improved Director' 4-4-0 No. 506 *Butler Henderson* built at Gorton in December 1919. The class was a development of the earlier '11E' 'Director' class. Externally the main visual difference was the side window cab in place of the 'cutaway' type of the '11E'. The biggest improvement was inside the frames, out of view and made the class more successful than it's already successful predecessor, this was the use of inside admission piston valves as against the earlier '11E' with outside admission. *National Railway Museum*

Drawing: courtesy SLS

1921, Class '9Q' (L&NER Class 'B7')

Boiler pressure: 180psi
Cylinders: (4) dia. 16in. x 26in. stroke
Wheel arrangement: 4-6-0
Coupled wheels: 5ft 8in.
Weight: Engine 79 tons 10cwt.
Tender 48 tons 6 cwt.
Tractive effort: 29,952 lbs

Class '9Q' 4-6-0 No. 73 built in June 1921. This class was reputed to be a little heavy on coal, but in a fireman's skilled hands they were comparable to other classes of 4-6-0 types of the day and were probably the most successful of the Robinson 4-6-0 type of locomotives with the class build continuing into L&NER days. However, the class was to become extinct soon after the formation of British Railways in 1948, the possible reason was the locomotives having four cylinders at a time when two were more economical to maintain.
National Railway Museum

Little and Large. Sacré outside framed Class '12AT' 2-4-0T No. 448B stands alongside Robinson Class '1A' 4-6-0 No. 440. When built in 1881 the 2-4-0 was originally fitted with a half cab but later converted to a full cab. It was reclassified '12AM' when it was converted for autocar services by Robinson. Later on it had the suffix 'B' added to its number when it came on the GCR duplicate list, it also had a Robinson chimney fitted. The locomotives were at first assigned for working on the MSJ&A lines replacing older engines and eight were built, all at Gorton. Coupled wheels were 5ft 6in; cylinder diameter was 16in. x 24in. stroke. The '1A' was built in August 1914 for mixed traffic use. A smaller wheeled version of the Class '1' ('Sir Sam Fay' class). Known as the 'Glen Almonds' after the name of the first of the class that was built in 1913 (No. 4). A total of eleven locomotives were built, nine in 1914 and the last in 1915. Coupled wheels were 5ft 7in., cylinder diameter was 21½in. x 26in. stroke
E.M. Johnson collection

Robinson Class '8M' 2-8-0 No. 422, built in June 1919, was converted as seen above to burn pulverised fuel in January 1920 from parts removed from locomotive Class '8K' No. 353 (No. 353 had a smaller firebox and was proven unsuccessful for these trials). In consequence, a new eight-wheeled bogie tender was built for the trial. *E.M. Johnson collection*

Robinson Class '11E' 4-4-2 No. 437 *Charles Stuart Wortley* was built in November 1913 and renamed about 1922 *Prince George*. These very handsome locomotives were the forerunners of the later '11F' (L&NER 'D11') Class 'Improved Directors' which became true to that name. *Authors' collection*

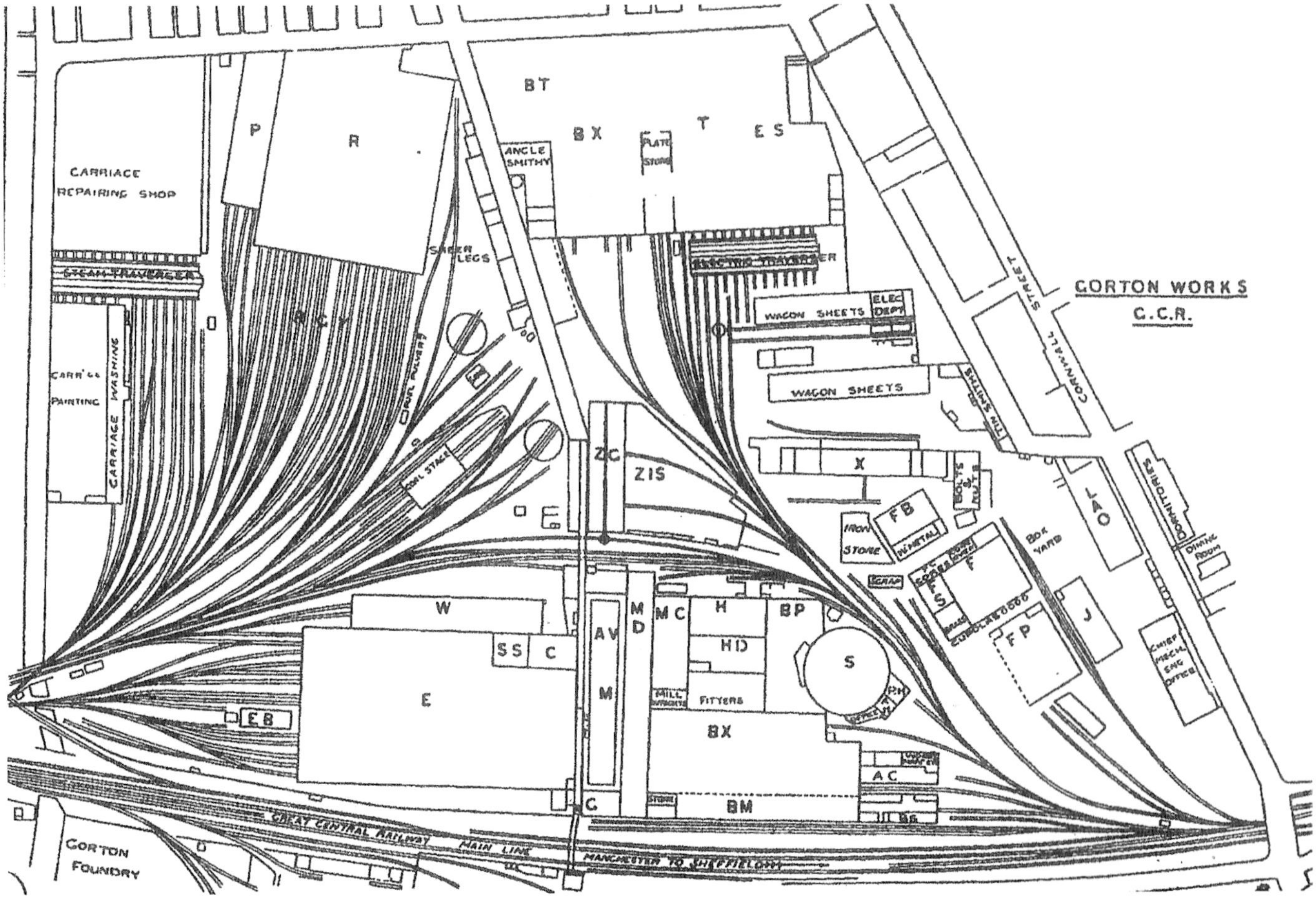

Author's revised I.L.E. drawing

Principal buildings:

AC – Chain proving shop
BC – Chain smithy
BP – Press shop
BS – Firebox stay shop
BX – Boiler shops
BM – Boiler mounting shop
C – Coppersmiths' shop
DSD – Dies for drop hammer shop
E/ Erecting shop
ES/ Locomotive stripping shop
F/ Iron foundry
FB/ Brass foundry
FP/ Plate moulding shop (plate foundry)
G/ grinding shop
H/ Forge
J/ Pattern & carpenters shop
M/ Machine shop
MD/ Machine shop
MT/ Tool room
P/ Paint shop
PH/ Electrical power house
R/ Running sheds
RGY/ Running shed yard
S/ Smithy
SS/ Spring smithy
T/ Tender shop
U/ Brass finishing shop
W/ Wheel shop
WMB/ White metal shop
X/ Permanent way shop
HD/ Drop hammer shop

Builders Plates *MLS collection*

The Great Central Railways First World War memorial Locomotive *Valour* is adorned with wreaths on its name plates and smokebox door on Armistice Day duties. Standing on platform 'A' at Manchester London Road it is preparing to depart for Sheffield. This annual event had railway employees standing trackside with their caps in hand and heads bowed as the train passed. On arrival at Sheffield Victoria Station the wreaths would be handed over to railway employees and a service held at the GCR memorial. This tradition continued well into L&NER days from first executed on the 11th November 1921. *E.M. Johnson collection*

CHAPTER FOUR
LONDON & NORTH EASTERN RAILWAY

With the formation of the L&NER on the 1st January 1923 as part of the 'Big Four', Gorton Locomotive Works joined Doncaster and Darlington as the principal locomotive workshops of the new railway company. However, from the very start it became evident that Gorton was going to be third in the L&NER pecking order. John G. Robinson was approached to be offered the position of the Chief Mechanical Engineer but he declined the offer due to his nearing retiring age, and, as noted previously Herbert Nigel Gresley was appointed to this position on John G.'s recommendation. Gresley, already a GNR man, decided that Doncaster was to be the principal works, with Darlington close behind. Gorton was not to fare favourably when it came to new locomotive construction. When it came to size Gorton was not the largest of establishments, there had been no room to expand in size since 1900 due to the highly industrialised neighbourhood it shared and with the high concentration of rows and rows of terraced houses whose occupants worked in that industrial environment, 'The Tank' was hemmed in. The carriage and wagon works at Dukinfield had helped a great deal when it was built in the first decade of the 1900s the space required was soon taken up though with mainly wagon repairs in the 1881 buildings on the other side of the locomotive running sheds.

For new locomotive construction, Gorton continued with the construction of their own GCR-designed engines. In the first year of the L&NER, 1923, the shops turned out ten of their Coronation 4-6-2T tank engines and seven '9Q' 4-6-0s. In 1924 only three of the '9Q' class were built. Between 1925 and 1928 forty Great Eastern Railway (GER) A.J. Hill designed Class 'N7' 0-6-2T passenger tank engines were built at Gorton. In 1932 Nigel Gresley ordered two of Robinson's Class '8H' 0-8-4 heavy shunting locomotives, these two engines were fitted with boosters to their trailing bogies to assist with starting heavy loads. No other new locomotives were built until 1938 and into 1939 when fourteen of Nigel Gresley's Class 'J50' tank engines were built. The last of these to be built was Numbered 615, later L&NER number 8985 in the 1946 renumbering scheme.

Gorton though did have one asset that could not be overlooked. That of the highly skilled work carried out at their iron foundry. Gorton was well-known as having the best foundries of the whole of the L&NER and its constituent companies with skilled founders being second to none. It was because of this that Nigel Gresley decided to use Gorton to cast the cylinder blocks for his three-cylinder locomotives. The castings for these locomotives were of a mono-block design, whereas all three cylinders were incorporated into one casting.

The following photographs show the castings and machining of the cylinder blocks as carried out at Gorton including the Class 'P2' 2-8-2 locomotive No. 2001 *Cock o' the North* that was equipped with Lentz Valve Gear, and other three-cylinder castings, mainly Class 'V2' 2-6-2s. A careful examination of the photos will show the centre cylinder at a different angle, pointing downwards (1 in 7 incline in the case of his pacific locomotives). This angle was to enable the centre cylinder connecting rod to clear the leading driving wheel as all wheels were driven from the same axle on most of his locomotives (the 'B17' and 'D49' Classes being the exception for his three-cylinder locomotives).

Above: In the middle of a 'pour', the founders are casting a Gresley three-cylinder mono-block. Gorton's foundry and its men were second to none in their expertise in the manufacture of large castings. Gresley's trust in Gorton to cast and machine the cylinder blocks lies testimony to the skills of the patternmakers, machinists, and foundry personnel alike. *National Railway Museum/MOSI*

Left: The start of a series of illustrations showing the machining of some of the Gresley three-cylinder mono-blocks. Here a radial arm drill is in use drilling into the top of the casting. *National Railway Museum/MOSI*

Opposite: A planing machine set up to machine the faces of the centre cylinder on a Gresley locomotive three-cylinder mono-block. Machine tool manufactured by Craven Brothers, Manchester. *National Railway Museum /MOSI*

Preparing to drill the outside cylinder cover bolt holes using a radial arm drill. The bolt holes are 'lined' up using a jig bolted to the casting. The radial arm drill is a product of 'Kendall and Gent Ltd' – Manchester.
National Railway Museum/MOSI

Upper: Boring out an outside cylinder on the three-cylinder mono-block.
Lower: Using the same machine tool. Milling the inside piston valve face on the mono-block. The angle of the inside cylinder perfectly demonstrates how the inside piston had to clear the leading coupled wheel to drive the centre axle. *both National Railway Museum /MOSI*

Upper: Boring out the centre cylinder of the mono-block, again, the angle of the inside cylinder as opposed the outside is clearly visible. *Lower*: Milling the flange faces of the casting. The machine tool used for the machining exercise on this and the previous page is the same machine, a very versatile piece of machinery. *Both National Railway Museum/MOSI*

Upper: A complete three-cylinder mono-block for a Gresley Class 'V2' 2-6-2 locomotive. No doubt the associated parts are test pieces to ensure the all fits perfectly before the finished mono-block is sent to Doncaster locomotive works.
Below: Gorton also cast the cylinder mono-blocks for the Class 'P2' 2-8-2 locomotives, this particular mono-block was for No. 2001 *Cock O' The North* which is the only one of the class fitted with Lenz rotary valve gear. A very intricate and complicated design, a credit to the skills of the pattern makers, foundry workers and machinists at Gorton. *Both National Railway Museum/MOSI*

Permanent way department - Points and Crossing Shop (P/way shop)

Two photographs not the best quality, but certainly worth an inclusion. The Points and Crossing Shop was located in one of the old MS&LR/GCR Wagon Sheet shops. The upper view looks west whilst that below is in the opposite direction. The machine shop was capable of turning out 1,000 points and the same number of crossings per year. The shop was equipped with a 5-ton overhead electric crane. The drawing on the next page gives an indication of the types of machines installed in the shop that were used to manufacture everything concerning the companies railway permanent way. The building was 261 feet long by 41 feet wide. A rail line went through the shop to convey the tracks outside on a small rail mounted truck, where they could be handled by the storage yards 5-ton gantry crane. *both Author's collection*

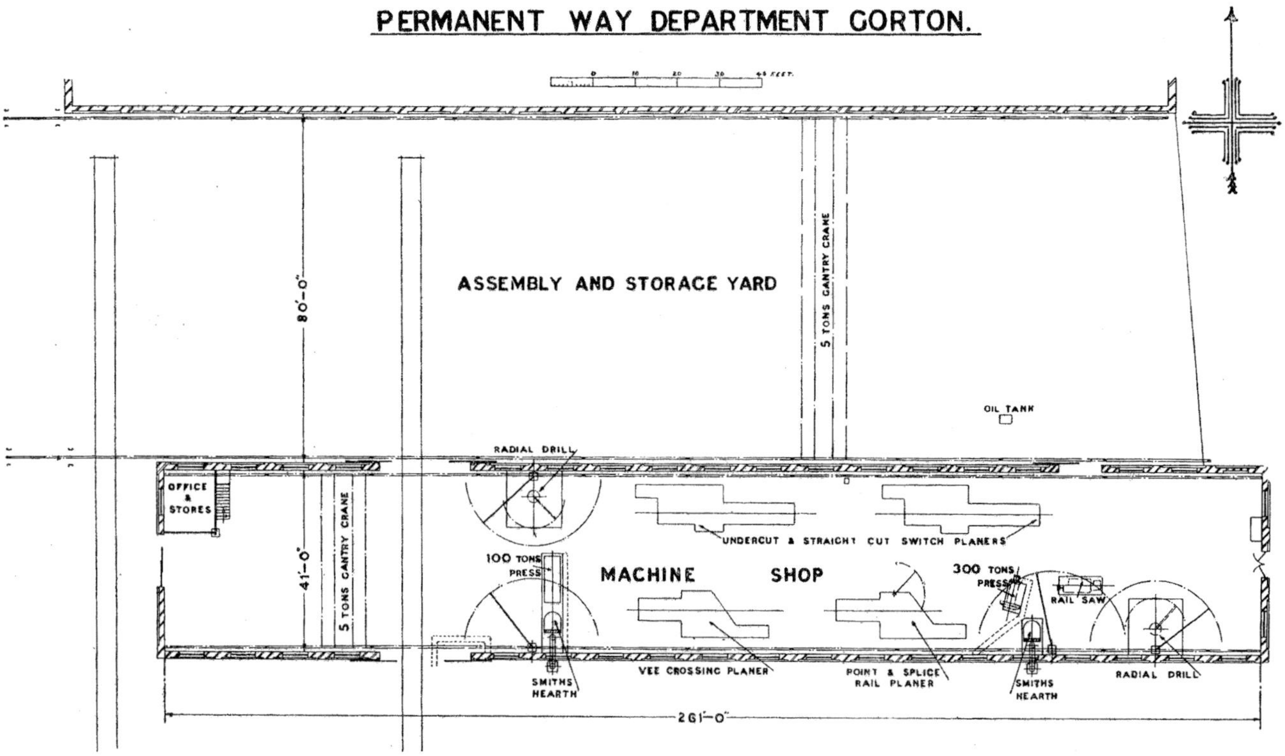

Plan of the permanent way shop at Gorton. *author's collection*

Guide Bridge station, Stockport Junction. An example of track crossing and point work manufactured at Gorton works in the 1930s. *author's collection*

Erecting Shop in the L&NER Period

No. 1 Bay seen on the 29th May 1935. Two ex-GCR 4-6-2 tanks are seen, No. 5168 is on No. 3 road with unidentified 'sister' engine on No. 1 road. Further down the bay are a mixture of locomotive types and a boiler and wheelsets. *N.L. Good*

A scene captured in 1936. Ex-GCR Atlantic 4-4-2 No. 5267, 0-8-0 'Q4' No. 5153 and 0-6-0 'J39' No. 2999 are in No. 2 Bay being stripped down for a overhaul. In addition to the wheels, the usual paraphernalia of locomotive parts including cab sections and a bogie frame are scattered around the shop floor. *N.L. Good*

October 1936, in the Erecting Shop the frame of a four-cylinder Class 'B7' (GCR '9Q') No. 5468 stands on the left-hand road in front of one of the four Cheshire Lines Committee Sentinel railcars receiving attention. Whilst on the right-hand road is a Gresley L&NER Class '39J' 0-6-0 No. 2712. Normally the L&NER Sentinel railcars carried names but those operating on the CLC just bore numbers, in this case Sentinel No. 602.

N. L. Good

'O4/3' 2-8-0 No. 6622 stands on the weighbridge in No. 5 Bay on No. 15 road. The weighbridge was later moved into the works yard after space was made following the removal of the old coaling stage after the completion of building the new coaling plant (the Cenotaph) in 1934. The removal of the weighbridge from the shop freed up movement along that section of the bay.

National Railway Museum

Viewed from the 'Lighthouse' signal box. This photograph just oozes railways as far as the eye can see. Dominating the scene is the cenotaph coaling tower with the main railway line facing up to Manchester. The signal box controls traffic in and out of the sheds and works at Priory Junction. The building to the extreme left is the Belle Vue sheds of the LM&SR. To the left of the coaling tower are the coal storage yard and further right still is the Openshaw Goods Depot. Behind the coaling tower is the massive railway yards at Ashbury's, once the Ashbury Carriage and Wagon Works. In Gorton's yard is a large array of rolling stock wheels and tyres. Though this is the L&NER period, the two locomotives are Robinson GCR designs being two GCR Class '8' (L&NER 'B5') engines. Look at the signals, what a sight. One can only wonder in awe at what this scene was like at this time. *W. Lees*

Locomotive Coaling Tower

The coaling tower was built on the west side of the Priory Junction bridges. The locomotive running sheds had no room to accommodate this type of facility closer as the tower itself covered just a portion of the large area required for this type of coaling plant. Associated to the coaling process were wet ash pits which covered a large area and were 280 feet long and situated about 300 feet away from the tower to allow for track layout. The plant layout also consisted of a sand dryer, three lines for full coal wagons and also ash disposal lines.

Directly opposite the coaling plant was the LM&SR Belle Vue shed, which had the old type of coaling facility involving coaling by hand tipping skips; their coaling personnel must have viewed their L&NER counterparts with some degree of envy.

When built in 1934 it must have been well received by all sections the running department, mostly the coal handlers and the shed planning staff. The original coaling plant in the sheds yard created a lot of congestion both with constant streams of locomotives queuing for fuelling and also the coal supply lines and ash disposal. The new Cenotaph plant was built quite a distance from the shed yard to the west of Priory Junction Bridges (the area around the over bridges was known as 'Over the Alps' for some strange reason!). A coaling plant of this type demanded a considerable amount of space and this area was able to accommodate it. The three roads to the north of the sand drier could hold fifty coal wagons. The wet ash pit was 280 feet long with two roads and ash disposal lines on either side pit. The road directly next to the three coal roads on the northern side was known (again for some unknown reason) as the 'Cheshire road'!

Built in 1934, Gorton's locomotive coaling tower was the second of the type to be built by the L&NER, this being similar in design to the first which was built at Doncaster. Coaling towers of this type were known as 'cenotaphs'. A study of the tower clearly shows a coal wagon on the hoist, one of the two winding drums clearly visible by the side of the operators cabin at the top of the tower. The counter weight for the loaded wagons is seen on the nearest side of the tower. The tower was designed to be able to coal up two locomotives simultaneously. *W. Lees*

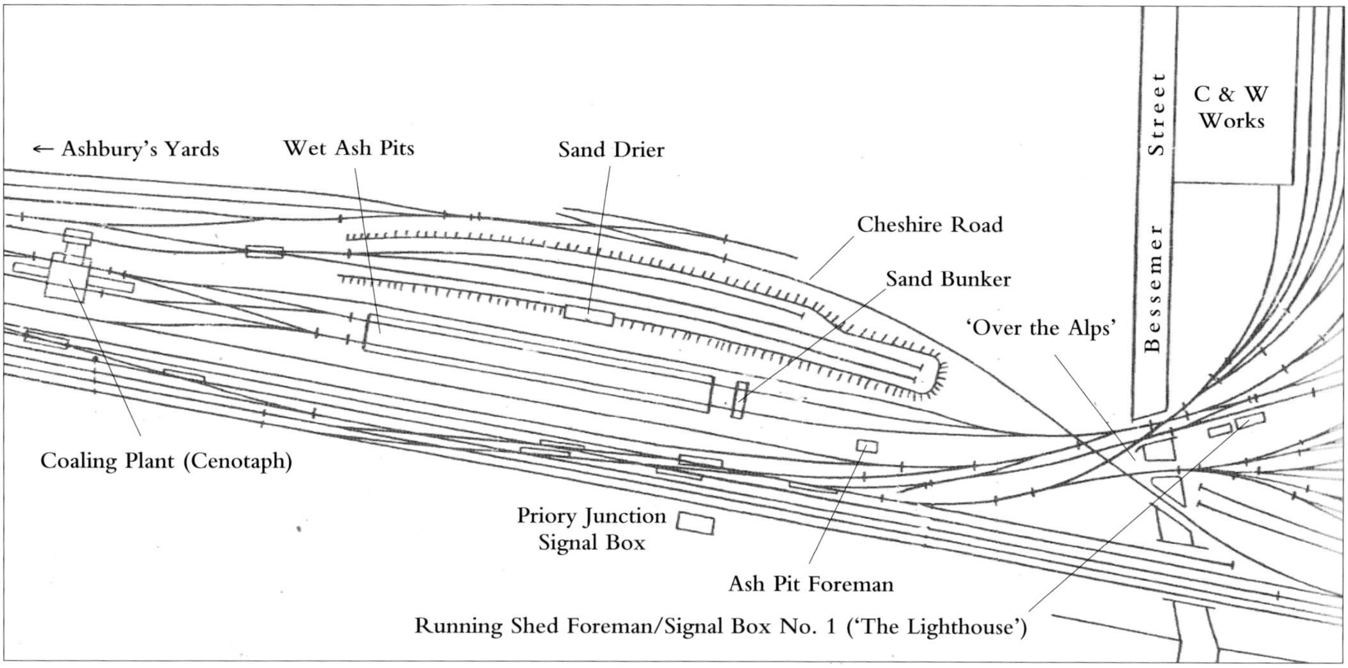

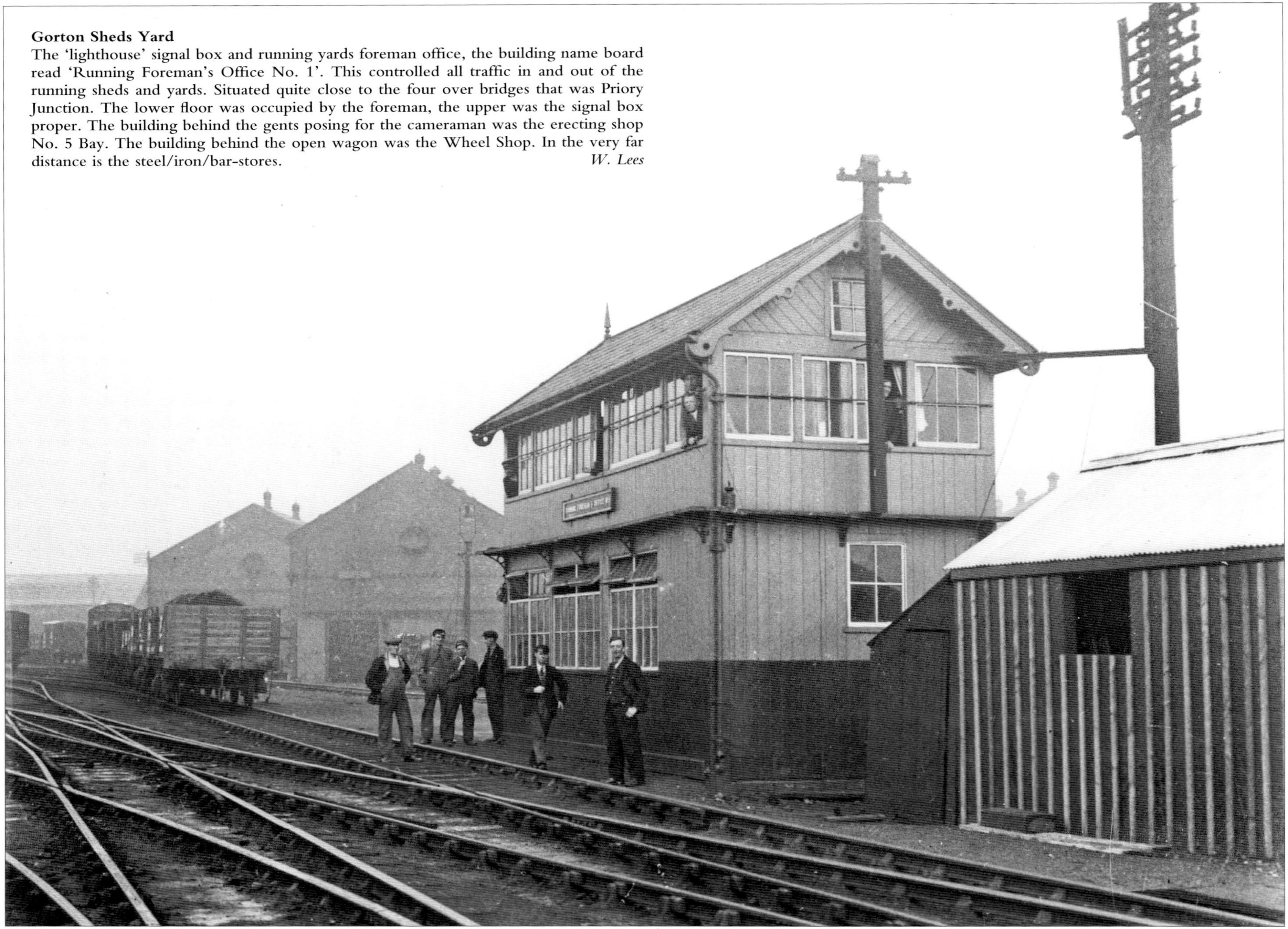

Gorton Sheds Yard

The 'lighthouse' signal box and running yards foreman office, the building name board read 'Running Foreman's Office No. 1'. This controlled all traffic in and out of the running sheds and yards. Situated quite close to the four over bridges that was Priory Junction. The lower floor was occupied by the foreman, the upper was the signal box proper. The building behind the gents posing for the cameraman was the erecting shop No. 5 Bay. The building behind the open wagon was the Wheel Shop. In the very far distance is the steel/iron/bar-stores. *W. Lees*

L&NER Locomotive Review

This review includes pre GCR types, not only Gorton's products but also locomotives that were to be found in Gorton Works and sheds during the L&NER period.

Now in L&NER days Parker designed Class '6B' 4-4-0 and now numbered 6466 and fitted with a weather shield for running tender first.. Originally Numbered 430 when built in 1877, a total of 27 were built, this engine being the eighth. Coupled wheels 6ft 9in. Cylinder diameter 18in. x 26in. stroke.

E.M. Johnson collection

Pollitt designed Class '13' 4-2-2 No. 968 displaying an early form of L&NER lettering. The second of the class of six to be built in May 1900. The original order was for ten locomotives to be built but Robinson reduced it to six as he knew that larger coupled wheeled locomotives would be needed for the London Extension. Note Robinson's colloidal fuelling plant at Gorton in the background.

E.M. Johnson collection

A Sacré Class '6B' 4-4-0 now with L&NER No. 6445 (MS&LR No. 445 built in January 1888). Now fitted with a Belpaire firebox, extended cab with no side window, and Robinson Chimney. *E.M. Johnson collection*

Robinson L&NER Class 'B3' 4-6-0 No. 6168 (ex-GCR Class '9P' No. 1168) *Lord Stuart of Wortley* stands outside Gorton Shed. The locomotive was rebuilt with Caprotti valve gear by Sir Nigel Gresley in 1929 in an attempt to reduce coal consumption marring its otherwise graceful (for such a large engine) appearance. Turned out in October 1920 the locomotive survived until September 1946. *E.M. Johnson collection*

Robinson 'Jersey Lily', L&NER Class 'C4' No. 1923 (GCR Class '8B') built in 1907 at Gorton as GCR No. 361. Gone is its magnificent GCR livery, brass number plates, burnished steel and the usual embellishments – this is L&NER days and the class has lost its position in the pecking order of things. *MLS collection*

Standing with a full tender over the wet ash pit at Gorton's coaling tower. Class 'D10' (GCR class '11E') 4-4-0 No. 5433 *Walter Burgh Gair*. Built at Gorton in 1913. *National Railway Museum*

Robinson L&NER Class 'D11' 'Improved Director' 4-4-0 No. 5511 (ex-GCR No. 511) *Marne* stands in Gorton's yard resplendent ex works in its L&NER livery in 1925. Fitted with an indicator shelter and fully coaled up and inevitably ready for trial runs.
P.F. Cooke/Rail Archive Stephenson

With just a whisper of steam from its cylinder blowdown cocks, Gresley Class 'B17' 4-6-0 No 2834 *Hinchingbrook* stands quietly in Gorton shed's yard. With a full tender of coal, the locomotive is probably ready for the 'off'. *MLS collection*

Standing in the shadow of Gorton's old coaling tower is Class 'J10' (GCR '9H') 0-6-0 with its L&NER No. 5125. The locomotive was built by Robinson at Gorton in May 1902 and numbered 125 to a design going back to the MS&LR days. The more famous Class 'J11' (GCR Class '9J') 0-6-0 locomotives (Pom-Poms) were a direct development of the 'J10's. *W. Lees*

Gresley Class 'B17' 4-6-0 No. 2846 *The Suffolk Regiment* stands under the shear legs in Gorton's running shed yard receiving attention to its centre and rear driving wheels. Note the large size of the lifting chains and hooks, all heavy physical work. *E.M. Johnson collection*

Ex MS&LR Class '4' 0-4-0 No. 511. Two locomotives of this class were purchased from Manning, Wardle & Co. of Leeds in 1883. After a series of number changes they ended up as L&NER Numbers 6430 & 6431 and designated into the L&NER classification 'Y2'. Both locomotives were taken out of service in 1931 having been used for dock shunting. *E.M. Johnson collection*

Thompson Class 'B1' 4-6-0 No. 1143 in green livery at Priory Junction where the lines lead in and out of the running sheds and works. Built by Vulcan Foundry in April 1947 the locomotive was withdrawn from service in February 1964 at Doncaster locomotive works. *MLS collection*

Gresley Class 'A1' Pacific 4-6-2 No. 2561 stands in Gorton's running shed yard having been sent from Doncaster works for running in. Built in May 1925 and later named *Minoru* after a thoroughbred racehorse that won the '2,000 Guineas' and 'The Derby' at Epson in 1909. The locomotive was rebuilt to Class 'A3' in June 1944 after nineteen years as an 'A1'. *Minoru* was withdrawn in December 1964

E.M. Johnson collection

Gorton Running sheds, 1925. A group of senior personnel look on as a Holden Class 'B12' 4-6-0 No. 8557 (GER Class 'S69') manoeuvres around the shed yard with its tender stacked to the gunnels in readiness for its return trip east after working the 'North Country Continental' from Harwich. *P.F. Cooke/Rail Archive Stephenson*

No. 8557 stands looking resplendent at the side of Gorton's double-sided coaling stage. It will be another nine years before Gorton has its new cenotaph-type coaling tower installed to the west of Priory Junction. *P.F. Cooke/Rail Archive Stephenson*

Robinson Class 'B8' (GCR Class '1A') 4-6-0 No. 5441. A class of eleven locomotives, they became known as 'Glenalmonds', the name given of the first of the class which was built in 1913. Four of the class were named. Not a very successful class in performance, they were a smaller coupled wheel version of the GCR Class '1' 4-6-0 'Sam Fays'. *MLS collection*

Edward Thompson's 1943 rebuild of Robinson Class 'B3' (GCR '9P') 4-6-0 No. 6166 (originally named *Earl Haig*). The locomotive was reclassified as 'B3/3'. Only the one 'B3' was rebuilt in this form as the locomotive suffered from cracked frames and such a drastic rebuild gave no advantage over Thompson's own 'B1' Class 0-6-0s. *E.M. Johnson*

Looking magnificent in its new L&NER guise on 33rd July 1933, Class 'D10' No. 5430 (GC Class '11E') *Purdon Viccars* stand proudly in Gorton yard with its tender full of coal. Erecting shop No. 5 Bay in the background. *Gordon Coltas Trust*

A panoramic view of Gorton's shed yard. This scene is in the second half of the 1930s. The gentleman, possibly a shed foreman is looking rather pleased with himself; the sheds now have a little more space. The old coaling stage has been demolished relieving the congestion that must have been a nightmare for locomotive movements. The new 'cenotaph' coaling plant has been located some distance way on the western side of Priory Junction, where there is ample space for that type of coaling facility. The twenty-road shed yard in the background is playing host to a mixture of home grown GC locomotives and L&NER types. A very busy place at this period in time. The large chimney is in the locomotive works on the opposite side of Wellington Street in the old smithy that was used when the carriage and wagon works was located there in 1879 in MS&LR days. *W. Lees*

Ernest Lambert

A brief biography of a GCR / L&NER Engineer

Ernest Lambert was born on September 23rd 1889. The family lived at No. 49 Jackson Street, just off Ashton Old Road in Openshaw. Ernest's father, Henry Spring Lambert, was a boiler inspector at Gorton, a craft that must have run in the family's veins as Henry's own father and two brothers, Tom Dick and Harry Spring, all worked at Gorton. Clearly, all such family connections must have had some influence on Henry and on his son's choice of career. A letter signed by the Gorton Works' Manager R.A. Thom and dated October 16th 1913, states in no uncertain terms that the Chief Mechanical Engineer (Robinson) has been extremely kind in allowing his son to serve his time as a draughtsman. Thom requests that Lambert Senior writes him (sic) thanking him for what he proposes to do. [NOTE: The late Alan Brown, who had an intimate knowledge of Gorton Works, related that Thom was universally referred to by his initials!]

Ernest's education and his CV make for interesting reading. From 1904-1907 he attended Wheeler Street Elementary School in Openshaw before moving on from 1907-1911 to Varna Street Elementary School in Gorton. Both schools would be classed as Primary schools today. From August 1911 to July 1915 he attended the Ardwick Central School in Devonshire Street. The school was sited to the south side of Hyde Road from what was then the Manchester Corporation tramway depot, premises still in use today by Stagecoach. Leaving school in 1915, Ernest Lambert began work on July 27th as an apprentice at Gorton Works. He describes his work at Gorton as working on locomotive cylinders and frames, repairs and new construction and millwrights' work. The pattern making department is also mentioned but no details are given. The GCR paid him £2 5s 6d per week for 47 hours work. With his eye on the future Ernest had obtained a bursary to enable him to study mechanical engineering at Openshaw Technical School in the evenings from 1915. The following year he moved to study at the Manchester College of Technology on Whitworth Street. His studies at the college are listed as an 'Engineers' Apprentices Day course in mechanical and electrical engineering'. Ernest aquitted himself well from the 'tech'. In December 1918 he was awarded War Savings Certificates by the college to the value of £3 2s in recognition of him having passed his second year examinations. These covered theory of machines, strength of materials, hydraulics, machine design and mathematics – comprehensive education indeed. A letter from the college principal dated July 28th 1919 advises him the H.M. Inspector will shortly be considering qualifications for candidates to study for an 'Advanced Course Certificate' but it is not known whether or not Ernest took up any further studies at this time. Clearly, he must have advanced through the works fairly rapidly to put his initials to an important drawing dated September 13th 1922. This was a 3-inch to one foot copy of a Class '8K' (L&NER 'O4') smokebox with superheater and is finished in colour-wash. The drawing was for the rebuilding of one of Robinson's 'Fish' engines. (Class '8', L&NER 'B5'). The deeper firebox required the boiler to be raised, something that completely altered the engine. By the 1930s Ernest Lambert was transferred to Dukinfield carriage and wagon works. As the decade progressed and war was looming, the Dukinfield site was being wound down. Ernest was offered a job at Doncaster, something he declined, not wanting to uproot his family. Instead he left the railway and went to work for the firm of Ferguson & Palin, electrical engineers and manufacturers of electrical switchgear in Openshaw. Despite mergers and takeovers, the company lasted into modern times; latterly part of the Alstom Group, Ferguson & Palin's works, which stood on Buckley Street in Openshaw, survived until 2002. Ernest Lambert retired in 1964 having worked part-time as a teacher of Technical Drawing at what was then Openshaw Technical School. He died on April 14th 1967.

Locomotive No. 184 (L&NER 5184 of Class 'B5') was the only example of the class to carry the '8K' ('O4') boiler, The remaining thirteen were fitted subsequently with the boiler used by Robinson on his '8A' ('Q4') 0-8-0; the rebuilding being undertaken between 1926-1936. No. 5184 itself was rebuilt again – also with a 'Q4' boiler – in December 1927. Similar modifications were carried out in L&NER days to Robinson's '8G' 4-6-0s ('B9'), though one of the class had been fitted with a 4ft 9in. boiler in 1910.

4-6-0 No. 184 the rebuilt 'Fish' engine of Class '8' (L&NER B5) No. 184 as rebuilt with a Class '8K' (O4) boiler as against a graceful un rebuilt example on page 108 of locomotive No. 186. Such a radical change. *E.M. Johnson*

Gorton Tank's last new steam build.
A magnificent action scene of one of the ten new Thompson designed 'B1' Class 4-6-0 locomotives (Nos. 61340 to 61349) under construction. Taken in the first year of Nationalisation it is probably one of the first two or three Class 'B1's built. Here the boiler is being lowered into its frame, two cranes being used for this lift operation. Terry Holtby advises that the second crane lifted via a special adapter fitted into the firebox door. No doubt somewhere the erecting shop foreman will be keeping an eye on the proceedings to make sure that all goes smooth with Gorton's new build under its new BR owners. *National Railway Museum*

CHAPTER FIVE
BRITISH RAILWAYS

On Ist January 1948 the L&NER was no more, as the 'Big Four' ceased to exist. The Transport Act 1947 brought the major railway companies in Great Britain under control of the British Transport Commission. British Railways was split into separate 'regions' with boundaries following a similar geographical pattern as their former big four areas of operation. Gorton locomotive works came under the new Eastern Region of British Railways. The North Eastern and Eastern Regions of BR now had three major locomotive workshops, Doncaster, Darlington and Gorton. As mentioned previously, during the big four days, Gorton played second fiddle to the other two works and this unfortunately was to continue. British Railways introduced new designs of locomotives in an effort to standardise their fleet and replace the existing classes as they became worn out. All major workshops in of the regions were given contracts to build allotted numbers of the new 'Standards'. The locomotive workshops just prior to 1948 was still building their own ex railway company locomotives to complete existing orders. One order that Gorton had was for ten Thompson designed 4-6-0 Class 'B1' locomotives. Construction of the 'B1's started in 1948 and was completed the following year. 'B1' No. 61349, the tenth on the order books was the last steam locomotive to be built at Gorton. All ten 'B1's went to Scotland.

In 1950 work started on building the new Manchester, Sheffield and Wath line (MSW) DC Class 'EM1' Bo+Bo electric locomotives, this construction lasted up until 1953. During the last year that the Bo+Bos were being built, work started on construction of the larger Class 'EM2' Co-Co electric locomotives. This work lasted until 1954 when, the last of the class, No. 27006 was completed. This 'EM2' was the last new locomotive that Gorton built, from now on Gorton's work consisted of mainly overhauls, repairs and rebuilds, work was also carried out on the manufacture of sub assemblies for BRs new fleet of diesel and electric locomotives that were being built both at Crewe and Derby locomotive workshops. In addition to all this more and more locomotives started to enter Gorton for cutting up. Anybody looking over the works yard and into the running sheds from the birdcage would see row after row of locomotives with a large 'X' daubed on them as they waited for their fate at the hands of the cutters torch. A train spotters Mecca.

The Smithy Roundhouse. The newish building nearest to the camera was the electrical substation supplying incoming power from the grid to the whole of the Gorton works complex including the running sheds and carriage and wagon works. The square building attached to the roundhouse was where chrome plating was carried out to all components. The chrome plating shop was also the unofficial hairdressers where you could get a haircut and buy your Woodbine or Park Drive cigarettes from Henry who worked in this shop. His barbers shop was behind a wooden screen hidden out of view from the 'gaffers'. *R. Whitehouse*

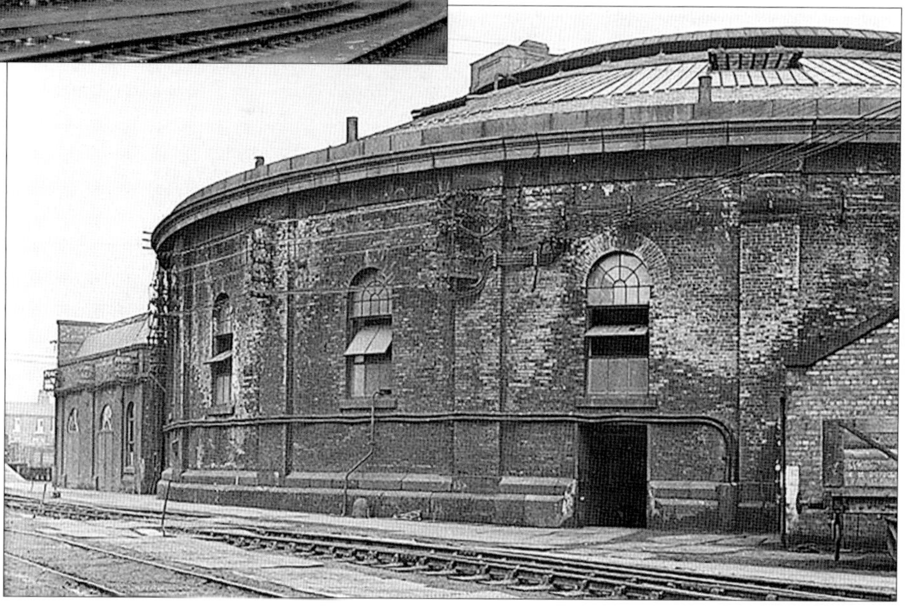

Looking south west to the smithy and the 'hairdressers'. Note the power reticulation cables from the sub station attached to the smithy wall. *W.A. Brown*

Boiler Shop. Still no ear protection during this era. The noise must have been deafening as the boilermakers operate their pneumatic riveting tools inside a locomotive firebox. These boilermakers would be performing this operation day in and day out, year after year peening over the hundreds of copper stays. *Manchester Libraries*

The Boiler Shop in early BR days. The firebox from Class 'O4/6' No. 63721 is being cut up, presumably for salvaging the inner copper firebox. The locomotive was rebuilt in 1944 with a Thompson B1 boiler. The round topped boiler is probably from a 'B17'. *National Railway Museum*

In the same boiler shop bay as above, boilermakers carrying out their work on a variety of boiler types. Note how the floor-boarding is removed to lower the boilers to a convenient working height further down the bay. The large jib at an angle at the end of the shop was for lifting the boilers into the riveting tower for riveting the longitudinal boiler barrels. Two superheater headers on the truck in the foreground will go further along to the boiler mounting shop for attention in the shop. The two storey building in the background was built after the Boiler Shop was extended and was home to the drawing offices, chain testing shop, Welding Shop, Copper Stay Shop and the Boiler Shop offices and stores.

Manchester Libraries

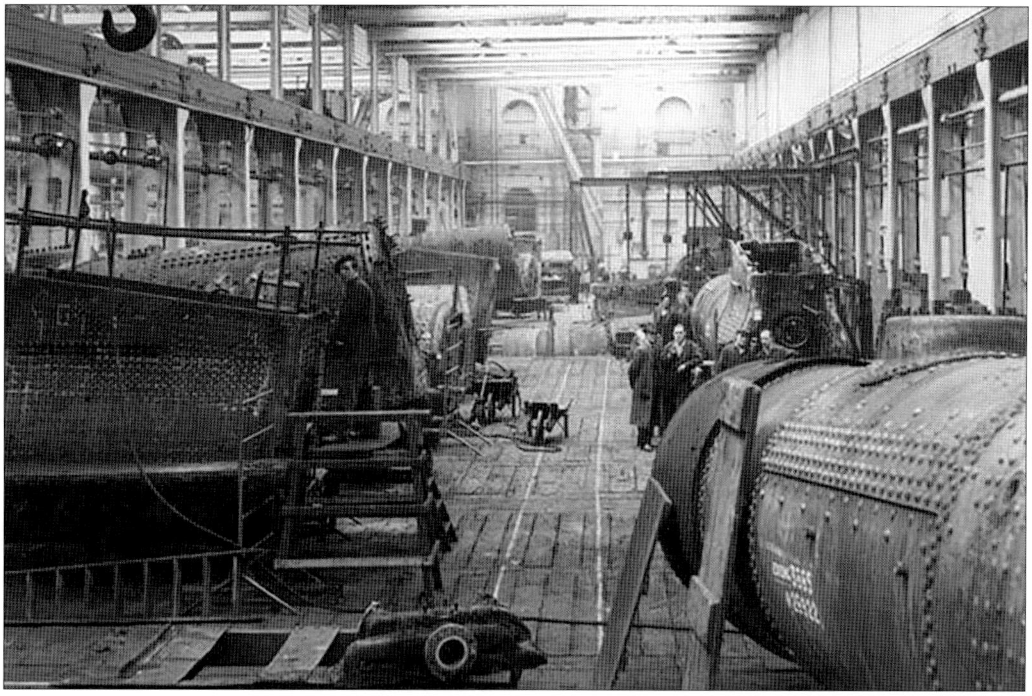

Looking in an easterly direction, two fireboxes receiving stay attention. *E.R. Lees*

Compare this photograph against the images from the GCR period. Perhaps approximately fifty years have passed between the two cameramen being in the Boiler Mounting Shop pointing their apparatus in the same direction. Nothing much has changed. Boiler mounting is still taking place. WD '8F' boilers now dominate the scene with perhaps one or two of the few remaining ex-GCR locomotive boilers. *J. Hillier*

Boiler shop No. 3 Bay. A scene of what appears to be a firebox being cut up. No doubt to retrieve the copper. Note the row of boilers to the left and two blurred figures at the side of the near boiler indicating a time exposure had to be taken to obtain the desired clear sharp image.
National Railway Museum

The Brass Finishing Shop in the 1950s was now occupying one of the former Wagon Sheet Shops. The shops' machine tools now more modern and thus taking up less space. The foreman's office can be viewed far right. It looks like it is lunch or 'brew' time judging by the men sitting down having a rest. The majority of the skilled personnel in this shop had their trade classified as 'Brass Finishers'.
courtesy Dorothy Lord

Wheel Shop. A close up of one of the wheel lathes shows the impressive size of the machines installed in the shop. The lathe is reconditioning a crank of a locomotive drive axle. In the background a lathe is turning the tyres of a wheel set. *G. Hilditch*

Wheel Shop looking east. The shop had one road leading into it and a cross road connecting it to the five bays of the erecting shop. The foreman's office can be seen at the far end. The gas rings for sweating on the tyres were at the west end behind the camera.

National Railway Museum

The Wheel Shop, this time looking west. The shop at this period was equipped with quite modern machine tools. At the far end, out of view were the gas rings used for sweating tyres onto their wheels. There are a mixture of axles and wheels to see including those from steam, 'EM2' and 'EM1' wheels. One of the two 6-ton cranes is at the far end. Adjoining this shop to the left is No. 5 Bay of the erecting shop. *J. Hillier*

The Danube looking north. This machine shop was alongside the main machine. The shop as indicated earlier was the area taken up by the original traverser that fed the twenty-one roads into the carriage and wagon shops, the nine roads into the 1847 erecting shop and two into the paint shop. The traverser was in the open air and was 365 feet long. Looking at the left-hand wall in the photograph, the arches that lead into the carriage and wagon shop (now the main machine shop) can clearly be seen. On the right-hand side the wall was raised up to support the new roof. Further down the right-hand wall were the arches into the erecting shop. The Danube housed mainly heavy and more modern machinery to the main machine shop. Planing machines and the larger milling machines were all located here. George Massey's large horizontal grinding machine which was used for grinding cross head slide bars is out of view behind the photographer as is the machine shop gauge room (1847 paint shop). The far end of the machine shop was extended in GCR days to form the inspection bay that ran transversely between both machine shops. This shop had a 15-ton and 5-ton overhead electric powered cranes installed. *J. Hillier*

The main machine shop looking north. This housed a large variety of both old and modern machinery, from small Herbert No. 2 lathes and mechanical saws up to large planing machines and double-headed boring machines, it was all here. Several fitting sections were also established in this shop. The tracks going across this shop and the Danube travelled between the erecting and boiler shops. Note the massive pillars supporting the roof, this shop was the original two-storey C&W shop and the upper storey level (now removed) can be clearly seen where the upper and lower support columns meet. The area that once formed the gallery around this shop when it became an erecting shop in the late 1870s is clearly evident. The overhead crane was of 15-ton capacity. Just before the cross rails and that is painted white for marking out and machining purposes is an articulated coupling which were used for connecting 'EM1' bogies together. Immediately at the front of the image is what appears to be lifting bracket, also painted in marking out white. *National Railway Museum*

Signifying its fate on the cab and tender side of Robinson Class 'D9' 4-4-0 No. 62302 is the dreaded 'X'. The date is 29th April 1950. Behind it are a row of similar GCR tenders waiting for the torch also. The locomotive was withdrawn the previous year but had to wait a while before being moved to Dukinfield for disposal. Of interest are its surroundings. It is stood next to the boiler mounting shop (this being the paint/ stock shed in 1848). This stretches a little beyond the 'lean to' which houses the safety valve test room. The stationary boiler was used for live testing the boilers after completion and for safety valves. The building beyond the mounting shop with the sloping roof is the 'Danube' machine shop, with the tall building behind being the main machine shop (original carriage and wagon shops) The Manchester to Sheffield main line is over the banking to the left. The bridge in the background spanning the line to Railway Street and Beyer, Peacock's. The sloping bridge is the birdcage traversing over the erecting shop and onto Widnes Street. *K.H. Cockerill*

Waiting for its turn to be cut up, Robinson Class 'J11' 0-6-0 No. 64308, oxy-acetylene bottles at the ready. This was one of the areas that locomotives met their fate in the works. Standing in the background is the original Peacock designed roundhouse which was converted to a smithy when the running sheds were built in 1877 on the other side of Widnes Street. The locomotive is standing at the side of the plate foundry. The gantry crane was used for lifting scrap metal to the main foundry furnaces (beyond the crane). Originally the old rolling mill used for manufacturing rails was on this site as well as the temporary locomotive shed used by the MR in the 1860s The square building in front of the ex roundhouse was the electrical substation for the works, running sheds and C&W shops. The large chimney was the main boiler/engine house used from day one until works closure. *I.S. Jones*

Taken from the top of the roundhouse (smithy) clock tower. The view looks east. The open wagons at the front of the photograph and under the crane gantry are where the ex scrap iron used to be stored and conveyed to the iron foundry. Immediately behind the wagons is the iron plate foundry where castings were poured for the rail plates, brake blocks etc. The low level building leading off the iron foundry at an angle on the right hand side is the iron casting fettling shed. The roof line behind the foundry is the two-storey patternmakers' and carpenters' shop. Behind the patternmakers building on the right hand side are the managers and engineers offices with the small garden. The company's telephone exchange is to the left of the main offices (known as the 'Top Offices'). Beyond the offices and on the other side of Cornwall Street is the canal depot. The two storey building is the depot's dry dock. To the far right near the top of the photo is the depot canal reservoir and settling ponds. The large building in the far distance to the top right is Varna Street School (Manchester Education Committee). It was at this school that the MS&LR employees children attended after the Company's own schools on the canal premises shut down. *J. Hillier collection*

Gorton's Last Erecting Shop – built 1890 – as it was in BR days

Every department whether it is a workshop or an office in any locomotive and carriage and wagon works, from the gatekeepers lodge to the paint shop, plays a vital part in carrying out the ultimate purpose of that establishment – to turn out locomotives and other rolling stock, either as new builds or repaired/overhauled machines, back into revenue earning service for the owning company. One department cannot function without the other.

One area of the works though does stands out to almost anyone with an interest in railways, it is here that a locomotive comes together as a finished product, the Erecting Shop. The thousands of components designed and manufactured in all the offices, departments and workshops come here to be assembled by the skilled personnel into a complete machine that will very shortly be back in traffic after it has been tested, painted, and had its trial runs. It is felt, therefore, that the Erecting Shop needs a more detailed mention.

Gorton had four Erecting Shops throughout its life. The last one was built in 1890 and is detailed here. This magnificent erecting shop was by far the largest. The adjoining Wheel Shop to the north side wall was added to the building in 1905. The shop was 480 feet long and 250 feet wide. It had five longitudinal bays 50 feet wide with three roads to each bay. An oddity of this shop was that the floor was approximately six feet lower than the adjoining shop floors (due to the lie of the land) apart from the first 60 feet leading from the machine shops and boiler shop which were at the same level as each other. This caused an inconvenience when the boilers were transferred from the boiler shop to the erecting shop. The Boiler Shop was on the opposite side to the machine shops to the erecting shop.

On leaving the Boiler Shop, completed boilers were mounted on a low truck on rail lines and moved across the Machine Shop via a capstan winding a rope and pulling the boiler into the Erecting Shop No. 1 Bay and onto the 60 foot section of the shop on the same level, commonly known within the works as 'The Stage'. From here it was lifted by the 40-ton crane and conveyed to its place if it was in No. 1 Bay. If a boiler was to go into the other bays, it was transported by the crane about 200 feet down the shop and placed on another low rail track mounted truck at ninety-degrees. These rail tracks went across all five bays transversely. This track also went from No. 5 Bay into the wheel shop so that wheels could also be moved to and from the Wheel Shop to all the bays in the same manner. The rail tracks also went through the south wall and out of the erecting shop. No. 5 Bay was somewhat shorter than the other four bays as the Copper Smiths Shop incorporated into part of No. 5 Bay at the east end of the shop. This shop was approximately 120 feet long by 50 feet wide.

The Erecting Shop offices were at the south-east corner of the shop accessed at the 'stage' and on the lower erecting shop floor. The works locomotive weighbridge was once situated at the west end of No. 5 Bay (No. 15 road). The weigh bridge was relocated at an earlier date to its own shop in the works yard close to the running shed turntable. During the 1950s the 5-ton crane in No. 4 Bay was moved over to the 'stage' end of No. 1 Bay. This no doubt for lifting lighter assemblies for and into the 'EM1/2' locomotives during new building work and repairs/overhauls to avoid using the heavier 40- and 50-ton cranes. The two 50-ton cranes were installed in No. 1 Bay later on in the shops years replacing earlier 40-ton cranes, this was to assist with the lifting of the heavier classes of locomotives, i.e. the 'EM1' and 'EM2' electrics. Extra crane rail support pillars had to be installed equi-spaced between the existing cast iron pillars to enable the new cranes to lift the heavier loads. The new pillars were of fabricated steel construction. This gave No. 1 Bay a total of four overhead cranes.

Another oddity of the erecting shop was that the shop at the west end when constructed was built over a drained reservoir that had been used as a water supply for John Ashbury's railway carriage and wagon works a little further to the west of Gorton works. This new erecting shop (as it was in 1895) was built partly over the cavity left by the reservoir and formed a 'storage area'. On a day during World War Two a crew of platelayers arrived in the shop and removed some of the wooden flooring from the section where the 'storage area' was situated, and flat bogie wagons were shunted into the shop. With the use of the overhead cranes several very large naval gun barrels were removed and placed on the wagons and shunted away. Perhaps these barrels had been stored there after Armstrong Whitworth's had closed down in approximately 1932. Armstrong's being involved with naval armaments and heavy industry had their large engineering company at the west side of Gorton Locomotive works across on the opposite side of Bessemer Street.

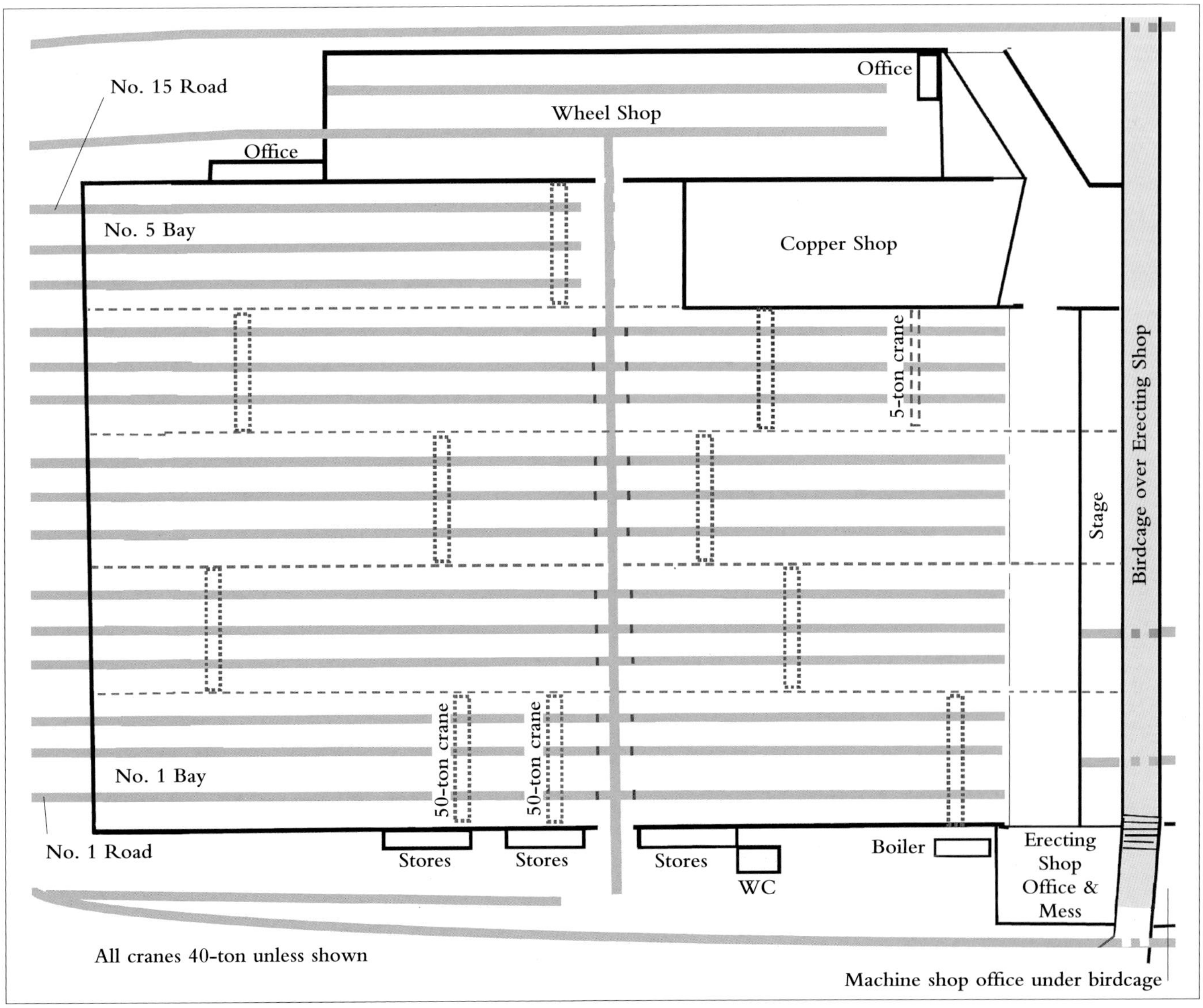

This plan of the Erecting Shop, Wheel Shop and Copper Smiths Shop predates the move that took place in one weekend during the 1950s when the 5-ton crane in No.4 Bay was transferred to No.1 Bay. The footbridge at the right-hand side of the drawing was the 'Birdcage' that crossed the over the works and main line to give access between Widnes Street in Openshaw and Railway Street in Gorton.

An image more than likely taken on a weekend as there is no activity in No. 3 Bay except for the roof and crane support columns having a new coat of paint. A mixture of what appears to be ex-GC and L&NER classes of locomotives are in the distance with a Riddles 'Austerity' Class 0-6-0 saddle tank nearest the camera and what appears to be the frame of an 'O4' alongside on No. 7 road. All looks nice and neat in this scene, not the usual clutter, has the works manager made a tour of the works and been not happy, or perhaps a VIP visit is on the cards. Note the 'Lister Auto Truck' in the foreground, a very common and versatile vehicle for moving lighter components around railway workshops. Many other industries in general used these vehicles and were in abundance both home and overseas.

courtesy D. Lord

No. 2 Bay. Viewed looking from one of the two 40-ton cranes. A mixture of ex-GC and L&NER types completes the scene in what appears to be an extremely busy period. Some locomotives receiving attention are 'O4' No. 63877 to its left in No. 3 Bay is 'A5' No. 69825. to the right is 'B1' No. 1281 (later 61281). To the right of the B1 is the frame of 'O4/8' No. 63575.

National Railway Museum

On the 18th October 1959 Class 'O4' 2-8-0 No. 63898 is receiving attention in No. 3 Bay. The locomotive was a Thompson rebuild with a B1 100A type boiler in 1944. *E.M. Johnson*

All is quiet in No. 1 Bay. Looking at the scene, steelwork is being laid out for the start of fabrication of 'EM2' frames. Construction is about to start. Down the bay, the locomotive body on No. 3 road will no doubt soon going to be lowered onto the 'EM1' bogies at the far end of the bay. *E.M. Johnson*

Sporting its 55G (Huddersfield) shed code and looking a little lonely, Class WD 'Austerity' 2-8-0 No. 90347 is shorn of its connecting rods. The AWS cable has been uncoupled also. Was it brought into the works like this or is a strip down about to start for repairs or overhaul? *MLS collection*

More 'Dubdees' accompanied by what appears to be an 'O4' in the next bay. With engine parts scattered all over the place in what appears complete disarray, it makes one wonder how the locomotives were all reassembled, not a problem though for the skilled personnel in the erecting shop. *E.M. Johnson*

No.2 Bay, July 1953. WD 2-8-0 No. 90423 on overhaul and has received a replacement boiler from class mate 90227. Receiving attention behind the WD are an '04' 2-8-0 and an 'N5' 0-6-2. *K. Field/Rail Archive Stephenson*

Gresley's huge six-cylinder Garratt Class 'U1' 2-8-0 + 0-8-2 No. 69999 stands on No. 6 road in No. 2 Bay in August 1952 undergoing conversion to oil burning. The locomotive was built 'over the road' at Beyer, Peacock Ltd and was fitted with two three-cylinder engines with Gresley derived motion similar to the GNR Class '02' locomotives. *K. Field/Rail Archive Stephenson*

Left: A crane driver's view of No. 1 Bay looking west with mainly ex-GC and L&NER types. Notice the locomotive wheel sets on the centre roads, this was a usual practice for placing them, either after removal or before refitting them back on the locomotive.

Below: In No. 1 Bay L&NER/BR Class 'O4/8' 2-8-0 No. 63688 stands on No. 2 road receiving a casual repair. The locomotive was rebuilt in 1944 with a Thompson 100A (B1) boiler and side window cab. Built in February 1918 and originally numbered 1670 by Robert Stephenson & Co. Ltd for the ROD and after seeing service in France, it returned to to the United Kingdom and after some time in storage it was taken into L&NER stock in December 1923.

Both J. Hillier collection

Doyen of the Class 'EM1's. Prototype Bo+Bo No. 26000 *Tommy*. Built in 1941, the locomotive commenced test running a year later on freight then passenger work over the MSJ&A system. The locomotive stands outside Gorton's erecting shop immaculately turned out from the paint shop in black livery, lined out in red. *C. Forest/Rail Archive Stephenson*

Right: No. 26000's nameplate *Tommy*. The inscription on the lower half of the plate explains why it was given this name. *C. Forest/Rail Archive Stephenson*

Class 'EM1' Bo+Bo DC electric locomotives

Almost immediately after the completion of the ten Thompson Class 'B1' 4-6-0 locomotives, Gorton commenced building the new Class 'EM1' (Electric Mixed-traffic 1) Bo+Bo 1,500 DC electric locomotives for the Manchester, Sheffield and Wath line (MSW). These had four-wheeled bogies with an articulated connection and all axles were powered by traction motors.

The prototype for these, L&NER No. 6701 was completed at Doncaster Works in 1941 but electrification of the Woodhead Route, together with construction of sixty-nine further locomotives, was delayed by the Second World War. No. 6701 was tested on a few sections of 1,500 V DC lines owned by the L&NER until in 1947 it was loaned to Dutch Railways to help with their post war shortage of locomotives.

The prototype locomotive had been assigned the classification 'EM1' in September 1945 and was renumbered 6000 in June 1946 It remained on Dutch Railways until 1952 when the Woodhead electrification was complete. It was renumbered to 26000 once returned to British Railways.

Between 1950 and 1953, a further fifty-six locomotives were built at Gorton to a slightly modified design but were still classified 'EM1'. There were to have been a further twenty-four built at Darlington but these were cancelled. Electrical equipment for the locomotives was supplied by Metropolitan-Vickers, who completed the final assembly of the locomotives at Dukinfield Works.

They were fitted with twin diamond-shaped pantographs and it was normal to run with both raised in normal Woodhead operation in order to maximise current collection under any weather conditions. Also at certain points on the Woodhead Line, notably in the vicinity of steam locomotive water columns, the electric overhead lines were as high as twenty feet above the tracks. The pantographs had to stretch to almost their full height to reach the wires at such points.

EM1 Class Named Locomotives

26000 *Tommy*	26051 *Mentor*	26057 *Ulysses*
26046 *Archimedes*	26052 *Nestor*	
26047 *Diomedes*	26053 *Perseus*	
26048 *Hector*	26054 *Pluto*	
26049 *Jason*	26055 *Prometheus*	
26050 *Stentor*	26056 *Triton*	

In 1950, No. 1 Bay in the Erecting Shop was utilised for the 'EM1' build, (and later the 'EM2'). In this view, the base frames for the bodies of the locomotives are being fabricated. A completed body is at the far end of No. 1 road with a half completed body in front of it. At the very far end are three steam locomotives receiving attention. As production increases on the new work all steam related work will be concentrated in the other four bays. A total of fifty-six 'EM1's were built at Gorton. A number of the class were fitted with electrically-heated boilers for passenger steam heating. Twelve locomotives later on received names, these being after characters from Greek mythology including the first named in the class *Archimedes* (following on from *Tommy*) the greatest inventor and mathematician of all time. The first steam locomotive built at Gorton bore the same name almost 100 years previously. *J. Hillier collection*

Two pairs of 'EM1' Class bogies are in view, those furthest away appear complete, already painted and no doubt prepared for use. The set nearest are still being fabricated with most sub- assemblies yet to be fitted. All looks nice and neat in this bay, free from the clutter of the usual scenes associated to railway workshops of this era, for how long though? No. 1 Bay from the start of the 'EM1' build was dedicated mostly for this class and the following 'EM2' Class. Later on, after the final 'EM2's construction had been completed, steam locomotives would start to appear on occasion in the bay again at the west end but the area at this end of the shop was dedicated for electric traction repairs and overhauls. The power cars for the Manchester, Hadfield and Glossop EMU power cars were usually overhauled in this bay also, (the trailer and driving trailer cars being overhauled in the carriage and wagon shops) but normally the usual heavy maintenance was carried at the carriage and wagon shops over the other side of the running sheds if no lifting was required. Reddish electric traction depot looked after maintenance and servicing for all DC stock. The odd guest would sometimes make an appearance, those noted were the Glasgow 'Blue' 25 kv EMUs that came down to Manchester after a series of problems were encountered to their electrical systems to be corrected by Metropolitan-Vickers. These units were normally sent to the old Dukinfield carriage and wagon works for remedial work but, if no space was available Gorton received them. Another surprise appearance late in 1962 was a 'Peak' Type 4 main line diesel electric locomotive, it probably came in for the rectification of some problem encountered whilst out on the road, the locomotive was only in the shop for a very short time. *J. Hillier collection*

Class 'EM1' locomotive construction. A very busy time in this bay, behind the almost completed 'EM1' body in the foreground, another one is starting to take shape. The bulkheads dividing the internal compartments are already in place whilst further down the bay another frame is perched on stands.
J. Hillier collection

A completed Class 'EM1' bogie stands in front of a new locomotive body in No.1 Bay ready for use. Looking at the end of the shop above the locomotive going right to left is the underside of the 'birdcage'.
B.K.B. Green/E.M. Johnson collection

Above and below: No. 3 road in No. 1 Bay, 1953. Class 'EM1' locomotives under repair, the wheel sets showing the large seventy toothed resilient gearwheels and the traction motors with their seventeen teeth (ratio 17/70). Traction motor nose bearings are scattered on the floor along with brake slack adjusters and other locomotive paraphernalia. 'EM1' traction motors adorn the second photograph whilst new 'EM2' cabs are being fabricated behind them whilst further back an unidentified DC electric locomotive is on stands with two others on No. 1 road. In the next bay a Class '04', 2-8-0 is receiving attention on No. 4 road *both K. Fields/Rail Archives Stephenson*

Gorton's Last New Build
Class 'EM2' Co-Co Electric Locomotives 1,500vdc - No's 27000 to 27006

Immediately on completion of the Class 'EM1' Bo+Bo electric locomotives 26001 to 26057 in 1954 the 'EM2' Class build started. The locomotives were rated at 2,800hp at 1 hour rating and 2,400hp continuous with a tractive effort of 45,000lb they were a larger development of the 'EM1' Class. Whereas the 'EM1's were designed for mixed traffic work, the Co-Co EM2 locomotives were designed specifically for express passenger work between Manchester and Sheffield (The Woodhead route). All the locomotives, including some of the 'EM1' Class, were given names from Greek mythology. The names given were from a suggestion to British Railways by the late railway historian and renowned author George Dow.

27000 *Electra*	27003 *Diana*	27006 *Pandora*
27001 *Ariadne*	27004 *Juno*	
27002 *Aurora*	27005 *Minerva*	

The 'EM2' differed considerably from the 'EM1' Class, with regards to the body and bogie design The 'EM1' bogies were based on a design from the original 1941 electric locomotive built at Doncaster to the design of Sir Nigel Gresley with steam age technology and knowledge in mind whereas the bogies for the 'EM2's were a new departure. The design had been proven very successful with the LM&SR/BR diesel-electric locomotives numbers 10000/1 as they were almost identical and were therefore an obvious choice for the 'EM2's. The 'EM2' Class were considerably longer than the 'EM1's to accommodate the Co-Co bogies and the extra equipment inside the body, i.e. an extra high voltage switch frame inside the HT compartment for the larger number of contactors to be used and an extra resistance compartment. The electrical equipment (apart from the traction motors) for both 'EM1' & 'EM2' Classes were identical, both coming from Metropolitan-Vickers of Trafford Park in Manchester and other suppliers.

After the closure of Gorton in 1963 the locomotives were sent to Crewe Locomotive Works for their overhauls and repairs, as were the 'EM1' Class.

In September 1969 all of the class were sold to the Netherlands Railways (NV Nederlandse Spoorwegen) following them being in storage at Bury Sheds for a short time. In the Netherlands they became Class 1500. Six were put into use with No. 27005, *Minerva* being scrapped and used for spares as this locomotive was in the poorest condition.

The locomotives were withdrawn in 1985/6. by the NS. Three have been preserved of which two have been repatriated. No. 27000 *Electra* (NS No. 1502) is preserved at the Midland Railway Centre at Butterley back in its original BR black livery and number (27000) although still fitted out as modified to NS condition. No. 27001 *Ariadne* is now preserved in NS condition as No 1505 on display at the Manchester Museum of Science & Industry (MOSI). No. 27003 *Diana* (NS No. 1501) is now preserved in the Netherlands in NS condition at Werkgroep.

The following selection of photographs were taken in No. 1 Bay of the erecting shop at Gorton during 'EM2' construction in 1953 and 1954. As they were the last locomotives to be built at Gorton, it is fitting to include a number of photographs of poorer quality which otherwise would never be seen again.

An 'EM2' base frame undergoing fabrication, it was clamped down in a large number of places to a jig in an effort to keep the frame true and square. In the foreground are lengths of channel and 'I' section steel lying in wait for the next base to be fabricated. *J. Metcalfe collection*

Above: Two views of No. 3 road in No.1 Bay looking west with an 'EM2' base frame in the process of being manufactured. A cab is next door, perhaps it is to be allocated to this frame when everything is completed. Further down the shop a locomotive is perched rather high up on stands.

Right: Two tradesmen are working on with what appears to be part of the flooring for a base frame. Pneumatic chisel guns appear to be part of their tooling for this particular exercise, no doubt being used to trim off 'leftovers' from the oxy-acetylene torches used to cut out the plate

all J. Metcalfe collection

Two images of 'EM2' Bogies undergoing fabrication. The bogies were almost identical to those of the LM&SR built diesel electric locomotive No's 10000/1. Drawings for the jigging up for fabrication obviously coming from Derby Locomotive Works technical department with possibly engineers from Derby also being on site for the first one or two builds. The upper photo showing the large number of clamps and fasteners involved with the welding/fabrication process. The lower photograph shows the two sides of the bogie frame, probably being aligned for cross member fitment. In view also are frame sides already cut out for further bogie fabrications. There is every possibility that these bogies are for the first 'EM2' (No. 27000) as in the background of following views are new bogies for an 'EM1' locomotive. If this is the case, then the date is 1953 as this is the year that both classes of locomotives were built new side-by-side (the last new build date for the 'EM1's).

both J. Metcalfe collection

Two more views in No. 1 Bay on No. 1 road showing the progress of 'EM2' bogies under course of construction. After inverting the bogie outer sides to their correct position the cross members and springing arrangement were fitted including brake cylinders. The upper photograph also shows new 'EM1' bogies already connected with their articulated coupling. This indicating that the bogies are for 'EM2' No. 27000 with the last of the 'EM1' locomotive construction taking place.

both J. Metcalfe collection

These views show No. 3 Road in No. 1 Bay, looking east. Here, 'EM2' Bogies are nearing completion, Showing the axle driven gearwheel, this, with the traction motor drive pinion would give a drive ratio of 17:64. The centre pivot assembly is yet to be fitted. The wheel arrangement on an 'EM2' loco was designated as Co-Co giving each axle a traction motor, i.e. six motors per locomotive, The '-' between each bogie indicating that the bogies were not connected mechanically. Meanwhile No. 2 Bay work is going on one of Gorton's works shunters, a Riddles 'J94' 0-6-0ST and also what appears to be a Class 'N2' 0-6-2T.

both: J. Metcalfe collection

Looking west on No. 3 road, a bogie that appears to be complete but, on a closer look it is not quite. The centre pivot, 'spider' is in place. A traction motor has been fitted, but as yet no cables for the motor. The traction motor gear case has been fitted, the bearing journal caps for the nose suspension of the motors have been fitted, the axle bearing journal covers are yet to be fitted, as are the bearing oil caps. Is this a 'trial fit' to check if all goes together as it should be? The rail line running at 90 degrees in the photo (L to R) was for transporting heavy objects, i.e., boilers, wheels etc. from bay to bay and also in and out of the Wheel Shop. *J. Metcalfe collection*

Again, No. 1 Bay, on No. 3 road. A look at an 'EM2' body being fabricated from both ends. The top view looks onto No. 2 end. With the side panels and roof still to be fitted, the various compartments can be identified. These are, left to right: the EMG and traction motor blower, boiler, resistance, high tension electrical, and SMG and traction motor blower, exhauster, compressor, and low tension electrical panel. Over in No. 2 Bay a 2-8-0 Class 'O4/6' No. 63718 and 2-6-4T Class 'L3' No. 69050 are receiving attention. The 'R3' above the 'O4's number indicates the position of boiler cladding, i.e. 3rd cladding from boiler front, RHS. *both J. Metcalfe collection*

Two photographs that are not of the best quality but certainly worth an inclusion. *Left*: A panel being marked out, cut and drilled probably for a bulkhead within one of the 'EM2's. Note the 'stage' at the end of the shop with step handrails leading up to it, the erecting shop office immediately to the right on the stage. Note also the large glazed doors at the end of the shop, these doors led into the machine shop. It is here that the boilers pass through the machine shop to and from the boiler shop. All work on 'EM2' locomotives came to a stop when this event occurred. The 40-ton crane is over the stage in its usual stance waiting for a boiler. Above the crane is the 'Birdcage' public bridge. *Right*: An 'EM2' base frame is receiving attention as it is being turned over by both of the fifty-ton overhead cranes. *both J. Metcalfe collection*

Taken late in 1954 – the final year that Gorton would turn out new locomotives. The 'EM2's will go down as the first of British Railways' main line class of electric passenger locomotives, entrusted (as with the EM1 mixed traffic locomotives before them) to the skills of Gorton locomotive works men and women. Who is with Joe Metcalfe as he is standing by the door of 27005? Perhaps a reader could tell us? On the extreme left of the photo, now 13 years old 'EM1' *Tommy* was now in the erecting shop for a very lengthy spell whilst having major rectification work. No. 27005 will end up in Holland following in *Tommy's* footsteps after British Rail no longer has use for her along with the rest of its class. *J. Metcalfe collection*

Time for a little more posing. Some of the new build crew stand proudly in front of No. 5. Joe Metcalfe stands to the far right, but who are his work mates? Is that Bill Lawless third from the right? One more Co-Co to build after this and the guys will go back on repairs and overhauls. With their experience on the electric locomotives they will probably stay working in No. 1 bay. The roof sections have yet to be fitted over the boiler and machinery compartment at No. 2 end. Check out the wheelbarrow, daubed with paint 'New Work' – the men making sure that this piece of hi-tech equipment is not stolen to go elsewhere in the shops.
J. Metcalfe collection

Tommy has muscled in for a better view of it in this photo as No. 27005 is lifted by the two 50-ton erecting shop cranes off its stands on No. 1 road, and across to its awaiting bogies on No. 3 road. In the right foreground are bogie centre assemblies, which when fitted to the bogies will soon grace the underside of the last of the class shortly after No. 5 has left the shop. The gent second from the right appears to be giving instructions to the crane drivers as both the cranes must work in unison to avoid any mishaps. *J. Metcalfe collection*

No. 27005 is now resting on stands on No. 3 road. The next exercise is to have its bogies rolled under for the body to be coupled to them. The traction motor in the foreground appears to be from an 'EM1' locomotive. A close examination of the photograph shows that the gent in the trilby watching the proceedings is making sure that all goes well, perhaps he is one of the erecting shop foremen, one of the Middlehurst family members perhaps.

J. Metcalfe collection

27005 now in the works yard, the number still only stencilled on the cab side as it awaits going to the paint shop to be painted in lined out BR black. Joe Metcalfe (centre) poses with three of his workmates. One more new 'EM1' to go and Gorton's new builds will come to an end. Later to be named *Minerva*, this locomotive did not fair too well when the class was purchased by the Netherlands Railways. It was broken up and used for spares for the remaining six locomotives in service over there.

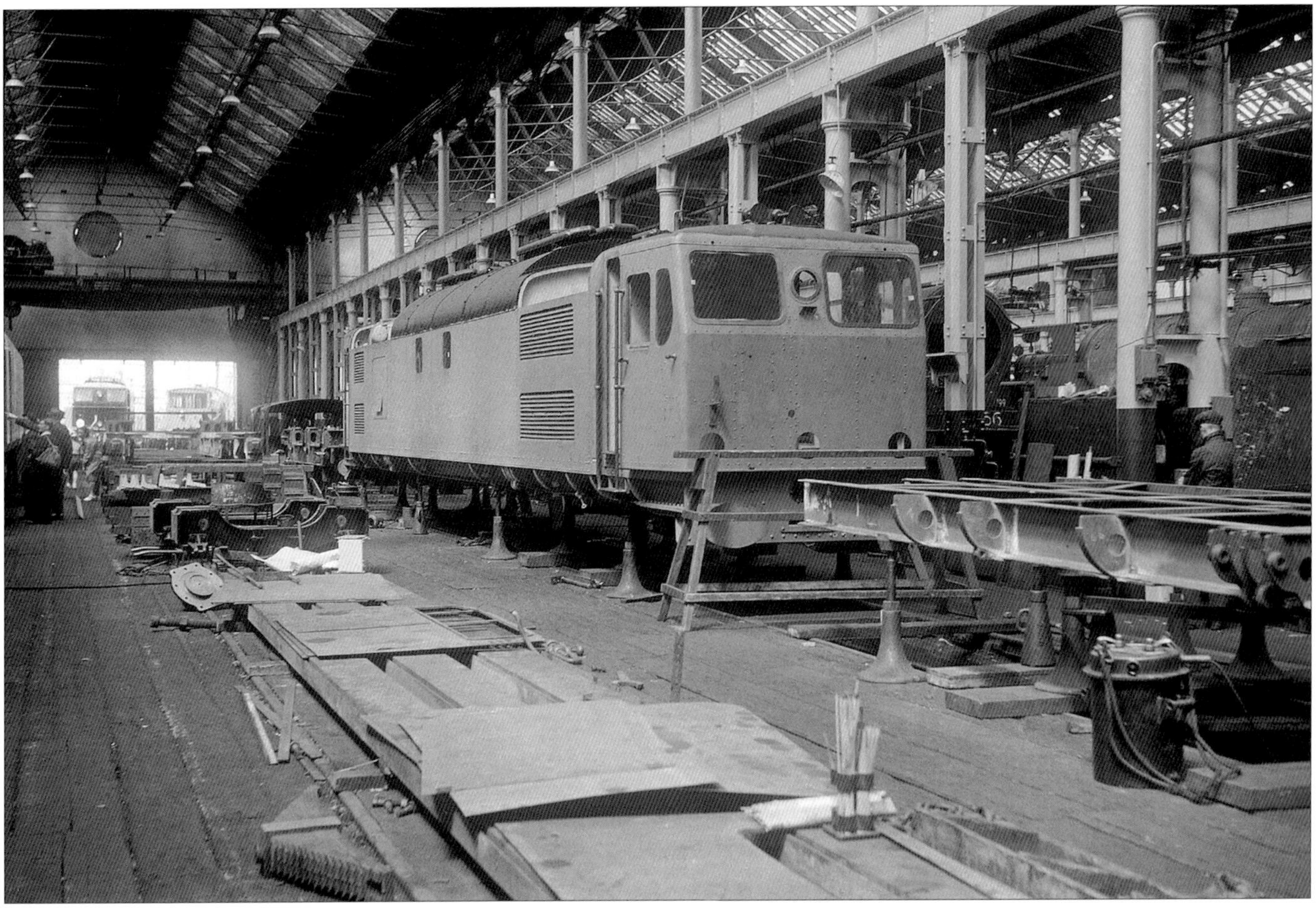

No. 1 Bay, July 1954. An 'EM2' is being fitted out on No. 3 road. A base frame for a 'sister' locomotive is in the foreground with what appears to be another of the class on the far left being sized up by a party of visitors whilst outside the shop is an unidentifiable 'EM1' or 'EM2'. In the foreground steel plating for locomotive fabrication work is lying out on the floor waiting to be worked on. Note the welding machine next to the locomotive base in the foreground, quite a common type in that era, a stack of welding rods are at hand waiting to be used once the visitors have passed by this area. Further down the middle road are large sub assemblies for the 'EM2' bogies. It can be seen that the 'EM2's were fitted from new with two horns at each end. The 'EM1' Class had only one when originally built but were similarly fitted with two progressively. Notice the additional steel fabricated intermediate support columns for the overhead electric cranes, for reasons explained earlier in this review. The first 'EM2' emerged from the works in December 1953 and the last, No. 27006 was turned out on New Years Eve 1954, was that date pure coincidence or a planned effort to turn it out for the New Year? From that date onwards, no other new locomotives would emerge from Gorton again.

K. Field/Rail Archive Stephenson

Two 'EM1' wheelsets stand waiting for attention as 'EM2' No. 6 body is being lowered onto its bogies. The two 50-ton cranes being inched down until they come to rest. Note the lamp head code. Certainly a locomotive fit to be at the head of a royal train. Perhaps the lamp targets were placed there in recognition by the erection crew knowing it is possibly the last new locomotive ever to leave the works. From now on all work will consist of repairs and overhauls and the increasing amount of locomotives that enter the works for cutting up.

J. Metcalfe Collection

J. Metcalfe collection

Class EM1 Bo+Bo No. 26034 pictured at Woodhead on a trial run ex works 1959.

Carriage and Wagon Works

The traverser at the carriage and wagon works in action. Parcels van No. M31153M makes an exit from Bay 3 (light carriage repair bay) on the south side of the complex following repairs, the bogies are all painted and ready for the road. The van was built at Derby in 1940/41 in a batch numbered 31109 to 31158. Dimensions 50ft x 9ft 0ins x 14ft $4^5/_8$ins. Rated to a carrying capacity of 12-tons. Still extant in 1968. When originally constructed, the traverser was powered by steam. *NRM C63174 (Upper) & C63715 (Lower)*

Carriage and Wagon Works. Viewed from the traverser in the lifting shop at the far north of the complex. The photographer probably has his back to the wheel lathe. The shop offices are at the far end of the photograph at the right-hand side of the view. *J. Hillier collection*

The same shop looking south along the wagon repair bays. *J. Hillier collection*

Plan of the Carriage and Wagon works

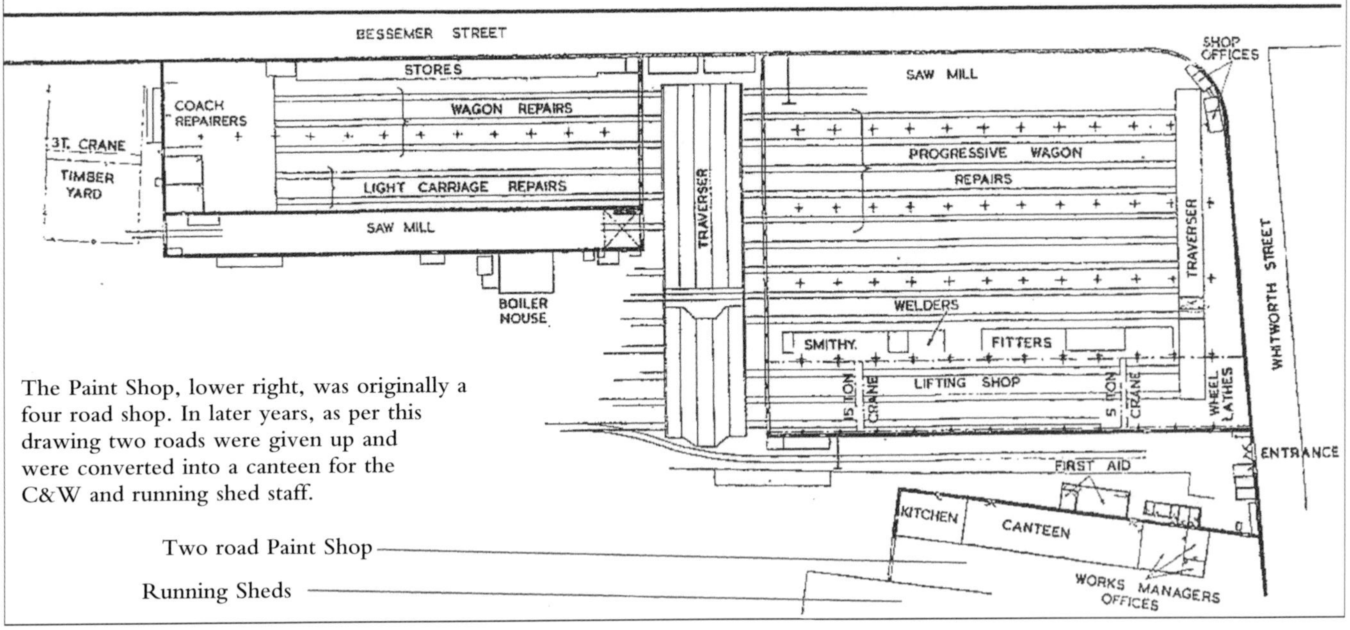

The Paint Shop, lower right, was originally a four road shop. In later years, as per this drawing two roads were given up and were converted into a canteen for the C&W and running shed staff.

These shops were the last C&W shops to be built at Gorton (1881) as an addition to the shops built in 1879 in the works on the east side of Widnes Street. When Dukinfield Carriage & Wagon Works was built in 1909, Gorton's 1879 shops gave up a number of their bays for locomotive work. These shops remained solely for carriage and wagon repairs until closure, all new coach and wagon construction being carried out at Dukinfield. *Author*

The Carriage & Wagon Works' underground wheel tyre profile machine. *J. Hillier collection*

Points and Crossing Shop – P'way Shop (Permanent Way Shop)

Compare this photograph to that on page 128, very little has changed in thirty years, the swing arm cranes now have electric hoist motors fitted. The 'Smith's' hearth is still extant with the 100-ton press positioned under one of the swing arm cranes. The radial arm drilling machine is still there, all the planers are still in use. The five-ton crane is at the west end of the shop. At this date, judging by the amount of rails in the shop, it is still an extremely busy shop. *J. Hillier collection*

Paint Shop

Above: *Butler Henderson* stands in the paint shop with a coach for company. When the locomotive came to the shop, a retired paint shop foreman had to be brought in to give his expert guidance as to how the painting should be carried out. Judging by the locomotive's appearance the ex-foreman did a magnificent job. John G. Robinson would fully approved and given his thumbs up. *E.M. Johnson*

Left: Painting the side of a MSW Class 'EM1' Bo+Bo electric locomotive. A nice warm and quiet environment to work in, apart from the odour of paint and varnish. *J. Hillier collection*

Charlie Cheetham and Joe Metcalfe have nipped over to the paint shop with some other workmates to pose in front of *Andy Capp*. *Andy* was painted bright yellow for the *Daily Mirror* newspaper to haul a couple of 'Andy Capp' specials. The locomotive was an ex LM&S Compound, Fowler Class '4P-A' 4-4-0 No. 41101. '*Andy*' retired from service shortly after its temporary star status and was withdrawn in late 1959.

J. Metcalfe

It is the 30th September 1950 and brand new 'EM1' No. 26001 is seen resplendently painted in the paint shop. Standing behind her is 26002 being prepared for painting and lining out. Also undergoing painting, probably after a major overhaul in the shop are Class 'B2' (rebuilt 'B17') 4-6-0 No. 61627 *Aske Hall* at that time a 31A (Cambridge) locomotive and Class 'B1' 4-6-0 No. 61150 of Sheffield (39B).

MLS collection

Gorton Works Yards

A view taken from the Birdcage looking east into the works yard. The Robinson 'Pom Pom' Class 'J11' (GCR '9J') 0-6-0 No. 64307, ferrying an open wagon loaded with coal and an old boiler between the works and the running sheds, looks to be in ex-works condition and probably just started 'running in'. The year is probably 1948, the locomotive carrying the sans serif BRITISH RAILWAYS on the tender and yet to be allocated to a shed. In the right background is the brass foundry. To its left is the steel laydown yard and further left is the permanent way shop with its outside gantry crane. The very tall building in the far distance is the old 'High Bank Mill' on Ogden Lane. Part of the mill at that time was used by Hugons of Atora Suet Pudding fame. Atora moved from the Ogden Lane site in 1974 and relocated to near Hartlepool. They now come under the 'Premier Foods' banner *MLS collection*

Waiting its turn to enter the erecting shop is Robinson L&NER Class 'B9' (GCR Class '8G') 4-6-0 No. 61473. It received its BR number in February 1949 but was withdrawn very soon after in May 1949. It was previously withdrawn in July 1939 but was reinstated. *Rail Archive Stephenson*

L&NER Class 'S1' 0-8-4 No. 69905 is also waiting for its turn to enter the Erecting Shop. A Gresley build in June 1932 to add to the four existing Robinson Class 'S1' three-cylinder locomotives. Behind the 'S1' is 'Q1' No. 69935 waiting its turn for shopping. *K. Field/Rail Archive Stephenson*

Another view of the Robinson Class 'S1' 0-8-4 No. 69905 waiting for shopping in 1949. *K. Field/Rail Archive Stephenson*

Standing in the works yard in August 1953, boiler fitted 'EM1' Class No. 26054. Built in mid 1952 it is quite likely the locomotive has not yet been out on the road as it is not yet complete – the pantograph heads are not fitted and a wiper arm is missing from No. 1 end drivers side window. The 1,500 volt system was also not completed as yet giving the fifty odd locomotives already built little work. The locomotive was later named *Pluto* from Greek mythology in line with several others of the class. *E. Fry Rail/Archive Stephenson*

Gresley's Garratt waiting to go in the shops. The headlight was fitted when the locomotive was transferred to Bromsgrove for banking duties on the notorious two mile long 1 in 38 Lickey Incline in Worcestershire. It did not remain there for long as the engine was found unsuitable for the job and problems with oil firing did not contribute to its performance. The locomotive was withdrawn in December 1955. Standing to the right of the Garratt is a Parker designed Class 'N5' 0-6-2T No. 69296 and to its left is a Robinson Class 'C14' 4-4-2. All this must be bewildering to the young child who is undoubtedly a member of a group of visitors. *K. Field/Rail Archive Stephenson*

Standing in the shed yard, fresh from the paint shop. Class 'Q1' 0-8-0T No. 69936. This class of locomotive was a rebuild by Thompson of the Robinson 'Q4' 0-8-0 tender engines 'Tinies'. The locomotive is awaiting for its return to Frodingham.
J.P. Wilson/Rail Archive Stephenson

Gresley Class 'B17' 4-6-0 No. 61600 *Sandringham* queuing up to go in the shops with an unidentified 'Pom Pom' close behind. *MLS Collection*

Two more 'B17's, No. 61631 *Serlby Hall* and class mate 61646 *Gilwell Park*, waiting to go into the shop in June 1951, both for repairs. *K. Field/Rail Archive Stephenson*

Another view of *Serlby Hall* and *Gilwell Park*, this time from the rear. No. 61646 looked to be in for a Light Repair according to the chalked note on the lower cabside. 'B17's became a staple diet for a long time at Gorton for repairs, overhauls, and rebuilds to the two-cylinder Thompson variant, the 'B2's. The two 'B17's No. 61659, *East Anglian*, and No. 61670 *City of London* both had their streamline casings removed during their spell at Gorton Tank for overhauls. *K. Field/Rail Archive Stephenson*

Gorton Men

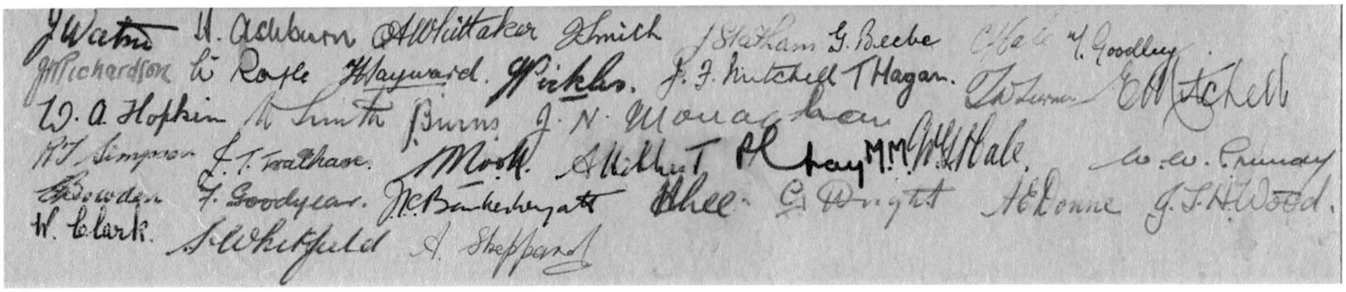

Gorton Tank's Foremen outing to Matlock in September 1955. Those signatories than can be deciphered are:
J. Watson; H. Ashburn; A. Whittaker; J. Smith, J. Statham, G. Beeber, C. Hale, T. Goodley
J. W. Richardson, W. Royle, H. Sayward, J. Pickles, J.F. Mitchell, T. Hagan, T.W. Turner, E. Mitchell
W.A. Hopkin, W. Smith, J. Burns, J.N. Monaghan
R.T. Simpson, J. T. Trathan, N. Nook, A. ??, M.M. McKay; W. G. Hale, W. W. Grundy
E. Bowden, F. Goodyear, ? Barker Wyatt, H. Lee, G. Wright, A. E. Donne, G.S.H. Wood
W. Clark, S. Whitfield, A. Sheppard.

Two very close and long time friends both in work and on the outside. Joe Metcalfe and Charlie Cheetham stand in the HT compartment of one of the MS&W electric locomotives in the erecting shop
J. Metcalfe collection

Staff from the drawing office congregate on the 'stage' for a group photo. This platform was used for daylight blueprint copying. To the right of the young lady is the Manchester to Sheffield main line with a Gresley locomotive heading toward Manchester. The tallest gent at the rear of the ensemble is Roy Payne. I wonder if any readers can put names to some of the other faces. *courtesy A Quirke*

Erecting shop. Four workmates pose between two Class 'EM1' locomotive bogies in the erecting shop. *J. Metcalfe collection*

The brake job – 1958/59. Back row, Jimmy Hindley, Jim-my Crompton, Bob Rhodes, Tommy Warren. Front row, Alf Carruthers, Jimmy Woodhouse, Jimmy Hinsley and Terry Holtby. *courtesy Terry Holtby*

Below: It is not known for definite what the occasion is but it appears that it is a Christmas function, judging by the cake surrounded by beer bottles in the erecting shop. Who is the gent with the tuba? Perhaps a musical interlude is about to take place. Would alcohol be allowed in the workplace in todays world? I doubt it, but then again, who knows, this after all was Gorton Tank.
J. Metcalfe collection

Below left: Parked outside the small north east entrance to the erecting shop by one of the birdcage columns, Brian Faulkner (at the wheel) with one of his mates pose for a photo on board their Lancing Bagnall 'Tug' truck, a design that goes back to the 1940s. Brian's older brother Harold was a fireman over at the sheds and in the early 1950s fired Gresley Pacific *Flying Scotsman* out of Gorton and on the Manchester London Road to Marylebone run just before the overhead was electrified on the Manchester to Sheffield route. Brian's younger brother, Bobby, started work at the Tank in the smithy (roundhouse) in late 1960 working on the 'Massey' steam hammers in 1961.

Below right: Brian and colleague again. This time supporting the birdcage column. Judging by the amount of people working there all from the same family, Gorton Tank was more or less a family concern!
both courtesy M. Johnson/Authors collection

Posing by Class 'O4' 2-8-0 No 63765, a group of erecting shop employees taking a break on what looks like a nice bright day. Dennis Corcoran, the gent with his leg stretched, out advises that the crew in the photograph worked on the weekend, carrying out repairs to locomotives reported with defects at the sheds. *courtesy D. Corcoran*

The 'Nutters Band'. The millwright shop's own musical ensemble. Can any old Tank employee or families recognise anyone in both of these photographs? *Pryce Williams*

Friday March 16th 1946 – Erecting shop

Gorton's most tragic day was on Friday, March 16th, 1946. During the course of that fateful Friday morning an employee (welder) was cutting off bolts using oxyacetylene equipment on a tank locomotive in the erecting shop, Whilst using the equipment the cylinder gas pipe and head caught fire. The foreman over the relevant section rushed over to help the employee on seeing the gravity of the situation, at that point the cylinder exploded. The usual practice at this period in time was to lay oxyacetylene equipment horizontal on flat trolleys. This caused the bottle to shoot down the shop horizontally like a rocket where it went as far as the shop as far as the crossing tracks crossing tracks. Two people were killed as the result of the explosion other people were seriously injured. The foreman who tried to help with the initial problem on the cylinder head was severely injured and lost a leg, he died ten minutes after arriving at hospital, he was the second of the first two fatalities. Three other men died later on as a result of their injuries, making a total of five people. One man who was seriously injured lost both legs but survived. The welder suffered head, back and leg injuries and passed away later. They were among nine people who were detained in hospital. Three of those detained through injuries were aged nineteen, sixteen and a very young employee aged fourteen, the fourteen year old youth (an erecting shop office boy) also lost both legs. At the inquest into the accident in Manchester, it was reported that the welder had a burnt pipe on his oxyacetylene equipment. After removing the burnt section of the pipe he reconnected it, and, when the nozzle of his torch was relit the pipe set on fire and travelled to the cylinder regulator and head, with the result being an explosion. The inquest verdict on the deceased was 'Accidental death'. Six ambulances attended the scene. Gorton works had not long before this event set up a first aid post within the works, and though such a horrific accident such as this was well above any first aid post capabilities, the nurse on duty was the heroine of the day in doing her upmost to give comfort to those that were the most seriously hurt along with all the first aiders in the works who rushed over to assist. If there had been no first aid post (it was not uncommon for engineering facilities not to have ambulance rooms first aid posts at this period in time) the suffering endured would have been considerably worse.

As a result of this accident, HM Inspector of Factories Mr J. H. Boyes with a colleague visited the works shortly afterwards and as a result of his investigations was adamant in his report that industrial gas cylinders had to be stored in a vertical position and this became an official recommendation. This instruction became law, not just within the railway industry but nationwide and had a rippling effect overseas also.

It was not part of the Inspectors scope of work, so it was not officially recorded but he did note that it was probable that one of those who lost their life was not actually an employee in the erecting shop but was there collecting bets from another department. The names of those affected by the terrible events of that day have been withheld. A book titled *Steel Wheels and Rubber Tyres* written by Geoffrey Hilditch also contains an eye witness account of that most tragic day.

British Railways Staff Association (BRSA). Once the GCR library and before that it formed part of one of the MS&LR schools and the old train crews barracks, now a social club open seven days a week with entertainment every Saturday and Sunday night. A favourite place for members and non-members alike. The club was affiliated to the local working mens clubs in the area. Both Harry Jewett Snr and Jnr played snooker there – both were great players. Harry Senior was a pleasure to watch and played competition snooker. Davy Jones of the Monkees fame was once reputed to have sung there! Him being a Gorton lad and, additionally his father worked at the Tank. Davy attended Varna Street School just a hundred or so yards from Cornwall Street and the works. An alternative to going into the canteen on a Friday lunch time was to go into the club to play bingo. Usually a foreman would shout out the numbers whilst the players and other club members, including the under 18s, all enjoyed a 'swift half' (or two). There was not much concern about having a drink and going into work in those days. Other activities of the club was fishing on the canal depot reservoirs. When the canal depot was in decline, the few who still worked (caretakers on essential services) at the depot would often sneak to the reservoirs and 'throw a line'. Is that Nick behind the bar, always topping pints up for the regulars who visited the snooker room, one could have a really cheap night out in the snooker room. *National Railway Museum*

CHAPTER SIX
THE FINAL YEARS

Now a nationalised industry, Gorton works faired just as badly as when it was in its L&NER period when it came to building new locomotives. Gorton, now part of the Eastern Region of British Railways, was given an order to build 10 of the Thompson designed 'B1' Class locomotives immediately into 1948. The locomotives were numbered 61340 to 61349 inclusive. The final B1 was the last new steam locomotive to be built at Gorton, this being in 1949. On completion of construction and testing they were all transferred to the Scottish Region and would never see Gorton works again. Under British Railways all locomotives sheds were given an identification coding system very similar to that which had been used by the LM&SR. Gorton shed was given the code 39A. All locomotives allocated to Gorton shed received this shed code, this being a small cast plate that was attached to the front of the smokebox door. In 1958 Gorton works and shed came under the auspices of the London Midland Region during regional changes to the railway network. The shed code changed to 9G on the first February 1958, with the code 9H for just a very short time before being 9G (perhaps for just a month or so).

In addition to the new 'B1' construction, Gorton now concentrated on repairs and overhauls to ex GCR and L&NER types. Quite a large number of Gresley Class 2-6-0 'B17's passed through the shops. The following BR review gives a pictorial account of the various types of locomotives that was dealt with in the shops. In the later 1950s and to closure, GCR types went through the works less frequently as they were replaced by later designs.

Thompson Class 'B1' 4-6-0 No, 61340. The first of ten built at Gorton. The class was first introduced in 1943. A total of 410 locomotives were built between British Railways, the L&NER and outside contractors. A very successful class, they were soon the preferred 4-6-0 type by the L&NER and as production increased the older classes of 4-6-0s started to be disposed of as they became worn out including the ex-GCR 4-6-0s. The chap in the centre wearing a white apron is Richard Hardwick – chargehand patternmaker and is mentioned elsewhere.
John France

Another view of Thompson's 'B1' No. 61340 just before leaving Gorton. Turned out in November 1948 and bearing 'British Railways' on its tender, the lion over wheel totem would soon be applied. After its running in turns it was sent directly to and based at Eastfield Shed Glasgow (65A) and later to Dundee (62B).
E.M. Johnson

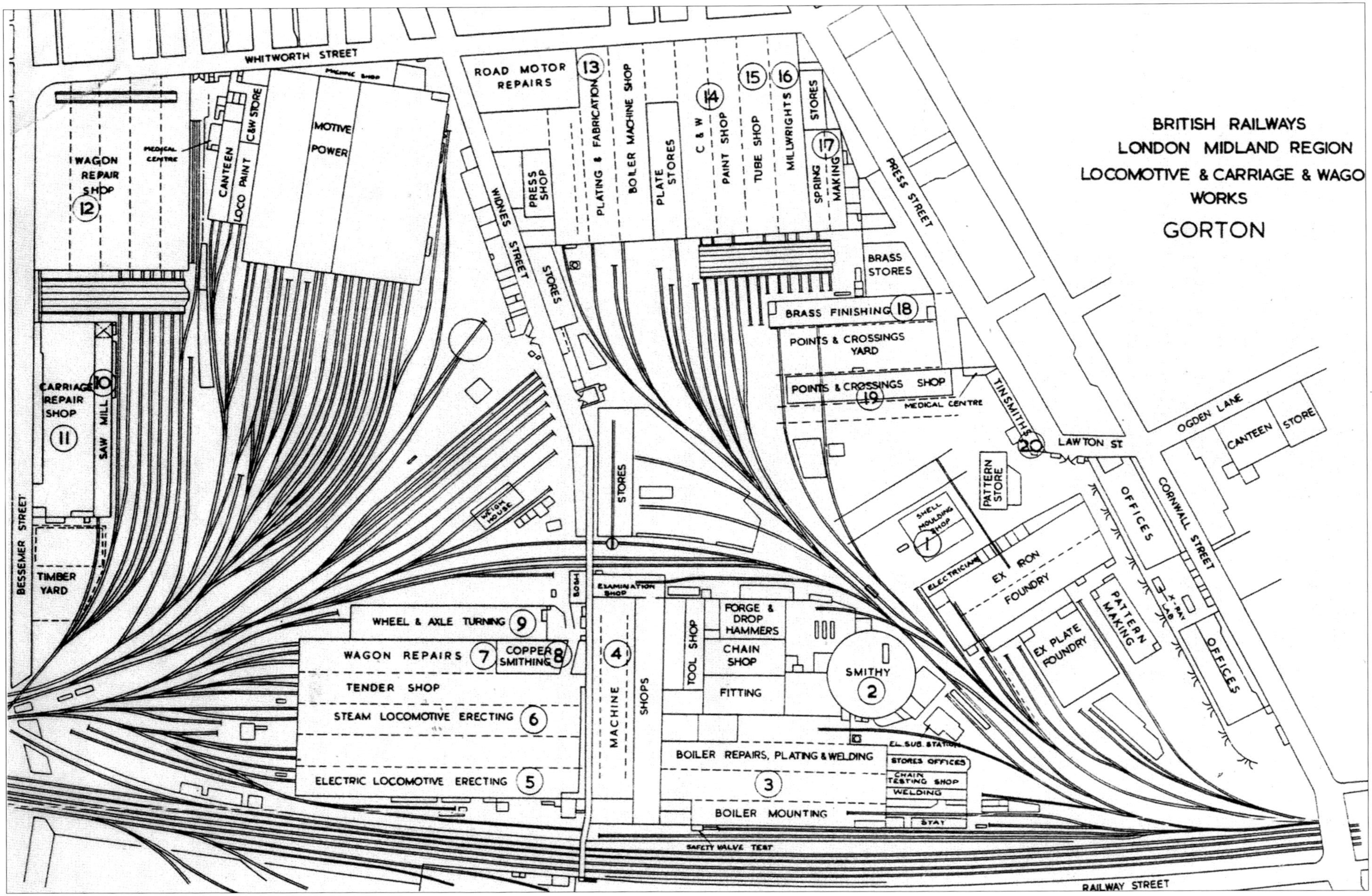

Plan of Gorton works in its late BR days. 1. Brass Foundry 2. Smithy 3. Boiler Shops (3 bays + boiler mounting shop) 4. Main Machine Shop 5, 6, & 7. Erecting Shop (5 bays) 8. Copper Shop 9. Wheel Shop 10. Saw Mill 11. Carriage Repair Shop 12. Wagon Repair Shop 13. Plate and fabrication bay 14. C&W Paint Shop (2 bays) 15. Tube Shop 16. Works main millwrights 17. Spring Shop 18. Brass Finishing Shop 19. Permenant Way Shop 20. Tin Shop (tinsmiths) 21. Wagon Shop traverser 22. Running sheds (20 roads) 23. Turntable 24. Running sheds offices - signing on - mess 25. C&W traverser 26. Traverser 27. Works main entrance, Lawton Street 28. Disused train crews barracks (used as stores) 29/ BRSA social club 30. Telephone exchange, X -ray and Photography dept. 31. Machine Shop (Danube) 32. Main boilers.

'A foreigner in the camp'. Resting on what is now its own shed at Gorton (now 9G) Fowler 'Crab' Class '5MT' 2-6-0 Mogul No. 42748 keeping company with a fellow LMR locomotive 'Jinty' Class '3F' 0-6-0 No. 47471. *MLS collection*

Parker designed Class 'N5' 0-6-2 (MS&LR Class '9F') first introduced in 1891 and built in batches up to 1901. Here, in its new BR identity No. E9288, numbered as such on the 13th March 1948 (soon to be 69288) stands in Gorton's yard next to Class J11 'Pom Pom' No. 4336. *MLS collection*

March 1948, just three months under public ownership Class 'Q4' 0-8-0 No. E3235 stands outside the weighbridge in ex-works condition. The locomotive will soon be renumbered 63235. Built at Gorton in 1909 as GCR Class '8A' No. 163, the class became known by the name 'Tinies'. When the '8K' 2-8-0 class were built a few years later that class became known as 'Bogie Tinies'. Later all became just 'Tinies'. *E. Fry/Rail Archive Stephenson*

Built in December 1946, LM&SR Ivatt Class '2MT' 2-6-2T No. 41203 stands outside the sheds at Gorton all spick and span with a bunker full of coal. Withdrawn in the second half of 1963, the locomotive had a relatively short life of just sixteen years. *MLS collection*

Standing on Gorton's turntable is 'O4' No. 63912. Judging by her condition it looks like she is fresh out of the paint shop and all coaled up, no doubt ready for running in trials. No transfers on the tender yet but the locomotive has its shed code fitted. The locomotive shed offices in the background with the works bar stores beyond over the other side of Widnes Street. *MLS Collection*

In very early BR days. Class 'O4/8' rebuilt with Thompson type BI boiler but otherwise still a Robinson locomotive. No. 63893 looks quite clean for an 'O4', that will soon change though when the locomotive goes back into service on freight and mineral hauling duties. *MLS Collection*

Class 'O4' 2-8-0 No. E3586 (soon to be 63586) stands outside Gorton's weighbridge. This is very early into the BR period. (February 1948) 'British Railways' on the tender but no 'Lion on wheel' transfer yet. The locomotive next door still in L&NER colours. The 'O4' looks like ex-works but that will soon change when it resumes its normal duties. *MLS collection*

Still in L&NER livery and with No. 1482 Class 'B4' 4-6-0 in early BR days. Originally GCR Class '8F' No. 1097 *Immingham*. A total of ten were built, all by Beyer, Peacock & Co. in 1906 to a Robinson design. No. 1097 was the last of all the Robinson 4-6-0s to be withdrawn (1950). Standing in the background is Gresley Class 'J39' 0-6-0 No. 64836. *MLS collection*

Gorton running sheds. The breakdown crew posing proudly in front of their new crane in early BR days. The running sheds administration buildings in the background.

Bert Lloyd/E.M. Johnson collection

August 1961. Looking in ex-works condition. Thompson Class 'O1' 2-8-0 No. 63873. stands outside Gorton shed. The locomotive was a rebuild of a Robinson 'O4' (GCR '8K') fitted with a 100A boiler, new cylinders and Walschaerts valve gear. This locomotive was also fitted with Westinghouse pumps for use on the Tyne Dock/Consett iron ore trains that used compressed air to operate the hopper doors.

D. Hampson/MLS collection

Foundry wall Gorton. The actual wording on the nameplate read ' VALOUR' 'IN MEMORY OF G.C.R. EMPLOYEES WHO GAVE THEIR LIVES FOR THEIR COUNTRY 1914 - 1918' *National Railway Museum*

Opposite: The Gorton 'Valour' memorial, showing the location on the foundry wall adjacent to the works main gates on Lawton Street. Further along the foundry wall is a large curved casting inscribed 'MS&LRCo.' was this plate over the original entrance to the works in 1847/8? It is believed that this plate was destroyed when the building was demolished. *National Railway Museum*

'VALOUR'

Great Central Memorial Locomotive Valour and Armistice Day.

GCR Locomotive No 1165 was the third locomotive built of Class '9P' 4-6-0 4-cylinder express passenger locomotive. The class was sometimes known as the 'Lord Faringdons' after the first built of the class. The locomotive was built in July 1920 and was named *Valour* in remembrance to those who fell during World War One. The nameplate was unveiled during a ceremony. With the forming of the 'Big Four' in 1923 the locomotive became Class 'B3' under the L&NER classification scheme and renumbered 6165 accordingly. It was further renumbered 1496 in 1946 but is generally recognised as being 6165.

The class of locos were very powerful machines although quite heavy on coal but enjoyed success hauling such prestige trains as the 'The Yorkshire Pullman' over Great Northern Railway metals.

On Armistice Day each year *Valour* was released from normal duties and headed a special train adorned with wreaths on the smokebox door and nameplates. It ran a special train from Manchester London Road station to Sheffield Victoria station usually accompanied by the works manager and wife and ex-servicemen. At Sheffield the wreathes were placed on the GCR Memorial.

After the locomotive was withdrawn from service in December 1947 one of its nameplates was mounted on a special memorial plaque that was attached to the foundry wall and situated close to the main entrance to the works on Lawton Street. The second nameplate was donated to, and is on view in, the National Railway Museum, York.

The Gorton memorial was located on the foundry wall so that it was on full view to all those employees entering the works to give a reminder of those who never returned from both major hostilities. On each side of the nameplate were cast brass plates with the names of GCR employees who had fallen in the Great War on the left-hand side and names of those of World War Two on the right-hand side. A third plaque was added underneath the nameplate inscribed: 'Also those who made the supreme sacrifice 1939 - 1945'.

On the Friday proceeding Armistice Day each year a small service was held at the memorial, this involved wreaths being laid on the base of the plinth, usually by the youngest female and male employee, followed by elder employees – no doubt one or two of the elder employees laying wreaths may have served in either of those terrible conflicts.

After closure of Gorton Works the second nameplate was fitted on a plinth at the then new St. Barnabas Church in Openshaw. A dedication service was held c1964, officiated by the Suffragan Bishop of Middleton, Manchester. Along with the nameplate were the two plaques with the names of the fallen that was also attached on the Gorton Foundry Wall.

Regretfully the nameplate was stolen from St. Barnabas Church sometime in the early 1970s. A reward was put out for information that would lead to its recovery but, as it has never been recovered. It is sad to think that the plate may have been melted down.

Does anybody know these two young teenagers? Dated approximately to the mid 1950s, Gorton's youngest female and male employees are laying wreaths on the memorial. This was an annual event which took place every Friday preceding Armistice Day. To the left of the passageway is the Accountants offices, the smaller building further on is the X-ray offices followed by the main offices (top office) furthest along the passageway.

National Railway Museum

From the youngest to the eldest. Wreath laying at the memorial. The medals proudly adorned by these gentlemen shows that they have given service to the major conflicts and no doubt is a poignant moment for them. The tall gent on the left was Vinson Gulliver (28 November 1887 – 7 August 1997). Vinson started his railway career at Trafford Park Locomotive sheds in February 1907 and retired in 1953. He lived to a remarkable age and was the oldest known living man in the United Kingdom at the time of his death.

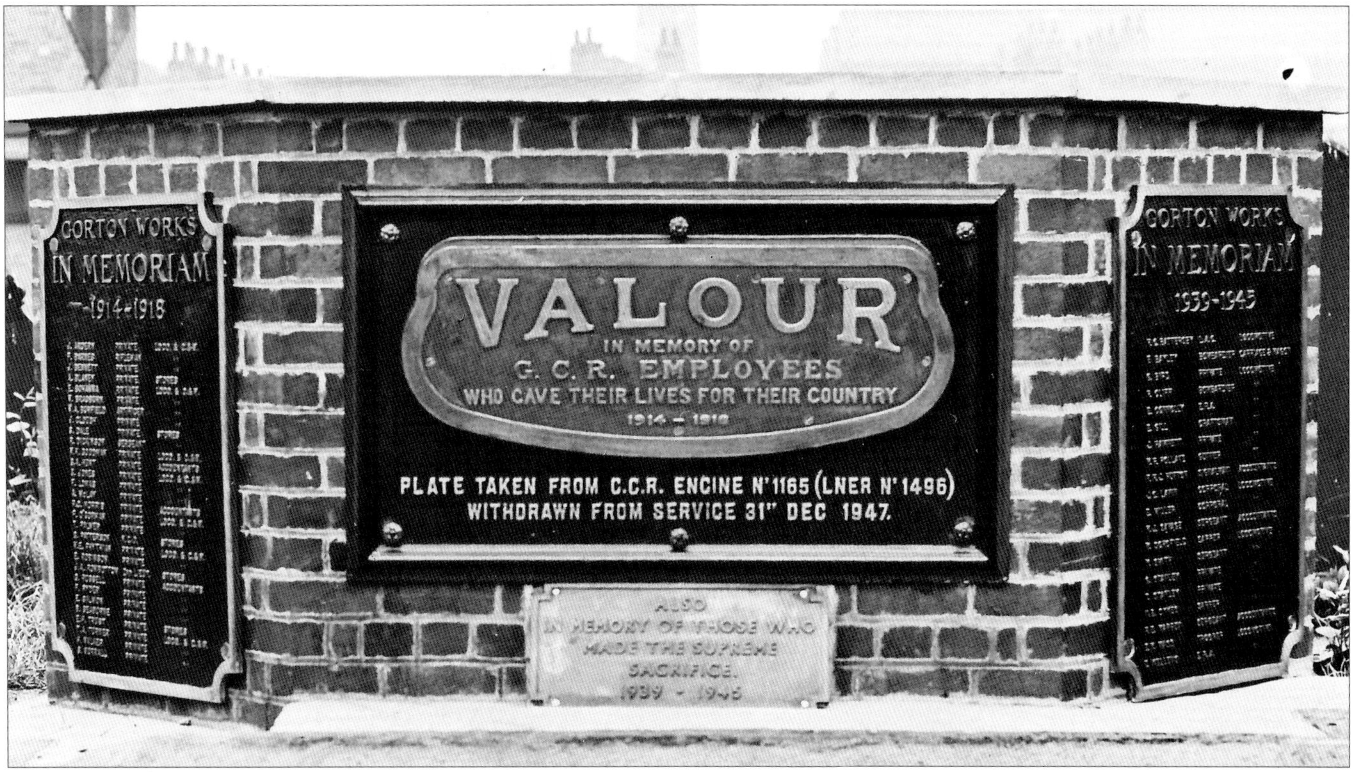

Above & below: 1964, *Valour's* nameplate that was attached to the foundry wall at Gorton now affixed to the plinth at St. Barnabas Church in Openshaw. The names of those that fell in the conflicts are attached to the plates that are angled off on both sides of the plinth. Photographs taken at the dedication service by the Suffragan Bishop of Middleton *J. Hillier collection*

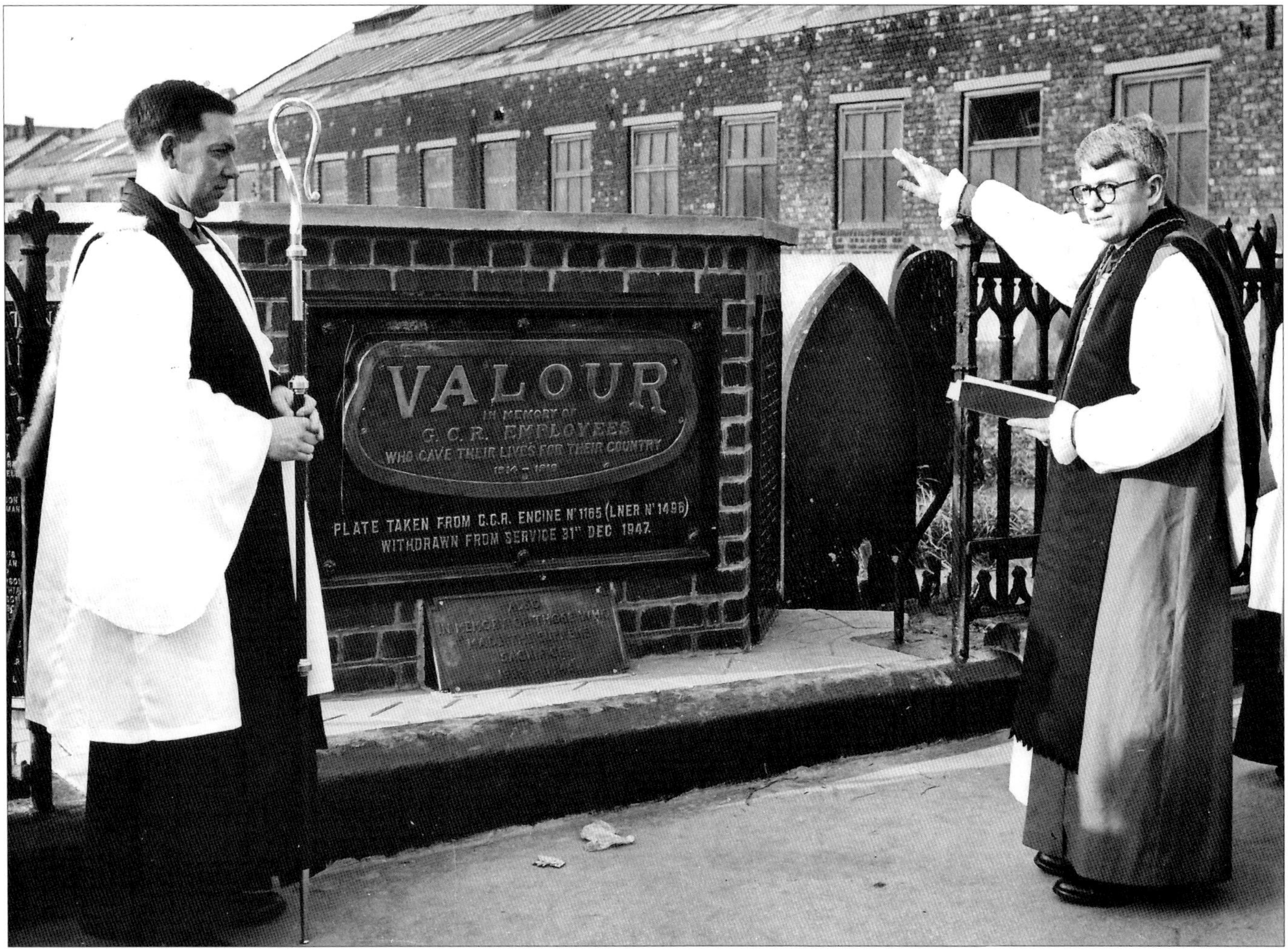

An exhibition for the apprentice training programme set up in the erecting shop The model of the 'EM2' was worked on in the gauge room in the Danube. Ironically at the side of the 'EM1' is a poster displaying a new Western Lines AC locomotive, first introduced in 1959/60. AC being the future way to go and the death knell to the MSW DC line.
National Railway Museum

Apprentices and Training

All departments within a railway workshop have to train new employees, the same applies in any industry. Gorton locomotive works was no exception. Young people, especially those of school leaving age require the necessary skills to carry them on into adulthood to take over those who reach retirement age, this is a natural process.

Whether the training is in offices taking on clerical rolls or hands on within the locomotive running department or in the workshops, it is imperative that the training is of sufficient capacity to carry out their everyday tasks when training is complete safely and be fully proficient.

Apprentices in the 1960s had to carry out a six year apprenticeship, 44 hours a week in the early part of this period, the school leaving age was 15. An apprenticeship to be fully skilled was this length of time due the many skills required to do their everyday work. This period is matched, probably more so by those who work in the locomotive running department in particularly locomotive drivers who, start off as engine cleaners and work up to be firemen and ultimately drivers, this takes quite a number of years to accomplish.

For apprentices at Gorton Tank, there was no formal training school such as the schools at Crewe, Derby and other large workshops. Practically all training was carried out on the job. The exception to this though was 'day release' where, apprentices could go to a technical college one day during the week during that school term as part of the apprenticeship. Before permission was granted for them to attend technical college, however, apprentices were required to attend evening classes in their own time to prove that they were serious about carrying out an apprenticeship. This was usually at Varna Street school in Gorton or Wheeler Street school in Openshaw and was for a full year of evening studies usually learning craft theory. On completion of the evening classes, and after obtaining a 'Pass' certificate with good attendance, then, day release was granted.

Apprentices attending day release usually attended Openshaw Technical College. The college had a reputation for training engineering skills second to none and no doubt gave a good insight to the theoretical and mathematical side of engineering that could have been missed on the shop floor. The colleges' workshops and machine shop was well equipped and gave students good training on their machine tools. The following pages illustrate apprentices carrying out some of the chosen trades that were necessary for the locomotive workshops to function.

A further view of the exhibition posters. The date must be 1960, displaying the work of apprentices that three years later would probably need transfers to other railway workshops. Note the Midland Pullman poster on the display. *J. Hillier collection*

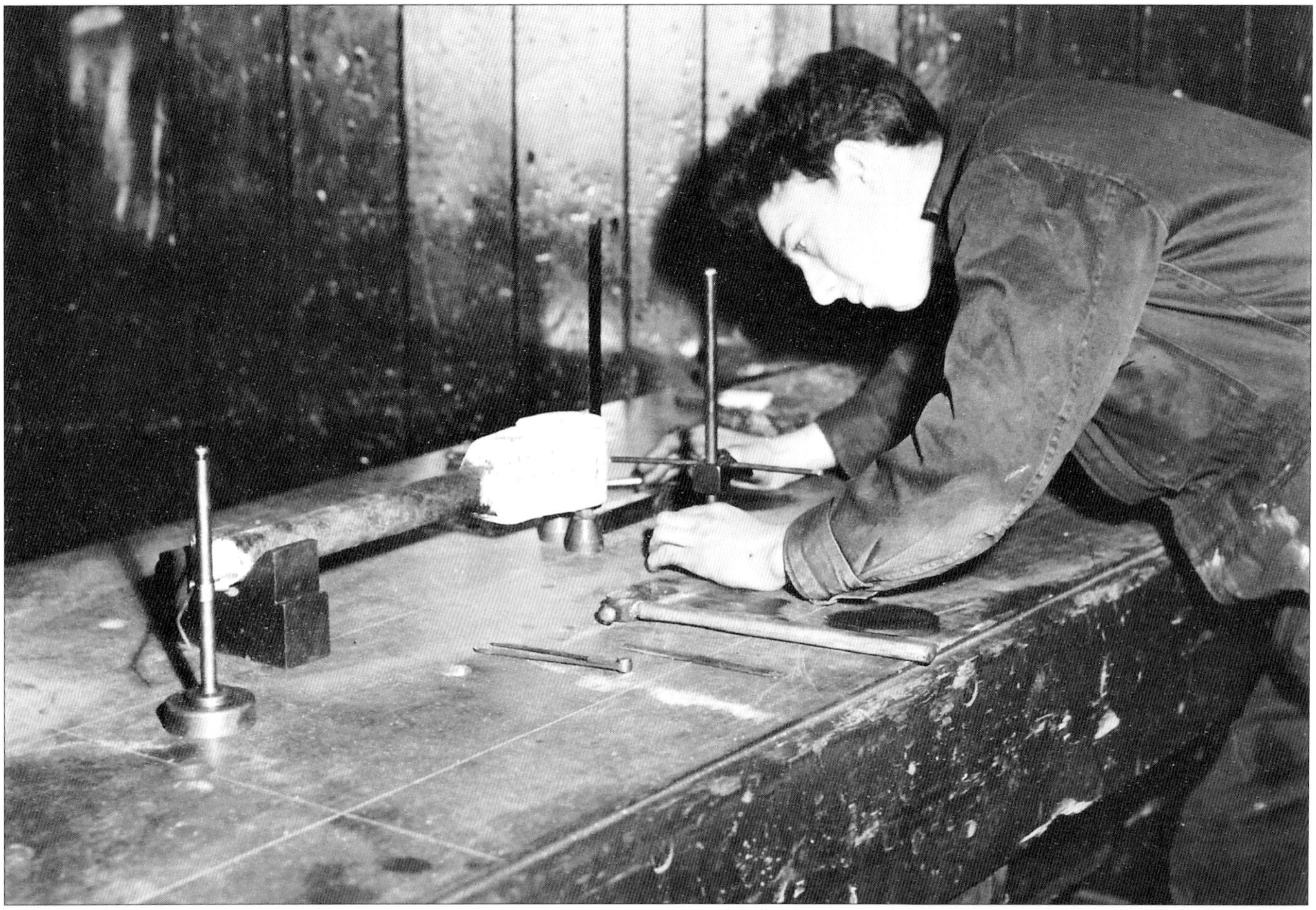

Above: Marking out block. The base of the scribing block to the left of the apprentice appears to be made from the outer section of a ball bearing race (a common practice at Gorton).

Right: Apprentice Tin Smith. Manufacturing an oil can in the tin shop. The tin shop manufactured lamps, cupboards and signal parts etc, including aluminium fabrication.

both J. Hillier collection

An apprentice carpenter assembling a window frame and assembling the finished frame in the workshops.

Above & right: In the brass finishing shop an apprentice brass finisher is assembling steam locomotive whistles. He must ensure that the seals are pressure tight to avoid any problems. *all J. Hillier collection*

Left: An apprentice brass finisher in the Brass Shop working on coaching stock door locks.

Below: Two views of the fabricating of fuel tanks for diesel electric locomotives being built at Crewe and Derby works.

all J. Hillier collection

Copper Shop: Apprentices, forming a copper steam pipe and brazing pipe couplings.

both J. Hillier collection

An apprentice turner machining bearing trunnions on a lathe and below measuring his work piece with a micrometer. *both J. Hillier collection*

Machine shop. Cylindrical grinding operation in use. Usually work of this nature was carried out by fitter-turners as part of their apprenticeship.

Machine Shop. Apprentice fitter working on a piston valve assembly.

both J. Hillier collection

Left: Carpenter / cabinet makers working on office furniture.

Above: Apprentice french polisher

Below: Cabinet maker planing a piece of wood, no doubt to fit in the specialised tool / equipment box he is in the process of making.

all J. Hillier collection

In the carriage and wagon workshops, apprentice coach builders carrying out repairs to a closed fruit van. Extensive repairs were still carried out at Gorton up to the works closure. *J. Hillier collection*

Apprentices in the carriage and wagon works. The work that they are involved with is converting coaches for working on the overhead wiring on the AC western lines electrification. *J. Hillier collection*

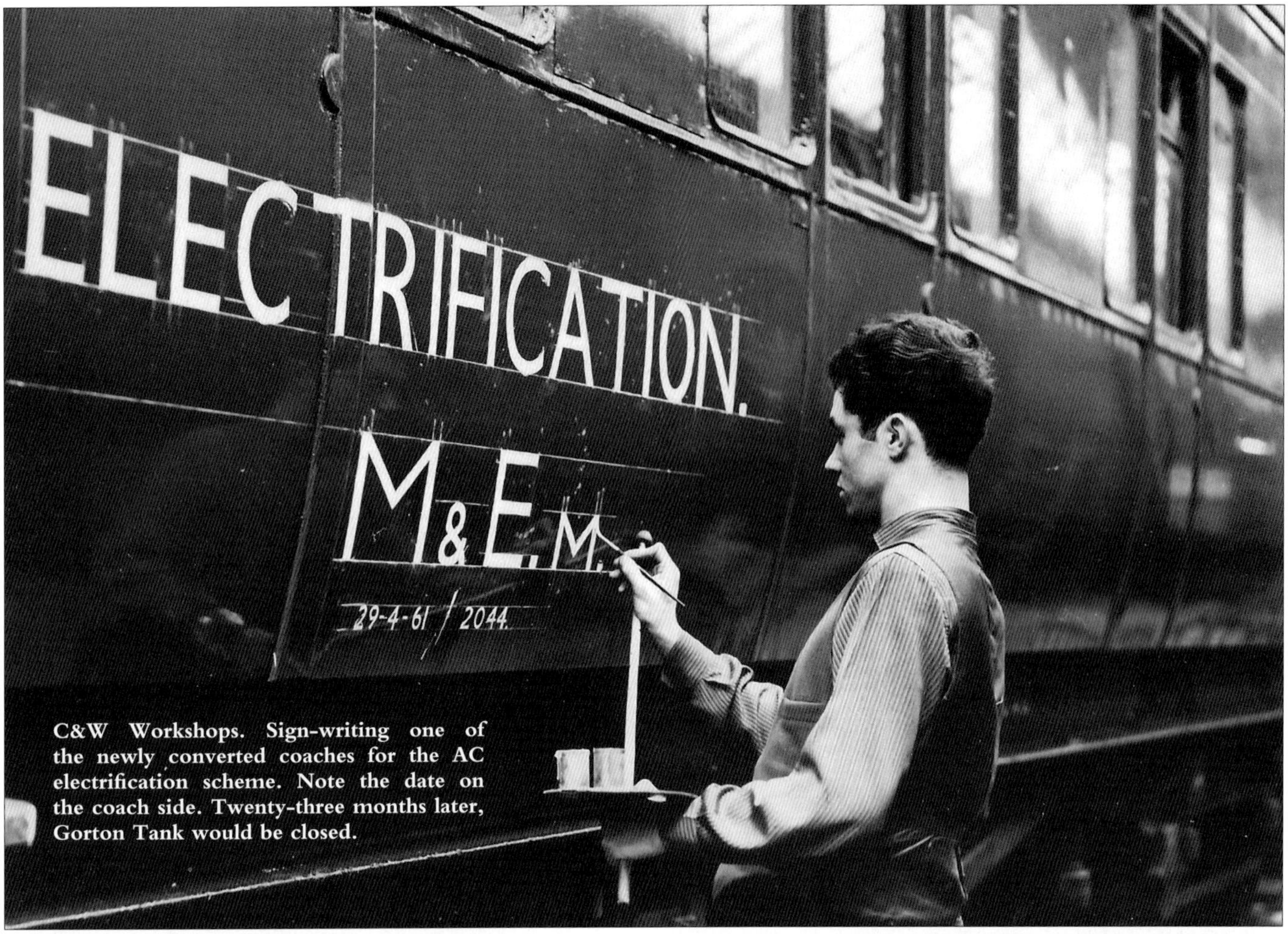

C&W Workshops. Sign-writing one of the newly converted coaches for the AC electrification scheme. Note the date on the coach side. Twenty-three months later, Gorton Tank would be closed.

Inside the HT compartment of a MSW electric locomotive, adjusting the 50volt LT contact fingers on one of the main contactor frames.

In the Erecting Shop, an apprentice electrician working on a MS&W electric locomotive master controller drum switch.

all J. Hillier collection

Erecting Shop. Adjusting a crosshead slide bar. Note the cylinder centreline wire. "*Keep your fingers out lad*"!

Erecting Shop. Fitting rubbing pad brackets to an EM1 bogie.

Apprentice fitter tightening up gravity feed pipework to an 'EM2' bogie in the erecting shop, No. 1 bay. Note the elaborate coil and leaf springing arrangement on these bogies, thus the main reason that the 'EM2's were such smooth riding locomotives. *all J. Hillier collection*

Erecting shop. Tightening up a piston packing gland on a Riddles '8F' 2-8-0 locomotive No. 90115.

Boiler mounting shop 'bluing' and scraping firebox flanges with the bluing plate on the trestle by his side. 'High spot blue' was not the actual material at Gorton, it was just terminology for 'red raddle'.

Apprentice blacksmiths in the roundhouse smithy. The work carried by the hammer drivers was carried out with quite a lot of precision which must seem hard to believe when one sees such cumbersome looking machinery and hand tools. The lady operating the hammer in this scene using her skills to ensure that the hammer hits the work piece former with the correct amount of force so as not to cause it to be miss-shaped and scrapped.

all J. Hillier collection

BR Class 'D11' 4-4-0 No. 62660 (GCR Class '11F' No. 506) *Butler Henderson* stored in the old Iron Foundry waiting to enter the erecting shop for restoration in 1961 for its new lease of life. *T. Quirke*

All spick and span after leaving the erecting and paint shops, now restored into its former GCR glory. The locomotive received an extensive 'cosmetic' overhaul whilst in the erecting shop (full working order came later). The locomotive was soon after exhibited at the Clapham Transport Museum. It is regrettable that only two of Gorton's steam locomotives were saved, this and GCR Class 'O4' 2-8-0 No. 63601 (GCR Class 8K). *J. Metcalfe collection*

Preservation

Robinson GCR Class '11F' 4-4-0 No. 506 (BR Class 'D11') *Butler Henderson*

It will soon be time for *Butler Henderson* to soon leave its birthplace, never to return. This is the handing over ceremony of *Butler Henderson* to the BTC. After a 'photoshoot' at Romiley it will be on its way south to London and the British Transport Museum at Clapham, where it would be on static display. The 'EM1' electric locomotive behind the gathering was possibly placed there so as to give a comparison between No. 506 of 1919 and the 'EM1' of the 1950s. Giving the handing over speech is the Works Manager Mr J.T. Hillier. Amongst the dignitaries and guests at the ceremony who are visible in this photograph are, M. Roy Payne, Mr T. Hagan, Mr C.F. Heath and Mr Clayton. Other guests are the supervisors from the works and administration offices. The Curator of the Clapham Museum, Mr J. Scholes, will accept the locomotive. *courtesy J. Hillier collection*

Presentation speech by Mr J.T. Hillier assistant works manager, Gorton Locomotive Works.

"Ladies and Gentlemen, it is my first duty to apologise for the absence of Mr A.E. Robson the Chief Mechanical and Electrical Engineer of the London Midland Region who has been prevented from coming and in the absence of Mr Barker-Wyatt, Works Manager, I have been deputed to represent him at this ceremony.

Most of you will be well aware that there was a national desire to preserve railway relics. As a result a consultative panel for the preservation of B.T.C. relics at the suggestion of the former chairman of the B.T.C. – Sir Brian Robertson, and the assistance of many representatives of interested railway societies were obtained and no doubt in all the years to come all this work of preservation will be appreciated in increasing measure.

It is, therefore, worthy of note that a Great Central Railway locomotive, *Butler Henderson*, which is here before you should be chosen as a representation of the 4-4-0 type for permanent preservation for this generation and those which will follow to gaze and marvel on in this changing scene of transport mediums – and naturally Gorton Works is proud and glad to be associated with this venture, typifying the clean line of G.C. designs. The passing of this locomotive like so many others marks the gradual decrease of steam power for locomotives, yet helps to illustrate the care taken in days when time was perhaps not so important but looks were essential.

Butler Henderson, one of the 'Improved Director' class, was built in 1919 and placed in service in 1920. Originally numbered 506 it was renumbered 5506 when the L&NER was formed and 62660 on the nationalisation of the Railways. The designer Mr J.G. Robinson, the Chief Mechanical Engineer of the Great Central Railway, and I know that numbers of you have worked under his jurisdiction and remember his work.

This engine was in the second batch of the 'Director' Class, ten engines having been built in 1913. As a point of comparison it had a tractive effort of nearly 20,000 lbs, approximately half of that of the Bo+Bo electric locomotives which you know were also built at Gorton. Its weight is 109 tons against the 89 tons of the Bo+Bo electric.

The 'Director' Class of locomotive was an example of successful running and service right from the commencement and, undoubtedly were J.G. Robinson's finest express design. They were designed to operate fast passenger trains on the Manchester/Marylebone route 212 miles, and this design so impressed Sir Nigel Gresley, Chief Mechanical Engineer of the L&NER that twenty-four engines of this class were ordered from private contractors in 1924 for service in Scotland.

The Manchester/Marylebone service was worked by the 'Director' Class until the 1930s when they began to be dispersed to other work, *Butler Henderson* included in this work after the grouping, hauling the Pullman Expresses on the Leeds/King's

Cross route during the comparative extensive trials of various types. Later this type was relegated to the C.L.C. and even there on some diagrams maintained a service of 200 miles.

Butler Henderson was withdrawn from traffic on the 5th November 1960, with a total mileage of 1,280,897 miles and now goes into honourable retirement and preservation – one of the examples of good design and craftsmanship.

It is a pleasure to note that in our company this afternoon are many who have years of association with these locomotives, indeed with this particular locomotive, including I believe more than one who fired and drove it on long journeys, in addition to those who built and later repaired it.

The restoration of the locomotive has meant quite an amount of research work and time to return it to its original detail but it has been both interesting and enlightening to conjure up the past and this is my opportunity and an appropriate time to thank all concerned for the enthusiasm, interest and energy put into the preparation for this handing over to Mr Scholes on behalf of Mr E. Robson, I therefore hand over to you as Curator of Historical Relics, British Transport Commission, for permanent care this locomotive – *Butler Henderson* with the trust that it will receive under your charge the same care and attention from the staff of Gorton Works and the Motive Power Department, and reflect their pride for all Time."

The following is the acceptance address by Mr J. Scholes to Mr J.H. Hillier, Assistant Manager, Gorton Locomotive Works:

"Mr Chairman, Mr Hillier, friends at Gorton, it is indeed a pleasure to me, particularly on this lovely late summer afternoon to be here in Gorton Works to receive this, yet another valuable addition to the Commission's collection of public transport relics which is already the largest of its kind in the world.

My personal pleasure in being here today with you is that I am a Lancastrian and proud of it, and although they have taken me to London to work amongst they say, the uncivilised people, it is a great pleasure to come back especially to my mother county, and strange as it may seem as I stand on this platform this afternoon to receive this relic I notice on the works plate 'Manchester', this again brings back more memories because my father had very strong connections with Manchester so that in a few moments when I come to tell you of the responsibility which has now been placed on my shoulders this, one of your achievements out of Gorton Works, will also be an added incentive to make sure that I look after it with the most utmost care.

It has been said amongst many people why should relics of British Railways or relics of any kind be kept, why are we spending time, why should we spend money, why should we use the staff to look after such things? Well to my mind today, living in a time when we have hardly time to breath, we are increasing our speed of movement every day, I think it does us good occasionally just to stop even if only for a moment to look back, not in anger but with pride at some of the achievements that we have done in this country, this England, this Britain of ours. We

The photographer has turned his camera around 180 degrees to look in a westerly direction with Mr J.H. Scholes, curator of Clapham museum giving thanks to Mr J. Hillier as he takes custody of *Butler Henderson*. Looking on behind the seated guests are members of the workforce, some no doubt having worked on the restoration. It looks like Ms Florence Ford is taking minutes of the proceedings. Looking at the floor of the rostrum there appears to be a number of redundant boiler plates being utilised for decking, nothing got wasted at Gorton! The two storey building in the background housed the copper stay shop, drawing offices, chain testing shop, small component welding shop and the stores and offices. The wooden building which appears to be painted for the occasion was the distribution office for parts and equipment to BR outstations. On reflection at this late date in Gorton's history, the hierarchy at the BTC in London under the guidance of Sir Stuart Mitchell must have by now pencilled in Gorton Tank for closure, little of this would be known by all celebrating his moment at the restoration of one of the finest designs of locomotive. *courtesy J. Hillier collection*

What a proud moment this must have been. Some BR staff from far and wide standing in front of one of Gorton Tanks finest express passenger locomotives 'D11' *Butler Henderson* now back to its former self as Great Central Railway Class '11F' No 506. Left to right are: Bill Grundy, Tommy Hagan, Bill Batters, W. Addison (Ret), E. Higginbottom, I. Baker, R. South (Ret), S. Whitfield, E. Bowden (Ret), T. Goodley (Ret), E. Garlick (Ret), R. Middlehurst, W. Hale (Manchester), W. Graham (Manchester), W. Cartwright (Doncaster), C. Hale (Ret), J. Statham (Ret), J. Wood, J. Andrew (Ret), F. Carter, C. Hesketh (Horwich), A. Owen (Crewe), J. Airey (Ret), W. Hopkin (Manchester), J. Hough (Crewe), W. Barker (Longsight), W. Clark (Doncaster), R. Hallan (Crewe), J. Smith (Horwich), A. Lane (Derby), A. Shepherd, A. Donne (Manchester), E. Gallimore (Crewe). *E.M Johnson*

are living in a period now of transition, I do not think anybody can actually predict what is in front of us, we do not wish to think about it, but in the last 150 years there has been a complete revolution in the way men have lived. We have had the so called industrial revolution which has brought about kinds of things which for 1,000 years before would have thought impossible and all these things have been brought about by one thing with which everything else would have been impossible, and that is transport, and when transport was found to be inadequate by the power of the horse someone had to find another alternative that would seem convenient and it came out of Britain and I for one am proud of it as they are all part of that gift to the world England has given one way or the another.

When you can look back, if you have the time, to the early days of the last century when the first locomotive was run on a rail in 1805, and then you add another 130 years or so on and look at the locomotive which broke the world record in steam, and a record that we shall always hold and always be proud of, it goes to show the development of the type of transport which has had a birthplace in this country, and which has been entirely due to the workmen of this country, the Engineers and the men under them. It would have been impossible without them. The craftsmen of all the different types of work that go into the making of locomotives, such as the one which face you here today, and we have reason to be proud of this achievement. We know that steam is out, we know we are one of the last countries in Europe now dispensing with steam but nevertheless we do not need to be worried about this to my way of thinking because a European said the other day to me. Britain has lead the world in mechanical and other engineering for so long she can afford to sit back for a little and get her breath back to take the lead back again in the next few years.

And so I think it is a good thing to have some concrete evidence of our heritage. Yours and mine. Our past achievement an encouragement for all that lies in front of us tomorrow.

There are also these relics which I have to look after and this, one of 70 or so Locomotives which I am going to care for in the next few years, and to have to care for them in public places where the whole world can see them for ever more. They represent also the craftsmen of this country of which I am personally very proud. Today with mass production it is necessary

Standing on No. 506's running plate and taking a firm hold of the handrail, Mr Scholes listens to John Hillier, as they have a chat and some technical information no doubt taking place.
J. Hillier collection

Posing like a film star, almost what she is. One of Gorton's finest – *Butler Henderson* stands at Romiley, Cheshire, prior to its travelling south to spend some time at the Museum of British Transport at Clapham in London where it will stand on static display from 1963 to 1972. It was subsequently moved to the Mainline Steam Trust at Loughborough on the closure of the former. Since then it has been restored to full working order and has run on the preserved Great Central Railway and also been on display at the National Railway Museum York.
J. Hillier collection

Gorton Tank's top yard on 22nd July 1962. Left to right (closest to the locomotive). Driver Vinson Gulliver, Herbert Wagstaffe, ?? , and Arthur Victor Davies. The gent with the soft hat on the right is Locomotive Inspector Ernest Calvert.
W.A. Brown, Eddie Johnson collection

Reunited, Barrow Hill. Dave Gosling on board No. 506. The last time I stood on the locomotive was in 1961 aged 17 working in the erecting shop on the locomotives brake rigging. Parked at the side of Butler Henderson at the time was preserved Peppercorn Pacific Class 'A2' 4-6-2 No. 60532 *Blue Peter*. *author*

to keep pace with the speed in which we live and the individual craftsman is disappearing fast and this is a sad thing to me, but the only means those craftsmen have of being immortalised in in the locomotives which they have restored in the various works on the B. R. system. Here at Gorton you will be able to eventually see, when we find a museum to house this engine, the caption saying that it was restored by the men at Gorton, and I shall be pleased to be able to point out that caption to 100,000 people who come from overseas to see our world famous collection and they will also be able to go back and say that it was a good thing that Britain was able to produce such worthy craftsmen as those, those who went out all over the world as the first locomotives went into Europe, into Scandinavia, Germany, Italy, so did the drivers go with them and well you may find there are families with curious names such as Smith and Jones, descendants of these men who went with the locomotives in the very early days.

It is indeed, Mr Hillier, to accept this locomotive from you and for it to be restored in the place where it was built by many of the men who helped in building her and certainly by their sons. I can assure you there will be many people in Gorton only to ready to come and see this locomotive and to be able to turn round and say Gorton still has craftsmen when the look on the wonderful restoration which you and your staff have done on this locomotive. I would like to take this opportunity of thanking Mr Barker-Wyatt who unfortunately cannot be with us today, and you Mr Hillier and those members of your staff who have helped in this wonderful restoration work. I cannot obviously name everyone of you who has lent a hand in this way, but perhaps you will allow me to mention one or two names to express my thanks – Mr J.T. Trathan, Mr B. Owen, Mr R. Payne, Mr R. Middlehurst, Mr F. Mitchell, Mr S. Saville, and those of their staff who have put such loving work into this restoration, but certainly not least is Mr A.E. Gallimore, Fore-man Paint Shop, and his old colleague, Mr J. Watson, who immediately came back and gave his knowledge and experience and helped in order to be able to get the right livery, because after all of the tremendous work which goes into restoring them correctly they would look nothing without a final overcoat which they must have and rests finally with the paint shop, and it is very nice for me to say from here, you have Mr Hillier still craftsmen who can paint straight lines and I have great pleasure in accepting this locomotive into our collection and museum."

Gorton Tank's contribution to 'Maglev'

In the late 1950s, Professor Eric Laithwaite the prominent and renowned celebrity electrical engineer who, apart from his famous work with gyroscope technology was continuing with his experiments at Manchester University on the principal of using linear motors as a means of propulsion and this led up to the idea of using this for rail traction. From this Eric Laithwaite set up a small manned vehicle on an 80 foot length of track at Manchester University and proved quite successful. From here, Eric Laithwaite and his team were given permission to carry out more work on the project on a full scale railway track in the Carriage & Wagon workshops at Gorton Tank on a 300 foot length of track in 1962. One of the simplicities of this linear design was that the wheels on the vehicle were not powered, the linear motor and aluminium rail did all the works (the aluminium rail being entirely passive), theoretically there were no mechanical or electrical moving parts involved, except for the wheels which were only there for the apparatus to move on. Braking was not required to stop the vehicle, electrical power to the motor was simply reversed until the vehicle stopped and then the supply switched off. Trial runs were carried out with the professor at the helm up and down the shops bay. The trials were a success and further development was deemed necessary to be carried out on a grander scale. The success of the demonstrations lead to the formation of 'Tracked Hover Craft Ltd' which, partly funded by the British Government, built a test track at Earith in Cambridgeshire where a large working model was built and demonstrated on the hover lift principle with linear propulsion with complete success. Maglev was born. Unfortunately, as is usual, the idea was not developed any further in this country. At this period in time the Beeching Plan was in full swing and the thoughts of the political climate was swaying to road transport. The government withdrew its funding and 'Maglev' in the country of its inception was dead, leaving its development to continue and flourish overseas.

Gorton Tank played host to Eric Laithwaite's linear motor powered vehicle trials in 1962. A linear motor powered test track and vehicle were erected in the carriage and wagon shop. Note the aluminium rail running down the centre of the 300 feet length of test track. The linear motors are positioned under the vehicle on either side of the rail. I doubt if HSE would have allowed the 440v three phase conductor rails to be so close to the person who sits on the apparatus in this day and age. The vehicle was able to achieve 30 mph in three seconds. *J. Hillier collection*

CHAPTER SEVEN
THE FINAL MONTHS

The date is Sunday, 3rd March 1963, the erecting shop is not the usual hustle and bustle that it once was. The shop now has half empty roads in the bays. Melancholy has crept in. The workforce is starting to diminish at an increasing pace. The younger employees are the lucky ones, they should be OK and find alternative work 'outside' if they do not apply for a transfer elsewhere within BR. This is difficult though as it may mean uprooting their homes and leaving friends, relations and neighbours. The young apprentices, no doubt still single are guaranteed to finish their apprenticeship and were given a choice of where to work to finish their 'time'. Longsight and Newton Heath sheds are close at hand, Crewe Locomotive works was only just over a hour away from Piccadilly travelling on the newly introduced Class '304' western AC lines electric multiple units, Derby Locomotive Works was further afield whilst Doncaster was geographically out of the question. A number of senior supervisory personnel were also offered and took jobs at Crewe. The older employees are not so fortunate, they may have to find alternative work away from their normal skills and trades. The powerhouse that was once East Manchester is also starting to feel a downturn in its local industries, this compounding employment prospects. Beyer, Peacock & Company 'over the road' was feeling the downturn and possibly some of their employees must have known that their future also was not rosy, along with other large industrial companies in the area.

Class 'EM1' Bo+Bo locomotive No. 26047 *Diomedes* stands in the shop undergoing an overhaul. This will be its last visit for an overhaul at Gorton, Crewe works will take over from now on to both this class and the 'EM2's. The Manchester - Hadfield - Glossop EMU sets would be going to Horwich for their overhauls. *J. Hillier collection*

No. 2 Bay, erecting shop, looking west. A Manchester-Hadfield-Glossop EMU power car No. 59404 stands before the camera on No. 4 road, The bogies are removed and the HT cubicles opened up, the pantograph has been removed all indicating that a major overhaul is underway. Further down the same bay an 'EM2' is resting on stands as is a 'EM1' with a 'EM2' bogie frame in front of it. The driving trailer and trailer cars being overhauled in the carriage and wagon shops.
J. Hillier collection

In No. 1 Bay *Fred Flintstone* appears to have just 'clocked off'. Down the bay an EM1/2 boiler is waiting to be installed. Traction motors and other electric pieces of equipment are resting on the shop floor behind the time clock. Towards the end of the bay, two electric locomotives are receiving attention. The date is the 3rd March 1963, just over a month to go before the works closure, a glance into the other bays which are nearly empty of locomotives indicates the diminishing workload at this time. *J. Hillier collection*

Ex LM&SR Fairburn 2-6-4T Class '4P' No. 42284 undergoing an overhaul on No. 1 road in No. 1 Bay facing the wrong way! All is quiet as it is a Sunday – no overtime any more. Gorton's days are coming to a close and work in the erecting shop is winding down. The locomotive was built in 1947 and withdrawn in December 1964, a very short life of seventeen years. Behind this engine is an 'EM2' electric locomotive receiving attention. *J. Hillier collection*

Riddles BR Class '9F' 2-10-0 No. 92210 in the erecting shop for repairs. 23rd April 1963. Built in August 1959 the locomotive had been allocated to Cardiff East Dock shed in September 1962 and in December 1963 went to Southall from where it was withdrawn in November 1964. Behind is another '9F' undergoing similar treatment. Seen in greater detail below that other '9F' appears to be No. 92149 which was shedded at Langwith Junction until withdrawn in June 1965. *J. Hillier collection*

No. 3 Bay and Stanier '8F' 2-8-0 No. 48520 is undergoing a major overhaul, this is the last such general to be carried out at Gorton and the last for the locomotive also. A couple of '9F's remain in the shop receiving light repairs and also an 'EM2' electric locomotive, these will depart within a few days after the '8F' and then the large erecting shop, the pride of the MS&LR and the GCR will see no more locomotives again after approximately 50,000 locomotives had passed through Gorton's shops in the 115 year history of the works since it opened in 1847. *J. Hillier collection*

Another view of No. 48520 on the same day, thirty days later it will be towed out of the erecting shop after receiving a paint touch up. The Riddles WD 2-8-0 in the background will leave the shop before the '8F'. *J. Hillier collection*

Overhaul complete, the '8F' leaves No. 3 Bay. The erecting shop now only has a couple of locomotives left undergoing light casual repairs. Those involved with the overhaul stand outside the shop to say their farewells. There are some smiles on a few faces but there must be a lot of uncertainty at the same time behind those smiles at to what their future holds. *Right: J. Hillier collection Below: Manchester Libraries*

J. Hillier collection

No. 48520 is towed ignominiously out of No. 3 Bay and into the works yard by one of the works type '03' 0-6-0 diesel mechanical shunters. The overhaul is now complete. In the cab is 63 year old driver Frank Hadfield of Ashton-under-Lyne with 43 years service on the railways. After steam tests she will be back on her way to Speke Junction shed (shed code 8C). Speke Junction shed itself closed in May 1968. Ironically No. 48520 was built by the L&NER Doncaster in 1944 for the Railway Executive Committee order. It remained on the L&NER on loan until it was transferred over to the LM&SR in 1946. Whereas the Robinson '8K' 2-8-0 locomotive was chosen for the ROD in World War One, the Stanier '8F' was the preferred locomotive for World War Two and followed in the RODs footsteps, both at home and abroad. The locomotive was withdrawn in September 1966 at its home shed and stayed there until it was cut up by Drapers in January 1967. On the locomotive departing the shops, Richard (Dick) Middelhurst the erecting shop foreman said that "*A thousand men here will probably remember this as the saddest day of their lives*", and, that was more than likely very true especially to the older long serving employees at the Tank, some of whom had worked there since leaving school 40 odd years ago aged just 14. *Above: J. Hillier collection Below: Manchester Libraries*

The last locomotives out of the erecting shop

A few days after the Stanier '8F' left the Erecting Shop, Riddles '9F' 2-10-0 No. 92161 was pulled out of the shop by one of the four works Class '03' 0-6-0 diesel mechanical shunters (No's. 2388/9/90/91). The '9F' was the last steam locomotive to leave after a light unclassified repair. Built at Crewe in December 1957 the engine was six years old at this stage, and was withdrawn at the end of 1966 she had a life of just nine years, such a waste of a perfectly good machine. Leaving the shop a week or so after was electric locomotive Class 'EM2' Co-Co No. 27001 *Ariadne* following a Light Classified Repair mainly to its bogies, now freshly painted. *Ariadne* is with us to this day after being repatriated from the Netherlands and is now on display in NS colours at the Museum of Science and Industry, Manchester. *J. Hillier collection*

The date is 4th April 1965. Gorton locomotive workshops on the other side of Widnes Street had been shut down for almost two years. Compare this panoramic photograph to the one on page 144. Little has changed since about 1935 as far as the sheds are concerned except the shed roof has been removed from roads 11 to 20. The locomotive types though over the nearly thirty years gap has changed significantly. Gone are the ex GCR and L&NER classes, the shed now comes under the LMR since regional changes in 1958, the Eastern Region shed code 39A has given way to 9G. The locomotives are now made up of a mixture a mixture of a Stanier Class '6P5F' 2-6-0, a number of Hughes/Fowler 2-6-0 '6P5F's (Crabs) designs and several Riddles WD 2-8-0 '8F's. Railway enthusiasts wander around and between the locomotives randomly, no guided tours during this era. Health and Safety in the present day would demand all such activities to be under strict guidance, especially in a locomotive running sheds. The sheds themselves have about twelve more months to go before they follow in the works footsteps.

MLS collection

A 1925 aerial view on the Gorton and Openshaw's main railway locomotive works. In Gorton, on the south side of the Manchester to Sheffield main line is the large locomotive building works of Beyer, Peacock & Co. Peacock's main administrative building was the two-storey building just to the right of the centre of the photograph. On the north side of the main line, in Openshaw is Gorton Locomotive Works. Directly opposite Peacock's administration building are the Machine Shops going off at an angle. To the left of the machine shops at right angles is the five bay Erecting Shop with the Wheel Shop joining it at the north end. Slightly to the north of the Wheel Shop – at its west end – is the old coaling tower (building with the 'whitish' coloured end). Further north of the Machine Shops are the stores (the light coloured building roof with a dark centre. Further north west to the top of the photograph are the Northern Shops comprising the locomotive stripping shops, Tender Shops, a Blacksmiths' Shop, Tube Shop and light boiler repair shop and Boiler Plate Shop. – these shops were the 1879 carriage and wagon buildings. Coming back down to the eastern side of the Machine Shops are the main boiler shops with the foundries just to the north near the engine/boiler house chimney. To the right of the chimney is the Roundhouse smithy, and to the right of the smithy are the iron and plate foundries, the brass foundry, pattern makers and carpenters' building with the main offices behind them. Going off to the north west of the Roundhouse and iron foundry are the wagon sheet shop (later the brass shop) and permanent way shops. Unfortunately the aerial photographer missed the running and 1881 carriage and wagon shops. *MOSI/SSPL*

Areas around Gorton Tank

The Birdcage

As a result of Gorton's last erecting shop being on the west side of Widnes Street it was necessary to build a bridge over the whole of the existing locomotive workshops to give the public a safer access between Widnes Street and Railway Street on the opposite side of the MS&LR main line and thus give unhindered rail access to the running sheds and the new C&W works. The footbridge was built in 1890 by Charles De Bergue & Company of Ancoats, Manchester to span the new erecting shop built in that year.

The bridge was a pedestrian walkway covered on the sides and over the top with strong steel meshing forming an archway and thus preventing unlawful public access to the works. The bridge aligned up against the original 1848 C&W shops on its western side. This bridge was soon to become known as the 'Birdcage'.

The Birdcage, GCR days, circa 1905. Looking south on Wellington Street (later Widnes Street) towards the sloping approach to the 'cage'. Immediately to the right behind the stone wall were the running sheds. On the left were (at that time), in the foreground a brass moulding shop, This was later demolished to make way for the main steel stores. Beyond the moulding shop chimney was the machine shop inspection bay. To the right of the cage were the erecting and wheel shops.
Manchester Libraries

Widnes Street looking north from the foot of the Birdcage. On the right is the locomotive works, On the left are the running sheds administration offices. Note the street gas lamps of that period in time.
Manchester Libraries

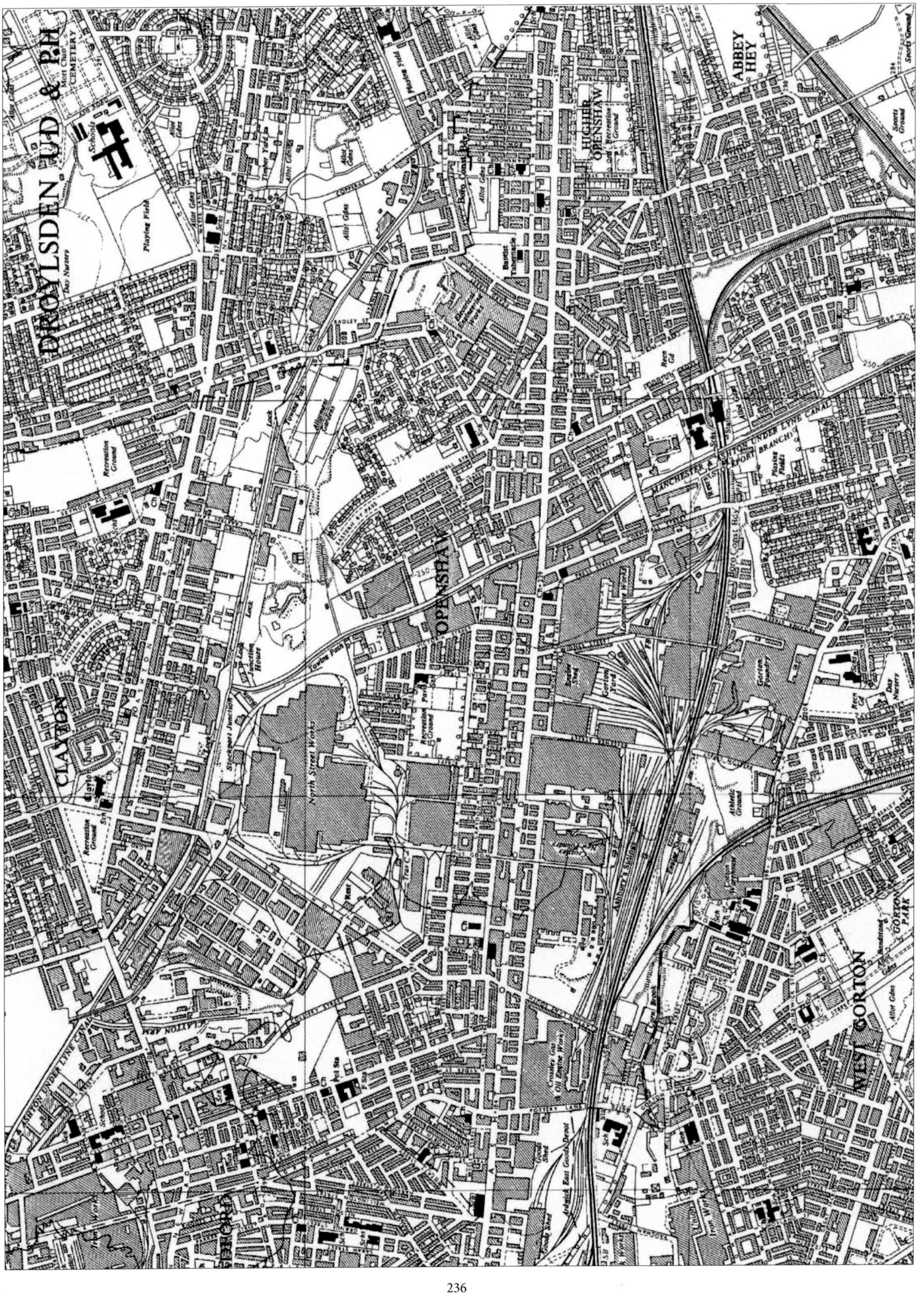
DROYLSDEN U.D. & P.H.
CLAYTON
OPENSHAW
HIGHER OPENSHAW
ABBEY HEY
WEST GORTON
GORTON PARK
North Street Works
Stockport Junction
MANCHESTER & ASHTON UNDER LYNE CANAL
CLAYTON ARM

Viewed looking south from the corner of Whitworth Street East and down Widnes Street. To the right is the wall of the running shed yard with the offices behind it. On the left is the 'Road Motors' department of the works, followed by the steel store. The 'Birdcage' can be seen in the far distance. The electric cables crossing Widnes Street fed the power supply to the running sheds and C&W Shops, the supply coming from the substation adjacent to the Smithy (ex Roundhouse).

Looking south into the approach of the Birdcage from Widnes Street. On the left of the cage were the Steel Stores (the moulding shop and its chimney of GC days since demolished) and the inspection bay of the machine shop. On the right and nearest to the cage is the erecting shop, further to the right is the wheel shop. The space between the wheel shop and the birdcage was, in early days, occupied by the gas works, which was moved over to the canal depot. The gates were for any supplies delivered by road to this section of the works. Note what appears to be a dip in the road on the right-hand side close to the entrance to the birdcage. Seen on the 1905 image, (page 235) it is still evident in this early 1960s photograph. This no doubt the location of a drainage grid. Perhaps this 'dip' could have been levelled somewhat in the intervening years. *both Manchester Libraries*

It was a particularly dull day when railway enthusiast Lee Burgess paid a visit to Gorton Tank and took this photo on the 28th August 1962 from the Birdcage looking over the works and running sheds yards on the west side of the 'cage'. Wagon loads of wheels bulging at the seams dominate the front centre of the photograph. The building to the left is the wheel shop built 1905 (the last major building built at Gorton). On the far right is the weighbridge. The coaling tower is in the far distance just to the left of the centre of the photograph. The building to the right of the view in the distance are the carriage and wagon shops built in 1881. Lee states that on that day he was 11 years old and took the photo with his Brownie box camera. Though a little blurred it is rather a good photograph considering the age of photograph and taken from such a basic type camera. He added that 'J11's, '39's and 'O1's were the order of the day and were clearly seen. How many locomotives have been 'copped' and numbers underlined in the Ian Allan ABC books from this viewpoint over the years? It must be in the high thousands. Lee remembered that his ensemble had tried to get into the works for a visit that day but was given a definitely 'no chance', the reason being that an experimental 'linear traction motor' was being trialled in the works and that the testing was a was supposed to be of a secretive nature.

Looking at Beyer, Peacock's Main offices from outside the boiler shop at Gorton Tank just over the Manchester to Sheffield main line. The steps leading up to the line overbridge and Birdcage can just be seen at the lower right hand corner of the photograph. The signage on Peacock's wall reads 'Beyer, Peacock & Co. Limited Locomotive Engineers & Blacksmiths'. In addition to the company being known locally as just 'Peacocks', it was known also to some as 'Gorton Foundry'. Beyer, Peacock's closed down three years after Gorton. Another locomotive works gone. Lack of orders resulting in its demise after a long and illustrious career supplying locomotives to all corners of the globe including Gorton Tank, just a few yards away directly over the main line, 'over the way'.
Manchester Libraries

Facing west towards Manchester with the Manchester to Sheffield main line behind the stone wall to the right. We are in Gorton here, on Railway Street. One of the main entrances to Beyer, Peacock's and the main office is on the corner of Froxmer Street that veers off to the left. Walking along the footpath on the right hand side to the very end of Railway Street would bring you to the steps leading upwards over the main line (just in view to the side right of the far office block, between the lamp posts and the wall), this bridge is the start of the Birdcage at the southern end. How many thousands of people have walked over the Birdcage in its long history? Pedestrians going to and from their destinations, railway employees on their way to the locomotive sheds to start their day or returning home, kids on bogie carts racing down the slope at the Widnes Street end.

Manchester Libraries

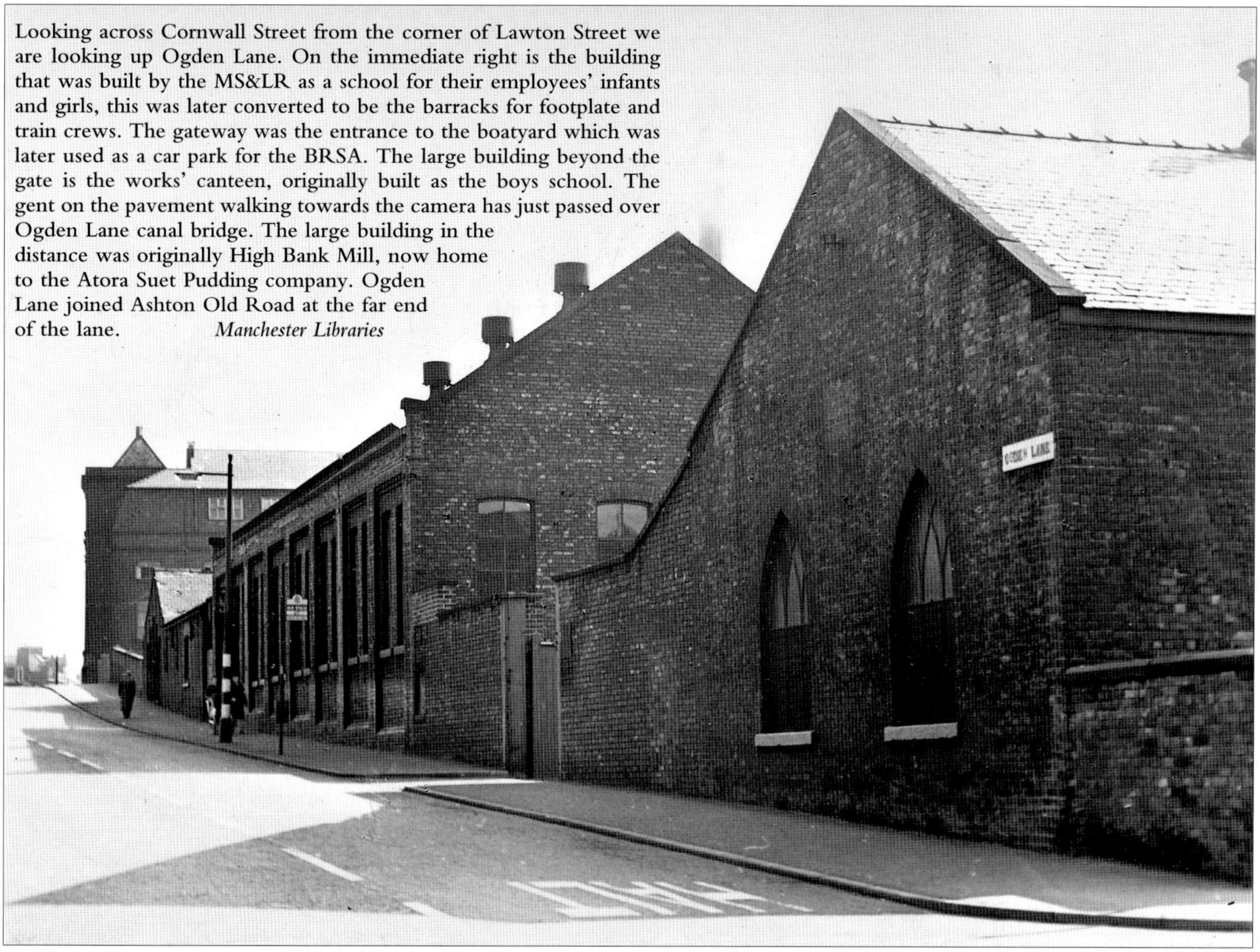

Looking across Cornwall Street from the corner of Lawton Street we are looking up Ogden Lane. On the immediate right is the building that was built by the MS&LR as a school for their employees' infants and girls, this was later converted to be the barracks for footplate and train crews. The gateway was the entrance to the boatyard which was later used as a car park for the BRSA. The large building beyond the gate is the works' canteen, originally built as the boys school. The gent on the pavement walking towards the camera has just passed over Ogden Lane canal bridge. The large building in the distance was originally High Bank Mill, now home to the Atora Suet Pudding company. Ogden Lane joined Ashton Old Road at the far end of the lane. *Manchester Libraries*

Priory Junction, just to the west of the Gorton complex. Photographed from Bessemer Street looking south. Four bridges in total, all four being built at different times as the works, carriage and wagon shops and running sheds expanded. The nearest bridge was built for access to the carriage and wagon works running sheds and shed yard, The next bridge to give access to the works (namely erecting shop) and coaling plant, going in the opposite direction. The third bridge carried a line to Ashbury's sidings from the main line. The largest furthest away bridge carried the Manchester to Sheffield main line. *Manchester Libraries*

Whitworth Street East. On the right of the photograph are the Shops at the northern end of the works. This is Openshaw. Row upon row of terraced houses for miles around. The industrial side of Manchester's once massive engineering area. This is the 1960s, all is about to change as industries, in particular the engineering industries shut down and literally thousands of people are starting to get laid off, including the 1,400 or so employees from Gorton Tank.
Manchester Libraries

Looking across Cornwall Street onto Lawton Street. Just in view on the left are the Works Accountants main office block. Going past the main office block is the Gatekeepers' office and the red double main entrance gates beyond. The flag painted on the wall was applied by local residents on the occasion of the coronation of Queen Elizabeth II on June 2nd 1952. Behind the wall the building with the louvered roof was the Tinsmiths Shop. The building with the chimney was the 'weighing hut' with the building behind the 'enquiry' sign being the pattern store with adjoining employees bicycle shed. The sign in the window is advertising the crowning of anther queen, this time the railway queen at Belle Vue Gardens in September 1952, followed by a fireworks display. Note: The unattended and unlocked bicycle! Would anyone be so brave today?
National Railway Museum

Have notifications of the impending closure of the works been distributed amongst the employees at this time? The gatekeeper points to the cameraman. Notice only the younger members of the group seem to raise a smile. Dark days are ahead are for the older gents as their future is uncertain in an area where employment chances are diminishing. Note *Valour's* nameplate attached to the old Foundry wall, just to the right of the gatekeeper.

National Railway Museum

Looking out of the gates with the gatekeepers' lodge (his little three-wheeler car that was usually parked there) on the right. Behind the lodge is a small section of the accounts offices. Looking across Lawton Street and over Cornwall Street are the rows and rows of terraced houses that was Openshaw in the 1960s. A very proud community of working class people. Next door to the shop on Cornwall Street was Malita's fish and chip shop with its little café. The rush at lunch time was to go either to the canteen, Malita's café or to the staff association for a 'swift half', or two perhaps!

National Railway Museum

A few scrapped locomotives

Starting in the late 1940s, going onto the Birdcage for a view of the works yard and running sheds one would have seen the row upon row of locomotives queuing up for their turn at the hands of the cutters torch. Below are just a few photographs of engines awaiting their fate.

August 1961. One of the works Class '03' shunters, diesel mechanical 0-6-0 No. D2392 appears to be moving condemned 'O4/1' 2-8-0 No. 63719 in Gorton's shed yard. The building to the right is the weighbridge, the large building is the steel/iron bar store which was on the other side of Widnes Street in the locomotive works. The 'O4' was built in September 1912 and withdrawn in August 1961 (approximate date of photograph). *MLS collection*

Marred by its hideous flower pot chimney, a once classic Robinson 'C14', built by Beyer, Peacock at the end of May 1907, awaits its fate in Gorton yard. Gorton's carriage and wagon shops are in the background. *Author's collection*

Kitson built Class 'J60' (GCR Class 'B') 0-6-0 No.8367. A class of four locomotives originally built for the Lancashire, Derbyshire and East Coast Railway (LD&ECR) in 1897. They received five different numbers in their long career. Their latter years were spent at Wrexham with one being transferred to Gorton as the works shunter. No. 8367 was withdrawn in September 1947. *E.M. Johnson/G. Harrop collection*

Robinson Class '1A' (L&NER 'B8') 4-6-0 No. 1350 *Sutton Nelthorpe* stands on the scrap line in 1947. Built in 1914 in a class of eleven locomotives, the '1A's were a smaller-sixed wheel version of the GCR Class 'B2' 4-6-0 (Sam Fays) and designed for mixed traffic work. Five of the class managed to survive into BR days but not long enough to obtain a number on the BR list. *E.M. Johnson/G. Harrop collection*

CHAPTER EIGHT
CLOSURE & DEMOLITION

Shortly after the works closed down in 1963 the whole of the site was demolished except for the running sheds, Staff Association (BRSA) social club and the Canal Depot. The running sheds remained in use until 1965. The canal was not in use and the Canal Depot itself was by now disused. The Staff Association club continued to be open until the running sheds closed, the Canal Depot complex was on essential services. The demolition contractors involved were G. & E. Robinson Bros. of Manchester (ironic that the name Robinson be used in the clearing of the site after all that John G. Robinson had done in the works development only to have his namesake destroy it). All useful equipment within the works was either transferred to other BR premises for further use or sold off to outside industries. The Birdcage was removed by the Longsight Breakdown Crane. The area once cleared made way for the New Manchester Smithfield Fruit and Vegetable Market.

Once the Offices of the CME, John G. Robinson and the Locomotive and Carriage & Wagon administration senior personnel. (Robinson's office far right). Already surrounded by demolition work the offices would soon be follow, as will the two story pattern and carpenters' shop to the extreme left of the photograph. The buildings behind the main offices on the right in the far distance were workshops and offices on the Canal Depot on the opposite side of Cornwall Street. *W.A. Brown*

Just at the time of the works closure, Pryce Williams from the millwrights' shop climbed to the top of roundhouse clock tower and took this unique photo looking to the north end of the works. From here the buildings that can be seen are, to the right with its gantry crane is the permanent way shop whilst behind are the series of bays housing the, L to R road motors, plating and fabrication shop, boiler machine shop, plate stores (the large building), a carriage and wagon repair and paint shop, tube shop, works mill rights and spring making shop.

Pryce Williams

GORTON TANK

Scrapped and forgotten: The 600 with no future

20/6/63

A SPECIAL Manchester Evening News INQUIRY

GORTON'S JOBLESS —THE 'OLD ONES'— NEED ACTION NOW

MEN without a future . . . this, it is revealed to-day, was the grim plight of 600 sacked when the Beeching economy axe closed Manchester's railway workshops at Gorton.

Chatting outside the Openshaw employment exchange are ex-Gorton Loco men William Heason (left), Ernest Harrison, and Harold Johnson.

Where are they now? What is being done for them?

There were 1,400 men at the works when the plan to close it in stages was announced.

A hundred were transferred to other railway jobs; 700 found work with private firms.

The 600 who were left? They are still vainly searching for work. They fear that they are in danger of becoming "the forgotten ones."

There is only one difference between them and the lucky 700 who found new jobs almost immediately.

• 'OLD ONES'

THEY have the same skill, the same experience. But they are the "old ones—the men nobody seems to want."

Nearly all the 600 are over 55. More than 200 of them are over 60.

HARRY BROOKS

A labour exchange official admitted: "Nobody could say the future looks very bright for them. If there was some improvement in trade generally there would be some hope, but at the moment the situation is not promising."

A situation which is tragic . . . and to-day the *Manchester Evening News* calls for urgent action to give these men some hope for the future.

These men have proved their skill in the years they spent at Gorton, establishing it as one of Britain's key railway centres.

They are willing to work. They have the health and capacity to wrok. It would be a waste if they were condemned to waste active years of their lives in idleness.

• BITTERNESS

ALREADY the bitterness which comes with the weary round of doing nothing is creeping in.

Harry Hughes, aged 54, of Evelyn-street, Reddish, Stockport, stepped out of Openshaw labour exchange and said: "There's still nothing doing. I've had enough already. I was a fitter at Gorton for 19 years, and had hoped to stay at my trade.

"There is nothing, absolutely nothing, for me in engineering. Now I am going after a job as a labourer on a building site. It will be better than doing nothing.

"It's nonsense to say I'm too old. I can give as good a day's work as ever."

• CHANCE LOST

HARRY BROOKS, aged 42, of Abbey Hey Lane, Higher Openshaw, was angry that the opportunity of keeping some men on at Gorton had not been taken.

"I'm an acetylene-burner," he said. "There were 80 scrap locomotives in at Gorton when the place closed.

"Breaking them up would have provided work for at least two years, for about 20 men. But they have been sent to Crewe, and you can bet if I wanted a job there I could get one—and it would be cutting up those same locos."

William Heason, of Vine-street, Gorton, and Ernest Harrison, of Battersby-street, Higher Openshaw, are both 63.

"It doesn't mean we want to stop work yet," they said. "But everybody seems to think we are too old."

Harold Johnson, aged 61, of Lees-street, Gorton, said: "After 47 years at the works I still think I can do a good day's work. I don't want to be left doing nothing."

• JOBS FOR YOUNG

THE 600 men are registered at 14 different labour exchanges, but their number dwindles slowly . . . too slowly.

Labour exchange officials think that employers, in face of the high unemployment and poor trade in the area, have done quite well in providing jobs for 700 of the ex-Gorton men.

But this has mostly benefited the younger workers. What is needed now is for employers to give urgent special consideration to the older men.

Old rail works are no more

BY A STAFF REPORTER

IT lies just off the main Manchester-Sheffield railway line, a dusty, derelict group of buildings that was the birthplace of thousands of steam engines.

But Gorton Tank Works, once the thriving nerve-centre of the Great Central Railway Company, no longer echoes to the whine of overhead cranes or the clanking of shunting engines.

There are no longer any tracks for engines to run on; the cranes are silent; the huge erecting shops where hundreds of men worked have been picked clean of every last nut and bolt.

For the works, built in 1850, is being razed to make way for a new market, planned by the new owners of the land, Manchester Corporation. The site will be clear early next year.

A SHOVEL

There are few indications that Gorton Works ever was part of a railway. Only a few remain—a rusty fireman's shovel, a pile of old sleepers, a mound of cinders.

Every few minutes the roof of the erecting shop will shudder as a train thunders past—drawn by an electric or diesel loco.

The sound of its klaxon seems to be a sneer at the end of the steam era. But for many inhabitants of the Ashton Old Road area, who built the electric trains at the works, the klaxon will always revive memories of the Great Central Railway.

'LITTLE HOPE' FOR WORKS

D.T. —— 23/5/63

RAILWAY CLOSURE

Daily Telegraph Reporter

The Minister of Transport, Mr. Marples, said in Manchester yesterday that he could hold out little hope of action being taken to avert the closure of British Railways' locomotive works at Gorton. It is estimated that 1,400 men will lose their jobs.

Mr. Marples made this comment after a meeting with the Lord Mayor, Ald. R. E. Thomas, and the chairman and deputy chairman of the corporation's development committee, Ald. R. Moss and Councillor R. A. Fieldhouse.

The Lord Mayor handed over a resolution of the city council expressing concern at the rise in unemployment and urging the Government to review the decision to close the works. Mr. Marples said: "I think there is little that can be done. It is virtually agreed that it will go through."

Mr. Marples's Visit—P9

What the Papers Said

On the announcement of the closure of Gorton Tank the news spread rapidly to the unions and tabloids, the most obvious being the *Manchester Evening News* newspaper and the local 'Reporter' group of newspapers. The *Manchester Evening News* in particular ran a substantial amount of headings. The following are just a few of the newspaper stories that appeared over that dark period in the life of Openshaw and Gorton and displayed the anger, concerns, fears, depression and also despair for the majority of those who worked there, for their families and also the local businesses that relied on the Tank. On the bigger picture dark clouds started to appear over the whole of this industrial area also, a decline in the engineering might of East Manchester started to show cracks as the downturn on the demand for its heavy engineering products started to recede. A walk down Ashton Old Road today is testament to the vastly different picture from that of 50 years ago.

To the left is the iron foundry (plate foundry section) with the two storey pattern and carpenters building beyond. Already demolished is the open sided shed that was used for fettling iron castings, namely brake blocks and track chairs. Immediately to the left is a corner of the main iron foundry. The large doorway on the left foundry building wall was made very late on in years and was opened out to run a track into the building for the storage of parts. This never eventuated as closure had been announced before the shop was utilised *W.A Brown*

Such a shame the photographer could not have positioned his lens more accurately through the wire mesh of the birdcage. Taken looking east, the view is of the works yard. Dominating the photo on the right hand side is the 'shell moulding' shop (brass foundry). Protruding out to its left are three windows of the pattern shop. More to the centre right is the permanent way shop. The gantry crane with a capacity of five tons to the left is the permanent way points and crossing yard, There was a gantry crane on either side of the 'P-way' shop. Almost hidden behind the wire mesh on the extreme left is the brass finishing shop. Extreme right to the brass foundry bordering the photograph is a small view of the iron foundry, which at this time housed the main electricians shops in part of the building. *Manchester Libraries*

The main machine shop, viewed looking north. The heavy columns and cross beams clearly showing where the upper light machine tool gallery used to be. The hook from the 10-ton crane hangs down laying idle, perhaps it may have a new lease of life if it is sold off before demolition takes place. The door at the far end of the shop led into the examination room which housed the 'bosh' dip tank which was used for cleaning locomotive parts.
National Railway Museum

The principal two-storey buildings joined to the main boiler shops as an extension. Originally built as two separate two-storey buildings, they were later joined together by a narrow single-storey building which eventually became the welding shop. The building to the left was home to the main drawing office on the upper floor and copper stay shop on the lower. A rail line ran through the centre of the shop to enable boilers to access one of the boiler shop bays. Protruding out of the building on the left-hand was a platform that was used for the process of daylight blueprint drawing copying. The building to the right was the boiler shop offices, stores and chain testing shop. The bay window bottom right once housed the works managers offices at the time when the works had resident chief mechanical engineers. After the reign of CMEs at Gorton, the manager relocated to the main offices and occupied the ex CMEs offices. To the right of the buildings is what remains of the smithy (roundhouse), now partially demolished, all that remains is the portal and clock tower. The small shed type structure in front of the building was the outstation materials office, this location is approximately just a few yards to the east of where the coking shed was positioned. Behind the materials office, the single storey building was the welding shop for smaller type sub assemblies. This welding shop was built later on, originally there was a bridge that connected the upper storeys of both buildings. Immediately to the left of the buildings and just in view in the far distance is the Manchester to Sheffield main line. Behind the clock tower is the works engine/boiler house chimney, having stood there since 1847 it stands in defiance of the wrecking ball that will soon send it crashing down. *W.A Brown*

A closer view of the boiler shop complex. The drawing office with its blueprint printing 'stage' protruding out of the wall. The copper stay shop was on the lower floor. Beyond the two-storey building are the boiler shops. Beyond the boiler mounting shop is the machine shop with its high pitched roof over the heavy machine shop bay (The Danube). Toilet block to the fore, all are now a deserted buildings. Not long now before demolition. *Manchester Libraries*

The cameraman, standing in No. 3 Bay of the Boiler Shop looking north, takes a photograph that looks insignificant. However, in the centre of the image behind the two crane support pillars is the base of the original engine house chimney with its ornamental beading around the upper edge of the base. The chimney was still in use to the very end of the works life. Further behind the chimney was the boiler house with three boilers and associated economisers and blowers.
National Railway Museum

From No. 2 Bay looking into No. 3. The north east corner of the Boiler Shop complex. Note the large swing-arm crane, this was the riveting tower where boilers were hung vertically to rivet the boiler plate seams with the assistance of a long anvil which had been removed by the date of this image. The air receiver was fed from the main air receiver outside the shop bay.
National Railway Museum

Boiler Shop No. 3 Bay. a view towards the end of the shop. Looking through the square doorways was the Danube Machine Shop and further still, through the arched doorways, was the main machine shop. *National Railway Museum*

Below: Boiler shop No. 2 Bay, again looking west towards the Danube and main machine shop. Now bereft of machinery and equipment bar the two 24-ton overhead cranes. *National Railway Museum*

Above: Erecting Shop. 1964. No. 1 Bay. Bereft of all equipment and machinery, one year after closure the shop is completely empty. In the foreground is the area that had the shop pits filled in at some point the 1950s so as to have a solid workshop floor for the assembly of bogies and ancillary equipment and to fabricate the frames for the 'EM1' and 'EM2' electric locomotives. The centre road was left intact to enable transporting boilers from the boiler shop after being conveyed from the boiler shop Where the pits starts further down the shop was the cross over track used for conveying the boilers to the other bays and wheel shop. This was the fourth and last erecting shop built at Gorton, built in 1890. *J. Hillier collection*

Right: No. 5 Bay of the Erecting Shop 1964. All empty except the 40-ton crane. *National Railway Museum*

No. 4 Bay, Erecting Shop. To the left of the photographer but out of view was the Copper Shop. Looking east towards the 'stage' is the ramp that was used for conveying small locomotive components to and from the machine shop. Looking through the door is the main Machine Shop with the 'Danube' Machine Shop beyond. The 40-ton crane rests idle underneath the gable of the shop and underneath the Birdcage. *National Railway Museum*

Erecting Shop. From the east end of No. 1 Bay looking north along the edge of the 'stage'. At the far end of passageway is the opening leading out to the Wheel Shop with the Copper Shop to the left. The Copper Shop was an extension of No. 5 Bay. Note the steel columns supplementing the cast iron columns supporting the overhead crane girders, these were an addition installed later on in the shops life when two larger 50-ton cranes were established in the bay, these being necessary for the later new and larger locomotive builds. A 40-ton crane stayed in this bay, mainly for the boiler lifts.
National Railway Museum

The 'Danube' Machine Shop, looking north. Most of the heavy machine tools were housed here on both sides of a central passageway. Once the open traverser from the late 1840s, it was converted into a machine shop in the very early GCR days and enclosed. To the near left, one of the arches lead into the Millwrights Shop. The whole of the left side was the original C&W works, whilst to the near right was the Paint Shop/stock holding shed with the original Erecting Shop further down the bay on the right.
National Railway Museum

Main Machine Shop. A shame that this photograph was not taken just before closure. Every apprentice fitter and turner started the first months of their 'time' here. Any apprentice fitter and turner reading this book will well remember this area quite well. Under the guidance of the two machine tool setters, Tommy Leach and Len Fanning, we all set to work on learning our trades on Ward Seven, Herbert 2C and Herbert 4C capstan lathes and centring lathes, turning out all manner of small components from 'whistle pins' to nuts, bolts, washers, rivets, stays and linkage pins. I started my apprenticeship on one of the two Ward Seven turret/capstan lathes situated very close to the stove on the 2nd of May 1960. One of the Herbert 4Cs was known as the 'Iron Duke' for some reason. There were usually about eight apprentices at any one time in this area. After several months training and learning the skills of turning and setting up lathes all apprentices were then sent to the 'brake job' situated to the east of the White Metal Shop. The brake job shop was the only shop that was used for its intended purpose the whole life of Gorton. The Danube Machine Shop is viewed through the arches and beyond through the first arch is the corner of the boiler shop with its time clock where we used to 'clock' in and out. Some names I remember at my time in this area are, apprentices Dave (Daz) Davenport, Eric Bond, Denis Wild, Barry (Sarge) Irvine, Geoff (Spike) Newton. Billy Howell, Peter Hodgson, Keith Ecclestone, Billy Ashton and Les Collinge. Also working on lathes in this area were turners Rosie McNight, Madge Rider, Lucy Watson and Elsie ???? A 'Manchester' mechanical saw was kept going full time by a tall gent called Sam ??? Cutting bars to length for the capstan feeds. The wash basin is visible extreme left where we scrubbed our hands after a good rubbing with 'Swarfega'. Through the arches were three large radial arm drills, to the left of these was a large Cincinnati horizontal milling machine. The rail line in the image was the track that was used for conveying boilers from the boiler shop to the erecting shop as described previously. *National Railway Museum*

The east end of the Wheel Shop. The foremens' office to the left. The central doors lead outside into the works yard at a point where the first gasholder was installed in the late 1840. Note the 6-ton overhead crane, it has been sol off so it can enjoy an extended life.

National Railway Museum

The Wheel Shop, looking west. The second 6-ton crane in this shop stands at the opposite end of the building. The erecting shop No. 5 Bay is to the left. The shop floor has had to be partially excavated to enable removal of the wheel lathes foundation bolts.

National Railway Museum

The Smithy being stripped of all machinery. The steam hammers have gone. Just the smiths' hearths and steam pipes remaining in the upper photo and only an air receiver in the lower picture as everything of any further use has been removed. Now, the Peacock designed roundhouse is waiting for the wreckers hammers and bulldozers to do their work. *J. Hillier collection & National Railway Museum*

November 21st 1965. Two and a half years after the works closed. Richard Peacock's famous Roundhouse is being demolished. Only half of the wall and the centre column are left standing. The supply distribution manifold is still on the column that fed steam to the large hammers. Such a shame that there are no sketches or photos of what the inside of the Roundhouse looked like in the days when it was housing the locomotives and turning them on that two road turntable. The plate foundry is just visible in the far background. *W.A. Brown*

Still on that November day in 1965 as the previous photograph. Looking into the Smithy. The portico to the Roundhouse. *W.A. Brown*

The end of the Roundhouse, courtesy of G. & E. Robinson, demolition contractors. Some of the construction details are clearly seen. *W. A. Brown*

Looking over the wall into the works from Cornwall Street demolition is well in hand. On the far left on the other side of the Manchester to Sheffield main line, Beyer, Peacock's works is still in business but only for about another eighteen months or so. The two-storey building on the left in Gorton works was the drawing offices, the chain testing shop, copper stay shop, foreman's office and stores. To its right, the three bays of the boiler shops have been demolished, only their gable ends remain. Behind the gables is the Danube machine shop, still standing. To its right, the Roundhouse (smithy) has gone but its portal, smithy office and clock tower remain. Further to the right everything has been torn down with the engine room / boiler house chimney still standing defiantly. In the far distance on the right the steel store roof is undergoing demolition. G. & E. Robinson were the main contractors for clearing the site, very ironic that their namesake J. G. Robinson built it to what it was. *MLS collection*

Left: Viewed from east end of the traverser, the carriage and wagon shop which in its final years was used for repairing coaches and also the MS&W EMU stock (later Class 506 sets). The shop was also used for converting coaches for use as overhead line construction work on the 25Kv ac western lines.

Manchester Libraries

Below: The C&W traverser pit facing west. To the left are the old carriage and wagon shops. Built in 1881 along with the building out of view on the right. The smaller buildings on the left, centre, were the running sheds. The building in the very far distance, centre, was the running sheds offices with the works steel store behind on the other side of the Widnes Street.

Manchester Libraries

Disposal of Machine Tools

Prior to the demolition of the buildings all machine tools of any worth were removed for further use. As British Railways had already started to close down other workshops, heavy machine tools were already were starting to become a surplus commodity and most likely there would be no need to relocate the equipment to their other works. Machine tools were therefore auctioned off to railway companies overseas or to other engineering concerns and, possibly, some to UK heritage railway workshops. There is no doubt that some machine tools were also were sold off for scrap. It is known that one of the centre lathes was sent to the Electric Traction Depot at Reddish a short distance away as the depot had no lathe of its own at that time. It is believed that some of the heavy lift overhead cranes went to Africa.

A wheel lathe from the wheel shop being checked over and surveyed for the means of removal. One of the contract companies involved in the removal of large machinery and equipment was the very well-known heavy haulage company Edward Beck & Son Ltd of Reddish. Becks was a large heavy haulage company, very highly regarded with a reputation for excellence and professionalism in all fields that they were involved with whether in dismantling large items of equipment, transportation of same and to installation projects. The wheel lathe was a product of Craven Brothers, makers of large machine tools and cranes and quite a large number of their products were evident around the workshops at Gorton. *Courtesy J. E. Beck*

Opposite: No. 5 bay of the erecting shop. A 'Noble and Lund' wheel lathe has been split into two and skated in the bay from the wheel shop next door by what can presumably be the Edward Becks Ford Thames Trader lorry. 'Nobles' were another manufacturer of large machine tools and were based in Gateshead on Tyneside. Unless the lathe was dismantled to more manageable pieces the lorry will probably be at its maximum load capacity. If power is still available, the overhead cranes will have no problem lifting the load with its 40 ton capacity overhead crane available. *Courtesy J. E. Beck*

EDWARD
BECK
& SON LTD
HAULAGE
TRADER
WJA 899
A 282

BECK
MACHINERY DISMANTLED & INSTALLED
COMPLETE FACTORY REMOVALS
ORDINARY & SPECIALISED TRANSPORT

Gorton running sheds. Post works closure

The date is the 5th July 1964, just over twelve months since Gorton Locomotive and C&W works had been shut down. but the running sheds were to linger on for two more years. Three of Sir William Stanier's ex LMS 'Jubilee' 4-6-0s, classified as 6P/5F, were seen at Gorton's running sheds having been withdrawn from Newton Heath. They were as follows: No. 45578 *United Provinces* withdrawn on the 30th May 1964 and cut up at T. W. Ward, Killamarsh, Sheffield (undated). Built by North British Locomotive Co. Glasgow. September 1934; No. 45710 *Irresistible* withdrawn on the 6th June 1964 and cut up at Central Wagon, Wigan on the 13th December 1964. Built at Crewe June 1936; No. 45737 *Atlas* withdrawn on the 30th May 1964. Cut up at T. W. Ward, Killamarsh, Sheffield (undated). Built at Crewe November 1936.

Why were they sent to Gorton? The two bound for Killamarsh would have made their last journey there along the Woodhead Route but for No. 45710 that seems illogical as it ended up at Wigan! The story from Newton Heath engine men was that their withdrawal coincided with a directive to remove all nameplates as they were becoming desirable as collectors items and were increasing in value and were becoming subject to theft. The plate removal was apparently carried out at Gorton because their premises were considered to be more secure. Interestingly though two of the locomotives still carried the smokebox number plates at this time.

'Jubilee' 6P/5F 4-6-0 No. 45578 *United Provinces*.

'Jubilee' 6P/5F 4-6-0 No. 45737 *Atlas*.

'Jubilee' 6P/5F 4-6-0 No. 45710 Irresistible.

Standing at the side of the weighbridge in Gorton yard. The date is the 20th June 1948. Six months under public ownership and Robinson four cylinder Class 'B7' (GCR Class '9Q') 0-6-0 No. 1383 stands behind an unidentified 'Sam Fay' Class 'B2' (GCR Class '1'). The 'B7' was withdrawn the previous month. The 'B7's were the most successful of all the Robinson 4-6-0 classes. Very similar in design to the Class 'B3' but with smaller coupled wheels they became very adaptable for all types of work from fast freight to excursions and semi fast passenger work. Reputed to be heavy on coal, if handled correctly they were just as just as fuel efficient as other similar 4-6-0 types. With the steel/iron bar store in the background, the photograph was taken from a very similar location as that on page 243, with a time difference of thirteen years. *MLS collection*

Gorton Tank club. (British Railways Staff Association – BRSA), Cornwall Street. The wooden porch was the entrance to the now closed down club. To the right it looks like a car breakers yard – with a scrapped Morris Marina car perched on a demolished building which was once part the District Locomotive Superintendent's domain. Further to the left along the street was once the GCR library with the train crews barracks. *MLS collection*

It looks like the only action in the shed at this point in time is a leaking water column. Once a hive of activity, all is quiet now The saw tooth roofline of the shed administration can just be seen lower left with the locomotive works northern workshops behind. The building on the right of the photograph is the steel/bar stores with the Birdcage barely visible in front of it.

Courtesy M. Sandals/ R. Whitehead collection

Surrounded by ex-Midland Region locomotives, enjoying a chat in the shed yard, Ron Whitehead and his mate Harold. It is 1964 and the works has already closed when this photograph was taken by a friend of Ron's. It must be on their minds as they are talking as to whether the sheds will be the next to go. A very predominant ex-LMS presence was evident at this late time in the sheds existence along with Riddles WD locomotives, soon they will be gone also. The locomotive running sheds closed on 14th June 1965, two years and fourteen days after the works.

Courtesy M. Sandals / R. Whitehouse collection

In the running sheds the machine shop tools was quite rudimentary. Two of the machine tools were the wheel lathe and a shaping machine. Wheels going onto the lathe for turning had to be lifted by chain blocks.

Note the writing on the dilapidated wooden hut behind the sheds rail mounted mobile crane, 'Don't put litter here', not appropriate anymore, the sheds and paint shop now completely empty. The photographer is probably leaning on a locomotive to take the photograph of this most depressing of scenes.

M. Sandals / R. Whitehouse collection

Running Sheds. The cutter's torch cuts up track near the turntable into manageable lengths for transporting to scrap metal facilities. In the right background are the running sheds administration buildings offices with its 'saw tooth' roof line. Beyond the offices are the locomotive works.

Both Manchester Libraries

Engineers boat *Joel* outside the dry dock. Built in 1918 for the Buxton Lime Company, the boat was bought out of service by the L&NER in 1926 and rebuilt in 1929 being fitted with an engine thus becoming the first motor powered boat in the L&NER fleet. This boat was replaced by a new boat in 1948 which retained the number 9 and name of the original. The boat is still with us today. The crew of the boat pictured are W. Potts, G. Challoner, W. Mcleng, Mr Mullins, Mr Lawton, Mr Lucas and Mr Muirhead. *H. Potts collection/Courtesy Canal and River Trust*

The Canal Depot – The forgotten side of Gorton Tank

Viewed from the top of the foot bridge that spans the Stockport Canal on a pathway that leads from Cornwall Street to Gorton Railway Station on Lees Street and the canal tow path which is below the photographer. The canal depot reservoir and the settling ponds dominate the photograph. Beyer, Peacock's clock tower is in the far distance on the left along with Beyer's main offices and part of their workshops just to the left of their tower. More to the right is the Gorton Tank complex with its clock tower now shorn of its ornamental roof. Part of Gorton's main offices (once the office of John G. Robinson) on Cornwall Street are to the right with the two-storey building forming part of the boiler shop buildings in far middle distance of the photograph. Hopefully the angler is keeping a watchful eye on the young child playing by the settling pond! The Manchester to Sheffield main line is down the embankment behind the wall to the left. The over bridge between Cornwall Street (in Openshaw) and Chapman Street in Gorton is on the upper far left. Just out of the frame on the left of the bridge is the 'Railway Hotel', no doubt a watering hole for both the 'Tank' and Peacock's thirsty employees. The reservoir was used regularly by the staff association BRSA members for a spot of fishing; one wonders how many fish 'got away'.

Looking at the broken windows in the now abandoned section of the depot buildings indicates this is now round about 1960. The canal depot in reality was the first part of Gorton Tank to face closure. A caretaker was all that was required now to carry out maintenance to essential services such as looking after the reservoirs which still supplied water for the locomotive works and sheds and their pumping systems. The electrical power supply was still needed and services for the BRSA club that occupied the premises on the Cornwall Street side of the complex. Looking beyond the depot are the works main offices (Top Office). In the far distance is the clock tower of the Roundhouse/smithy with the chimney of the engine room and original boiler house still standing proudly, sadly it will not be for too long. The stand-alone building just to the right of the centre of the photograph was once the Locomotive Superintendent's residence.

both Manchester Libraries

Above: Taken from the canal overbridge that was also accessed from a pathway on Cornwall Street to Lees Street and Gorton and Openshaw railway station and passing Varna Street school. The scene here is of total dereliction. The canal depot and canal completely overgrown with foliage.

Below: A view taken inside the depot yard. The large doors, half boarded off, were the entrance to the dry dock and boat repair shop. The adjoining buildings housed a saw mill, engine house, pump house, mortar mill, Smithy, blacksmiths' shop and carpenters' shop in addition to the gas house and purifying house as the gas holder was once on this site also. Out of view on the site was the works canteen and BRSA club house, these being the old MS&LR schools and train crews barracks. Now all is derelict and vandalised. *both W.A. Brown*

In the 1930s, the canal depot under its L&NER owners was still a busy place repairing and maintaining its own fleet of boats which were necessary to keep the canal and its infrastructure in operation. The canals around east Manchester, in particular the Ashton Canal, were in a slow process of decline in terms of their usefulness but, they were not finished yet.

Left: L&NER engineers narrow boat No. 15 *Flora* is moored up in the depot arm outside the dry dock. Herbert Potts and E. Lawson are standing at the stern of the boat behind the engine room. *Flora* was originally a horse boat built in 1858, it was shortened to 58ft in 1896 and was still in existence in 1946.
H. Potts Collection/Courtesy Canal and River Trust

Joel again, still moored in front of the dry dock with her crew but this time the photographer is on board. Such a shame that the Kelvin 9hp engine is not more visible. Notice that the dry dock is flooded showing a reflection of the buildings windows in the still water.
H. Potts Collection/Courtesy Canal and River Trust

Joel now in the dry dock. Not very often that a narrow boat can be seen from this position, giving a good view of the outline of the hull. The dock floor is clean and orderly, a little bit different to the locomotive shops. Notice the access steps at the end of the dock.

Above: The rudder and stern of *Joel* whilst in the dry dock.

Left: A view from above of *Joel* in the dock receiving attention.

all H. Potts Collection/Courtesy Canal and River Trust

Above & Left: *Joel* again. Above is a close-up of the engine room compartment. There are various men around it, Mr Lucas is stood in front of the engine room, behind it are A. Langton, G. Challoner, W. Potts and W. McLeng. The view to the right shows the Kelvin engine in more detail.

Now in British Waterways days (nationalised at the same time as the railways), the replacement *Joel* built in 1948 at the Gorton canal depot. The boat, seen here, is fairly new at Audenshaw on the Ashton Canal in its new British Waterways colours. Steering is Jim Hirst of Gorton depot. Jim steered both of the *Joel's* in his time. The depot's maintenance fleet included goods carriers, stone carriers, weed cutters and dredgers. Additionally, there were eight iron-built ice breakers which came under Gorton's jurisdiction. Some boats were horse-drawn to the end of their days. There are several boats still in existence, two of the boats are moored at the Ashton packet boat company, quite close to their original home base.

All Photos: Courtesy R. Tansly/ J. Pitman collection

Narrow boat *Violet*. Built in June 1857, the boat was number 11 in the depot's boat fleet. She is pictured here displaying her L&NER engineers identity. *Violet* was still in existence as late as 1946 at the good old age of 89. *L&NER*

Posing under the depot's overhead crane gantry are some of the workshop staff. These include Mr P. Taylor, E. Lawton, W. McLevis, L. Burgess, F. Moulton, F. Leigh, A. Williams, A. Shawcross, T. Challenor, E. Hyde, W. Higginbottom, A. Langton, J. Mullen and J. Sherratt.

Circa 1950 the canal depot still has some life in it, though by 1960 it was more or less derelict. The boat in the dry dock is more than likely *President*, a steel fabricated motorised vessel. The author visited the depot in around 1950, when aged five, with his father who worked there before he moved to the Marple Depot when there was very little work remaining.
courtesy D. Kitching

Looking out from the dock arm to the canal proper under the hump back bridge. The large building on the opposite bank is High Bank Mill.
courtesy D. Kitching

Top Left: Narrow boat No. 9 *Joel*. The replacement for the 1929 boat, built in 1948 at the Gorton Tank canal depot. This boat and *Maria* now both reside at the Ashton Packet Boat Company at Guide Bridge.

Lower Left: Narrow boat *Maria*. It is unconfirmed but it is quite possible that this boat was a replacement for the original built and was built in 1915 by Jinks Yard of Marple for £155. The original *Maria* was built in July 1854. *both Author*

Above: Engine room of *Joel*. Kelvin paraffin engine. *Author*

Two of the eight ex-Gorton canal depot maintenance department iron ice breakers at the Canal and River Trust Museum, Ellesmere Port waiting for restoration. *both courtesy J. Pitman*

Captured from the site of the Stockport Branch of the Ashton Canal, had this photograph been taken fifty or so years ago, the photographer would have had to stand in about five feet of water to take it. It is now a public foot and cycle path leading from the Ashton Canal proper and Hyde Road to the south. The humpback bridge was part of the towpath which spanned the 'arm' leading into the canal depot basin and dry dock. On the other side of the bridge there is now a small housing estate and prior to that, there was a coal yard. Featured above is the keystone of the bridge but whose head is sculptured into it? *both Author*

In ex-works condition. Robinson Class '8K' (L&NER Class 'O4') 2-8-0 No. 63724. Sitting on the running board, John Duncan poses for a photograph with a fellow apprentice.

CHAPTER NINE
THROUGH THE LENS OF AN APPRENTICE'S CAMERA

It is most fortunate that engineering apprentice John Duncan, when working at Gorton in the late 1940s and early 1950s, took a very keen interest in the railways and was able to take quite a number of photographs with his 1914 folding camera inside and around the works. Given that he was an amateur photographer with such an old camera, and how expensive 116 roll film was in those days it is pleasing that he has been able to make these photographs, which were taken for personal use, available for us to see today. Some images are very good, some not so brilliant, but, are included as they would probably never be seen for people to enjoy if not added. Quite an amount of John's locomotive photographs are of GCR vintage, even a few are survivors of the MS&LR. With this in mind the locomotive images show them in a basically run down condition and eking out their last few years before the inevitable, especially with some attaining the ripe old age of fifty or more years. Robinson's 4-6-0 designs were withdrawn en masse after the Second World War. His 4-6-0s were never a resounding success, though some could be on par with some of the products of other pre BR railway companies if handled correctly. The 'B7' Class (GCR Class '9Q'), being very versatile could have soldiered on for a few more years but with their reputation for being heavy on fuel when not in expert hands, this probably being one of the deciding factors in their relatively early retirement, that is, if thirty odd years is 'early'.

The captions on the photographs were quite brief, as John described them. A few more detailed descriptions have been added on some of the images for a better understanding where necessary.

John Duncan having a rest on the right hand eccentric rod of Gresley Class 'B17' 4-6-0 No. 61605 *Lincolnshire Regiment*. Maybe trying to do a 'Buster Keaton' perhaps?

Johnny Duncan on board a Class '9J' 0-6-0. John spent a lifetime on the railways after completing his engineering apprenticeship. Following retirement (he is now in his 80s) he became very active in the railway heritage field becoming involved with the Bulleid WC Class 4-6-2 'Light' Pacific locomotive BR No. 34092 *City of Wells*.

Above: Robinson GCR Class '9L' (L&NER Class 'C14') 4-4-2T No. 7748, later given the BR number 67448. Such a shame that these attractive little 4-4-2 tanks had to suffer with the addition of the flower pot chimneys. Behind is a Thompson 'B1' 4-6-0. The 'C14' was built in 1907 and withdrawn in the second half of 1959.

Left: Ernie (surname unknown) from the brass shop 'ejector section' working on Robinson Class 'D11/1' (GCR Class '11F') 4-6-0 No. 62660 Princess Mary in Gorton yard, ex-works. The locomotive was the fifth member of the class to be built and was turned out from Gorton in May 1920 and numbered 510 by the GCR, renumbered 5501 by the L&NER, then 2664 in the 1946 L&NER renumbering scheme and finally 62664 by BR. The 'D11s' will go down as John Robinson's finest and most successful passenger locomotives. Thankfully the first built of the class No. 62660 *Butler-Henderson* has been preserved to its former GCR livery for all to admire.

Just prior to BR days. Sat in the cab of a Robinson Atlantic Class 'C4/4' (GCR Class '8B') 4-4-2 No. 2901, could this perfectly groomed young man (no doubt courtesy of Brylcreem) possibly be dreaming of what it must have been like to drive one of these GCR classic locomotives. Built in December 1903 by Beyer, Peacock and numbered 194, the locomotive was withdrawn in November 1959 at Gorton and cut up a month later.

GCR Class '9A' (L&NER Class 'N4') 0-6-2T No. 69234. It appears that some type of work is being carried out in the smokebox. Perhaps the wheel barrow is the mode of transport for a fitters' tool kit! The locomotive had a long life in service of exactly 53 years.

Above: Can any ex-Gorton person reading this book identify these two men? Names are forgotten after fifty five or so years.

Above left: Standing alongside Gresley Class 'B17' 4-6-0 No. 61605 *Lincolnshire Regiment*.

Above right: Testing a Ross pop safety valve. The noise must be horrendous and there was no hearing protection in this era for the gentleman as the safety valve is blowing off. The valves were tested in the wooden 'lean to' at the side of the boiler mounting shop (known in the works as 'the drum' with its stationary steam raising boiler).

Right: Mates, Peter Barrow and Les Hadfield take a short break and pose alongside an unidentified Class 'C13' 4-4-2 in Gorton yard.

1949. Gorton's last new steam build. Thompson Class 'B1' 4-6-0 under construction in No. 1 Bay in the Erecting Shop. The locomotive will be numbered 61349 on its completion.

Freshly painted, Thompson Class 'B1' 4-6-0 No. 61225 appears to be receiving some attention behind the rear right side coupled wheel. Built in August 1948 and allocated to Gorton, 39A. The locomotive was withdrawn in mid-1965, a working life of just eighteen years. Such was the hurry for British Railways to eliminate steam locomotives and introduce diesel and electric traction to the railways.

Covered in snow in late 1950, 'Streamlined' Gresley Class 'B17/4' 4-6-0 No. 61670 *City of London* stands outside No. 2 Bay of the Erecting Shop. Chalked on the cab side is 'For Sec 6' where it would be under the watchful eye of Zac Baker, the section six foreman. Once the locomotive has gone in from the cold it will undergo a transformation. Defrocked of its streamlined casing it will receive a general overhaul and emerge out of the shop complete with a Thompson 100A boiler in April 1951, as seen below.

This image is not from the camera of John Duncan, but as the theme from these couple of pages are on the topic of the B17 streamliners it is worthwhile including it here – June 1949 and streamlined B17 61659 *East Anglian* in the works yard waiting to enter the erecting shop. When it emerges it will be de-streamlined after a major overhaul and classified as B17/6. *R. Fysh/MLS collection*

Standing outside No. 3 Bay of the Erecting Shop is a rare visitor to Gorton. Sentinel Class 'Y3' 0-4-0 shunting locomotive BR No. 68169. Behind the Sentinel is a Class 'O4' 2-8-0, No. 63755, stood on No. 10 road waiting to go into No. 4 Bay. Chalked on its cab side is 'Keep off - LR' (LR – light repair).

Thompson Class 'B1' 4-6-0 No. 61190 appears to be alone at this end of the shed yard. Newly painted and no doubt ex-works. Originally bearing No. 1190 when first built in May 1947 it became 61190 in 1948 under the British Railways numbering scheme. The locomotive was withdrawn mid-1965. The running sheds offices can be seen behind the tender and the west end of the sheds further away to the left of the smokebox.

Originally numbered 183 by the GCR when first built by Beyer, Peacock, Robinson Class '8' (L&NER Class 'B5') 4-6-0 stands outside Gorton shed bearing its L&NER number. The locomotive never received a BR number as it was withdrawn from service at Mexborough on the 12th June 1950 and was observed shortly afterwards at Gorton awaiting its fate. The photograph was probably taken at this time.

Peppercorn Mogul Class 'K1' 2-6-0 No. 62020 being turned on Gorton's turntable. Built in August 1949 by the North British Locomotive Company in Glasgow, thus the locomotive would be relatively new at the time it was photographed. The 'K1' was a development of the Thompson 'K1/1' .

Robinson 'O4' (GCR Class '8K') No. 63907 stands in Gorton yard in the company of another unidentified 'O4'.

APPENDIX ONE

COMPLETE LIST OF LOCOMOTIVES BUILT BY GORTON LOCOMOTIVE WORKS 1858 to 1963

Manchester Sheffield & Lincolnshire Railway to 1898
Great Central Railway to 1923
London & North Eastern Railway to 1948
British Railways Eastern Region, later London Midland Region to 1963 (works closure)

CLASS	TYPE	BUILDER	YEAR	NUMBERS
5	0-6-0 Tender	MS&L	1858	6, 7
5	0-6-0 Tender	MS&L	1859	36, 53
1	2-4-0 Tank	MS&L	1860	23, 24
			1861	No New Builds
8	2-4-0 Tender	MS&L	1862	67
23	0-6-0 Tender	MS&L	1862	28, 29
13	0-6-0 Tender	MS&L	1862	63
1	2-4-0 Tank	MS&L	1863	12 (70), 20
	(Rebuilt 1892/3 to Class '1A')			
8	2-4-0 Tender	MS&L	1863	76
13	0-6-0 Tender	MS&L	1863	21
8	2-4-0 Tender	MS&L	1864	96
1	2-4-0 Tank	MS&L	1864	9, 123
	(Rebuilt 1892/3 to Class '1A')			
13	0-6-0 Tender	MS&L	1864	54, 51
1B	2-4-0 Tender	MS&L	1865	10, 17
24	2-4-0 Tender: Pass	MS&L	1865	180-185
24	2-4-0 Tender: Pass	MS&L	1866	186, 187
23	0-6-0 Tender: Goods	MS&L	1866	91, 92, 200-207
1	2-4-0 Tank	MS&L	1866	208, 209, 211
	(211 Rebuilt 1892/3 to Class '1A')			
1	2-4-0 Tank	MS&L	1866	210
1B	2-4-0 Tender	MS&L	1866	11 (47), 13 (79)
8	2-4-0 Tender	MS&L	1866	77 (47)
24	2-4-0 Tender: Pass	MS&L	1867	55-59, 85-87, 152, 153, 256-261
24	2-4-0 Tender: Pass	MS&L	1868	262-267.
1B	2-4-0 Tender: Pass	MS&L	1868	14 (80), 31
8	2-4-0 Tender: Pass	MS&L	1868	2
1B	2-4-0 Tender : Pass	MS&L	1869	32, 33 (81)
10	2-4-0 Tender: Pass	MS&L	1869	74, 75 (2), 94 (151), 95, 97 (27), 98 64 (90)
18	0-6-0 Tender: Goods	MS&L	1869	22*, 78*, 157
18	0-6-0 Tender: Goods	MS&L	1870	1*, 5, 16*, 19*, 35, 38, 41*, 52*, 72*, 73*, 88*, 156*, 158*
18	0-6-0 Tender: Goods	MS&L	1871	8*, 43*, 61 (53)*, 93, 154*, 160 (17)*, 40*, 42*, 66*
8	2-4-0 Tender: Pass	MS&L	1871	65, 68
18T	0-6-0ST: Goods	MS&L	1871	271, 272, 273, 274, 275, 276, 277, 278 279, 280
	* = Subsequently fitted with saddle tanks and reclassified Class 18con			
18	0-6-0 Tender: Goods	MS&L	1872	281,-295 (307), 296, 297 (966), 298-303
18	0-6-0 Tender : Goods	MS&L	1873	304-310
18T	0-6-0ST: Goods	MS&L	1873	336-341
12	2-4-0 Tender: Pass	MS&L	1873	311-320

CLASS	TYPE	BUILDER	YEAR	NUMBERS
18	0-6-0 Tender: Goods	MS&L	1874	321-335
18T	0-6-0ST: Goods	MS&L	1874	344-345, 342-343
6A	0-6-0 Tender	MS&L	1874	346, 347 (397), 348-352
6A	0-6-0 Tender: Goods	MS&L	1875	353-355, 133
12A	2-4-0 Tender: Pass	MS&L	1875	356-362 (319) 363-365
18T	0-6-0ST: Goods	MS&L	1875	366-374
6A	0-6-0 Tender: Goods	MS&L	1876	375-394
24	2-4-0 Tender: Pass	MS&L	1877	71
6A	0-6-0 Tender: Goods	MS&L	1877	395-398, 105 (399), 168 (155)
6B	4-4-0 Tender: Pass	MS&L	1877	423-434
6B	4-4-0 Tender: Pass	MS&L	1878	435-444
6B	4-4-0 Tender: Pass	MS&L	1879	445, 446
6B	4-4-0 Tender: Pass	MS&L	1880	4, 129, 129
18T	0-6-0ST: Goods	MS&L	1880	411-416
12AT	2-4-0 Tank: Pass	MS&L	1880	23, 24
6C	0-6-0 Tender: Goods	MS&L	1880	3, 30, 34
6C	0-6-0 Tender: Goods	MS&L	1881	458-468
18T	0-6-0ST: Goods	MS&L	1881	417-422
12AT	0-6-0 Tank: Pass	MS&L	1881	447-452
6C	0-6-0 Tender: Goods	MS&L	1882	469, 472-491
14	2-2-2 Tender: Pass	MS&L	1882	399 (104)
6C	0-6-0 Tender: Goods	MS&L	1883	492-499
14	2-2-2 Tender: Pass	MS&L	1883	500 (105), 501 (106), 502 (107), 503 (108), 504 (109), 505(110), 506 (111), 507 (112), 508 (113), 509 (114), 510 (115)
6C	0-6-0 Tender: Goods	MS&L	1884	513 (6), 514 (7), 515(31), 516 (32), 517 (33), 518 (35), 519 (36), 520 (37), 45, 46
12A	2-4-0 Tender: Pass	MS&L	1884	39, 44, 48, 49, 146 (212), 147 (213)
6C	0-6-0 Tender: Goods	MS&L	1885	521 (88), 522 (470), 523 (471), 524 (500), 531 (501), 532 (502), 533 (503) 534 (504), 535 (505)
7	0-6-0 Tank	MS&L	1885	525 (10), 526 (11), 527 (12), 528 (13), 529 (14), 530 (15)
12A	2-4-0 Tender: Pass	MS&L	1885	539 (159), 540 (160), 541 (161), 542 (162), 543(163), 544 (164), 545 (165), 546 (166), 547 (167), 548 (168), 549 (169)

CLASS	TYPE	BUILDER	YEAR	NUMBERS
12A	2-4-0 Tender: Pass	MS&L	1886	550 (170)
6D	2-4-0 Tender: Pass	MS&L	1887	10 (506), 17 (507), 79 (509)
6A1	0-6-0 Tender: Goods	MS&L	1887	551-553
6DB	4-4-0 Tender: Pass	MS&L	1888	37 (508), 89 (510), 400(511)
6A1	0-6-0 Tender: Goods	MS&L	1888	163 (549), 166 (550), 554-560
9	0-6-0 Tender: Goods	MS&L	1889	568-573
9A	0-6-2 Tank: Goods	MS&L	1889	161 (512), 165 (513)
3	2-4-2 Tank: Pass	MS&L	1889	574-579
3	2-4-2 Tank: Pass	MS&L	1890	580
9A	0-6-2 Tank: Goods	MS&L	1890	173 (514)
2	4-4-0 Tender: Pass	MS&L	1890	562-567
3	2-4-2 Tank: Pass	MS&L	1891	581, 582
9C	0-6-2 Tank: Goods	MS&L	1891	7 (515)
2	4-4-0 Tender: Pass	MS&L	1891	682-684
9A	0-6-2 Tank: Goods	MS&L	1891	601-603
9C	0-6-2 Tank: Goods	MS&L	1892	47 (516), 171 (517)
2	4-4-0 Tender: Pass	MS&L	1892	685-687
3	2-4-2 Tank: Pass	MS&L	1892	584
3	2-4-2 Tank: Pass	MS&L	1893	583, 585
9D	0-6-0 Tender: Goods	MS&L	1893	639-644
2A	4-4-0 Tender: Pass	MS&L	1894	688-693
9E	0-6-0 Tender: Goods	MS&L	1894	738-740
9E	0-6-0 Tender: Goods	MS&L	1895	741-743
11	4-4-0 Tender: Pass	MS&L	1895	694-699
9F	0-6-2 Tank: Goods	MS&L	1895	200, 536, 756
9F	0-6-2 Tank: Goods	MS&L	1896	201A(54), 202A (21), 203A (25), 757-762
11A	4-4-0 Tender: Pass	MS&L	1897	268, 269
5	0-6-0 Tank: Goods	MS&L	1897	882-893
	(Number 889 originally built as Class '5' with Crane 0-6-2 type. Converted 12/01/1918 to Class '5' 0-6-0 type when the Crane was removed)			
11A	4-4-0 Tender: Pass	GCR	1898	270, 852-861
9F	0-6-2 Tank: Goods	GCR	1898	204A (51), 205A (173), 206A (189), 207A (251)
9F	0-6-2 Tank: Goods	GCR	1899	894-909
9F	0-6-2 Tank: Goods	GCR	1900	910-924
13	4-2-2 Tender: Pass	GCR	1900	967-972
9H	0-6-0 Tender: Goods	GCR	1901	74-77, 79-84, 90, 94-101, 103, 116, 117
9H	0-6-0 Tender: Goods	GCR	1902	118,-126, 130-132, 134, 141, 172, 174-176
	Note:- number 134 Fitted with special Boiler on 22/02/1908 and reclassified Class '9M'. Converted back to 9H on 18/12/1924			
9K	4-4-2 Tank: Pass	GCR	1903	171, 178, 179, 188, 190, 191, 193, 199
9J	0-6-0 Tender: Goods	GCR	1903	177, 197, 202
9J	0-6-0 Tender: Goods	GCR	1904	204, 207, 208, 217, 220, 232, 233, 240, 241
9K	4-4-2 Tank: Pass	GCR	1904	2, 9, 18, 20, 27-29, 47, 50, 55
	Steam Motors	GCR	1904	1, 2
8D	4-4-2 Tender : Pass	GCR	1905	258
9K	4-4-2 Tank: Pass	GCR	1905	114, 115, 310, 357, 359, 453-457
	Steam Motor	GCR	1905	3
9J	0-6-0 Tender: Goods	GCR	1906	281, 282

CLASS	TYPE	BUILDER	YEAR	NUMBERS
8D	4-4-2 Tender: Pass	GCR	1906	259
8E	4-4-2 Tender: Pass	GCR	1906	364, 365
8B	4-4-2 Tender: Pass	GCR	1906	260-262, 358, 360-363
5A	0-6-0 Tank: Goods	GCR	1906	89, 157, 321, 538
5Acon	0-6-0 Tank: Goods	GCR	1906	60, 61
	(Fitted with condensers)			
9J	0-6-0 Tender: Goods	GCR	1907	283-309, 311-318
9J	0-6-0 Tender: Goods	GCR	1908	319, 320, 322-329
9J	0-6-0 Tender: Goods	GCR	1909	16, 330
8A	0-8-0 Tender: Mineral	GCR	1909	39, 44, 48, 49, 62, 63, 159-164, 212, 213, 356
9J	0-6-0 Tender: Mineral	GCR	1910	947-955
8A	0-8-0 Tender: Mineral	GCR	1910	401, 956-965, 1174-1179
8A	0-8-0 Tender: Mineral	GCR	1911	1180-1182
9N	4-6-2 Tank: Pass	GCR	1911	23, 24, 165-170, 447, 448
8K	2-8-0 Tender: Mineral	GCR	1911	26, 69, 93, 331-335, 996
8K	2-8-0 Tender: Mineral	GCR	1912	102, 133, 155, 346-355, 400, 402, 403, 405-408
9N	4-6-2 Tank: Pass	GCR	1912	128, 129, 449-452
1	4-6-0 Tender: Pass	GCR	1912	423
1	4-6-0 Tender: Pass	GCR	1913	424-428
11E	4-4-0 Tender: Pass	GCR	1913	429-438
8K	2-8-0 Tender: Mineral	GCR	1913	375, 376, 378-385
1A	4-6-0 Tender: Mixed Traffic	GCR	1913	4
8K	2-8-0 Tender: Mineral	GCR	1914	386-399, 271
5A	0-6-0 Tank:Goods	GCR	1914	277
1B	2-6-4 Tank: Goods	GCR	1914	272, 273
1A	4-6-0 Tender: Mixed Traffic	GCR	1914	279, 439-446
1A	4-6-0 Tender: Mixed Traffic	GCR	1915	280
1B	2-6-4 Tank: Goods	GCR	1915	274-276, 336-340
1B	2-6-4 Tank: Goods	GCR	1916	341-344
1B	2-6-4 Tank: Goods	GCR	1917	345, 366-370
9N	4-6-2 Tank: Pass	GCR	1917	371-374, 411
9P	4-6-0 Tender: Pass	GCR	1917	1169
8M	2-8-0 Tender: Mineral	GCR	1918	412-415, 417-419
8N	4-6-0 Tender: Mixed Traffic	GCR	1918	416
8K	2-8-0 Tender: Mineral	GCR	1918	(ROD) 2002-2004
8K	2-8-0 Tender: Mineral	GCR	1919	(ROD) 2005 (1), 2006 (5), 2007 (8)
8M	2-8-0 Tender: Mineral	GCR	1919	10-13, 420-422
11F	4-4-0 Tender: Pass	GCR	1919	506
11F	4-4-0 Tender: Pass	GCR	1920	507-510
9P	4-6-0 Tender: Pass	GCR	1920	1164-1168
8M	2-8-0 Tender: Mineral	GCR	1920	14, 15, 17
8M	2-8-0 Tender: Mineral	GCR	1921	19, 22
8N	4-6-0 Tender: Pass	GCR	1921	52, 53
9Q	4-6-0 Tender: Mixed Traffic	GCR	1921	72, 73, 78, 465, 466
9Q	4-6-0 Tender: Mixed Traffic	GCR	1922	467-474
11F	4-4-0 Tender: Pass	GCR	1922	501-505, 511
9N	4-6-2 Tank: Pass	GCR	1923	3, 6, 7, 30, 45, 46, 88, 154, 156, 158
9Q	4-6-0 Tender: Mixed Traffic	GCR	1923	475-482
9Q	4-6-0 Tender: Mixed Traffic	L&NER(GC)	1924	5483, 5484, (Last numbers in GC series)
N7	0-6-2 Tank: Goods	L&NER(GC)	1925	409, 421, 426, 456, 457, 460, 464, 471, 473, 475

CLASS	TYPE	BUILDER	YEAR	NUMBERS
N7	0-6-2 Tank: Goods	L&NER(GC)	1926	826-830, 832-834, 837, 838, 850-853, 865-868, 870
N7	0-6-2 Tank: Goods	L&NER(GC)	1927	873, 2632-2637
N7	0-6-2 Tank: Goods	L&NER(GC)	1928	2638-2641
			1929	Nil
			1930	Nil
			1931	Nil
8H	0-8-2 Tank: Goods	L&NER(GC)	1932	2798, 2799
			1933	Nil
			1934	Nil
			1935	Nil
			1936	Nil
			1937	Nil
J50	0-6-0 Tank: Goods	L&NER(GC)	1938	599, 600, 602, 605, 606
J50	0-6-0 Tank: Goods	L&NER(GC)	1939	584, 585, 587, 590, 595, 598, 608, 611, 615
	(Note:- No. 598 was the thousandth locomotive built at Gorton)			
			1940	Nil
			1941	Nil
			1942	Nil
			1943	Nil
			1944	Nil
			1945	Nil
			1946	Nil
			1947	Nil
B1	4-6-0 Tender : Pass	BR	1948	61340, 61341
B1	4-6-0 Tender: Pass	BR	1949	61342-61349
EM1	BO+BO Electric	BR	1950	26001-26003
EM1	BO+BO Electric	BR	1951	26004-26024, 26029, 26030
EM1	BO+BO Electric	BR	1952	26025-26028, 26031-26051
EM1	BO+BO Electric	BR	1953	26052-26057
EM2	CO-CO Electric	BR	1953	27000
EM2	CO-CO Electric	BR	1954	27001-27006
			1955	Nil
			1956	Nil
			1957	Nil
			1958	Nil
			1959	Nil
			1960	Nil
			1961	Nil
			1962	Nil
			1963	Nil
	Gorton Locomotive Works closed 31st May 1963			

Extracted from Mechanical Engineers Office – Gorton. From notes superbly written by the late Mr Allan Brown, member of the Manchester Locomotive Society and **the country's leading researcher of the Great Central Railway.**

APPENDIX TWO

THE FINAL YEARS

Following the completion of the construction of the EM1 Bo+Bo and 'EM2' Co-Co MSW 1500Volt dc classes of electric locomotives in 1954 it become apparent that no new locomotives were to be constructed at Gorton. By the mid 1950s it was also announced that British Railways was going to embark on a massive modernisation plan where the building of steam locomotives was to cease, on completion of the construction of the British Railways 'Standard' Classes of steam locomotives being built at other workshops, and that electric traction was ultimately going to be the new form of motive power with diesel locomotives being the intermediary step until the whole system was electrified. For electric traction, British Railways were looking at the continental voltage for locomotives, where, 25,000 Volts ac current was becoming more and more adopted for mainline work. This put the new MSW 1,500 Volt dc electrical system out of favour for future use and thus the decision was made to cut the number of new 'EM2' locomotives to be built to just seven instead of the planned twenty-seven. The Manchester to Sheffield line (Britain's first electric main line) was destined to be a 'one off' system. Following this, on the 1st March 1960, Ernest Marples appointed Dr Richard Beeching into the position of the new Chairman of the British Railway Board, which was to replace the British Transport Commission from June of the same year. Dr Beeching's job was basically to make the railways become profitable. Gorton Locomotive Works along with quite a number of other locomotive workshops was soon to come under review. The Beeching report put shivers down the spine of the whole of British Railways. Tens of thousands of railway jobs and thousands of route miles of railway line were destined to be lost and thiswas to leave a bitter taste in the industry for a long time. This was particularly so at Gorton where Beyer, Peacock Ltd, 100 yards or so away on the other side of the railway line from Gorton Tank, were given the job of building a number of the fleet of 'Hymek' diesel-hydraulic main line locomotives for British Railways, whilst BRs own Gorton Works was left in the cold and under threat of closure.

One year on following this 1962 review, Gorton Tank would be closed.

During the final years the works, with regards to production, carried out the general and casual repairs of steam and the MSW dc electric locomotives at the average rate of seven per week, as well as heavy repairs to approximately eighty wagons per week. Ancillary activities carried out involved the fitting out of AWS equipment to two locomotives per week. The fitting out of vacuum braking equipment to wagons was also carried out to about twenty-five per week. Work was also carried out on special conversions to coaching stock for AC electrification work to approximately three coaches per week.

At that period, the works were also involved in the manufacture of steel and aluminium fabrications for diesel locomotives being built at Derby and Crewe locomotive works. Points and crossings were still being fabricated in the Permanent Way Shop at approximately twenty assemblies per week to the Chief Civil Engineers requirements.

Whilst this was being carried out, the works were engaged in cutting up/scrapping of old life-expired steam locomotives on a large scale as the British Railways Modernisation programme of building its fleet of diesel and electric locomotives gathered rapid momentum.

APPENDIX THREE
SUMMARY OF STAFF, MARCH 1962

By 1960, the number of Personnel in the Locomotive and Carriage and Wagon Works stood at a total of 1,953. This was comprised of:

CM&EE's Department	
Managerial	4
Professional and Technical	14
Clerical	61
Workshop Supervisory	72
Nursing Staff	3
Wages Staff - Conciliation	23
Workshop	1,566
Canteen	12
TOTAL	1,755

Accountant's Department	
Salaried Staff	97 (CME)
Workshop Staff	5
Stores Department	
Workshop Staff	71
Salaried Staff	25
TOTAL	198
GRAND TOTAL	**1,953**

APPENDIX FOUR
THE PRINCIPAL SHOPS POST NATIONALISATION

The following is a review of the activities carried out within the various shops:

PATTERN SHOP

This shop shared the same building as the Joiners Shop. Work that was carried here consisted of maintaining locomotive, carriage and wagon, permanent way, and other plant and equipment patterns.

In addition some of the staff prepared and fitted foot boarding for the steam and electric locomotives.

Equipment in the shop consisted of sanding, planing, mortising and moulding machines. The shop also had a 'Wadkin' timber miller. Area 125ft x 25ft

SHELL MOULDING SHOP

This shop was formerly the Brass Foundry.

The shop manufactured shell moulded carriage and steam heater pipe couplings (machined at Wolverton and Gorton), gravity valves for same, coupling rod bushes, electrical terminals for Wolverton-built coaches and other electrical details for the Electrical Traction Engineers overhead line maintenance schemes.

Capacity output at this time was 1,000 steam heat couplings per week, 60 bushes, and 600 gravity valves etc.

Only one 'Moulder' was still employed at this period mainly for emergency purposes.

Shop Equipment included:

2-ton overhead crane
2 x 600 lb Bauman Melting Furnaces
Shell and Core Moulding Plant.

SMITHY

The Smiths' shops comprised several sections and included the General Smithy, Chain Smithy, Upsetting section, Drop Stamping section, Die Sinking Shop and Forge.

The general smithy was housed in the old seventeen road locomotive roundhouse (of 1847 vintage) where locomotives were repaired during that early period.

Included in the smithy equipment were a 'Hancomatic' profile cutting machine, two flash butt-welding general purpose machines, three 'Atomic Hydrogen' arc welding sets (for welding steel chains) and a hydraulic press.

Other principal equipment in the various shops were:

2-ton 10cwt forge hammer
6 x drop stamps, from 25cwt to 5cwt
10 x steam hammers ranging from 15cwt to 5cwt
4 x Upsetting machines (3½ inch to 1 inch)
Blacksmiths' furnaces.

Lifting equipment for the Eastern and North Eastern Regions and outdoor machinery was made and repaired there.

WELDING SHOP

The Welding Shop was a small shop with the main purpose of carrying out light welding jobs.

Each individual welding booth was equipped with an Electric Arc Welding set supplied from an eight operator generator. Each booth was served by an individual 2-ton overhead hoist.

This shop also housed metal spraying equipment.

MAIN BOILER SHOPS

The main Boiler Shop consisted of four bays (one bay – Boiler Mounting Shop – was part of the old paint and stock shed of the 1850s.

All heavy repairs were carried out to boilers in these shops, including the fitting of new fireboxes and copper firebox welding. The shops had also manufactured complete boilers in the past, but this practice was no longer carried out as steam locomotive production was phased out at Gorton in 1949.

The Boiler Shop had its own maintenance team, employed mainly on repairs to pneumatic hand tools and oxy-acetylene equipment and hoses.

The equipment in the shop bays consisted of:

4 x 24-ton overhead electric cranes each in the two centre bays
1 x 15-ton and 1 x 5-ton crane in the 4th bay
1 x 100-ton and 1 x 55-ton boiler barrel gap riveter (hydraulic)
2 x boiler plate bending rollers.

MACHINE SHOP

The machine shop formed part of the original C & W shops of the 1850s and the traverser runway of the same period after it was covered over to form a work shop (as mentioned in earlier chapters). The shop was in two main bays. Both bays held a very large number of machine tools for carrying out practically every machining process for locomotive repairs, and included milling machines, lathes, planing, boring, radial arm drills, shaping, slotting, boring machines, capstan lathes, grinding machines and presses etc. The heaviest machine tools were installed in the bay affectionately known as the 'Danube' which was the location of the of the original traverser. The white metal shop and various fitters departments and sections also came under the control of the machine shop. The north end of the shop comprised the 'Bosh', (where locomotive sub parts/components were acid cleaned in dip tanks after removal from locomotives in the erecting shop, and examined prior for attention in the machine shop fitting bays).

The machine shops also had its own millwrights section, tool room, and jig & template room, which served various areas of the works as required.

Main machine shop bay 1 x 10-ton overhead crane.

Heavy Machine Shop Bay (Danube) 1 x 15-ton and 1 x 5 ton overhead crane.

Bosh – Examination Room 2 x 5-ton overhead cranes.

Tool Room / Fitting Shop 1 x 5-ton overhead crane.

COPPER SHOP – COPPER SMITHS

In the late 1950s, early 1960s parts of this shop was turned over to the manufacture and fabrication of aluminium fuel tanks, battery boxes, sand boxes, cable ducting and other small detailed work for diesel locomotives under construction at Derby and Crewe Locomotive works.

The remainder of the shop still provided its intended use for all copper pipework for steam and MSW Electric locomotives. Also pipework for maintenance to 'Outstation' departments.

Equipment included:

1 x 37-ton pipe bending machine

1 x 37-ton hydraulic press

Aluminium welding was with a 'Saturn Surge Injector Unit' and a 'Rowan Arc Unit'.

BOILER MACHINE SHOP/FABRICATION SHOP

This shop was the main shop for larger fabrication work. The work that was carried out here dealt mainly with steel fabrication work, also an amount of aluminium fabrication work not carried out by the Copper and Tin Shops. During this period there was a high concentration of fabrication of radiator tanks, fuel tanks, battery boxes and other details associated for the construction of diesel locomotives at Derby works.

This shop also was the machine shop for the machining of locomotive barrel plates and fabrication details.

Equipment included:

5 x overhead electric cranes ranging from 25-ton to 5-tons.

2 x plate bending machines

1 x edge planing machine

Several radial arm drilling machines.

Several welding sets, including 'Saturn' surge injector unit for welding aluminium.

PRESS SHOP

The heavier press work, such as boiler firebox plates (steel and copper), smokebox fronts (doors) and other thick/heavy duty platework, was carried out in this shop. Rail bending was also carried out for the Civil Engineer here.

Equipment in the shop included:

1 x 300-ton triple ram hydraulic press

1 x 100-ton hydraulic press

1 x 5-ton overhead crane.

TUBE SHOP

Locomotive boiler tubes were repaired in this shop. Tubes, large and small were rumbled, repaired and new ends welded on, belled, screwed and cut to length. All this on a mass progressive repair flow line system. All secondhand tubes from Doncaster Works were sent here for reconditioning where possible. Maximum output of tubes per week was 2,500 small tubes and 300 large reconditioned tubes.

Equipment included:

5½ inch dia. tube butt welding machine

2½ inch dia tube butt welding machine

1 x 15-ton overhead crane

1 x rotary tube heating furnace.

SPRING SHOP

The shop was laid out on a progressive repair system with roller conveyors which was capable of dealing with approximately 100 locomotive and 200 wagon springs per week.

Equipment in the shop comprised of:

1 x large oil fired spring tempering and annealing furnace

1 x 'Pels' cropping machine

1 x Hydraulic stripping press

1 x Buckling press

1 x 30cwt overhead electric crane

1 x 5cwt overhead electric crane.

BRASS FINISHING SHOP

The Brass finishing shop was involved with the manufacture of all brass components and other parts. All components removed from locomotives passed through a cleaning system prior to examination.

In addition to the manufacturing, repairing and assembly of items, work was also carried out on steam heating couplings and vacuum pipe couplings for the carriage and wagon construction programmes.

Production of rail bonds for the electrification scheme was also carried out with a capacity of 1,700 per week.

The Shop also had facilities for the repair and testing of all pressure and vacuum dial gauges.

Equipment in the shop comprised mainly of brass machining lathes, milling, shaping and drilling machines. Also installed were caustic and acid cleaning boshes.

PERMANENT WAY SHOP

This shop manufactured and assembled flat bottomed rail points and crossings for the Civil Engineers Department. Production rate was approximately thirty assemblies per week.

Incorporated in the shop were automatic gas furnaces for heating rails prior to bending into shape.

Other equipment included:

4 x rail planing machines.

1 x 5-ton overhead electric crane.

Outside the shop was a large storage and assembly yard which included a 5-ton overhead electric gantry crane.

TINSMITHS SHOP

The 'Tin Shop' manufactured and repaired various lamps and lamp parts, oil cans etc. Light sheet metal work also was carried out for various areas of the works. Aluminium cupboards for diesel Bo-Bo locomotives, steel sand boxes for Co-Co locomotives and steel sub assemblies and air trunking for diesel shunters which were under construction at the time at Derby locomotive works.

Gas and electric welding was carried out in this shop.

A minor novel feature of this shop was the use of a T.T.3 Pneumatic rivetting tool for pup rivets.

SAWMILL

The production sawmill produced all timber requirements for the Carriage & Wagon stock repairs. The timber was fed from a timber storage yard which was covered by a 3-ton gantry crane spanning 60 feet outside at the south end of the shop.

4 cutter and a 5 cutter combined surfacing and thickening machines was used in this shop.

There was also equipment for sharpening and reconditioning all Cutters and Saws.

Note: a jobbing saw mill was also installed in Wagon No. 1 shop and a small wheelwrights under the sawmill foreman was situated in the locomotive section of the works

ERECTING SHOP

The erecting shop was a five bay shop originally with three roads per bay, (fifteen roads total). The shop was 480 feet long and 250 feet wide, 50 feet width per bay.

An additional road transverse to the shop was used to convey boilers to the other bays and wheels into the wheel shop via a bogie. This road was approximately 100 feet from the Eastern (Machine Shop) end of the shop.

The erecting shop, along with the wheel shop, was built in 1900 and was the last of the main principal shops built on the Gorton complex. When built, the erecting shop was primarily for the purpose of building and repairing Locomotives. During the late 1950s and into the 1960s up until closure the Erecting Shop was sub-divided into various sections as the overhaul of locomotives started to wind down:

Erecting Shop – No. 1 Bay.

Overhaul of MSW dc electric locomotives.

Locomotive output – One general overhaul and two casual repairs per fortnight.

Equipment in No. 1 bay included:

Facilities for both mechanical and electrical repairs. Electrical repairs were jig assembled prior to refitting into the locomotives.

5,000 volt flash testing unit

Industrial vacuum cleaning plant

Electric heating oven

Heavy duty welding plant.

2 x 50-ton overhead electric cranes

1 x 40-ton overhead electric crane

1 x 5-ton overhead electric crane (This crane moved over from No. 4 bay in the 1950s).

Erecting Shop – Nos 2 and 3 Bays.

Concentrated on the overhaul and repairs to steam locomotives. Mainly existing ex GCR and L&NER classes of locomotives and British Railways WD 2-8-0 and Standard '9F' 2-10-0 locomotives. Space permitting, 'EM1' and two classes of locomotives were occasionally overhauled/repaired in this bay on No. 1 road in No. 2 Bay.

Main equipment in No. 2 and 3 Bays included:

Locomotive frame optical alignment and instruments (spread across the two bays)

Cylinder alignment and boring tools

Portable pneumatic drilling machines, welding/cutting equipment etc.

2 x 40-ton overhead electric cranes per bay.

Output approximately five locos and tenders per week

Erecting Shop – No. 4 Bay.

Concentrated on the overhaul and repairs to locomotive tenders. Some staff also employed in the manufacture of radiator shutters and fuel tanks for diesel locomotives that were at that time under construction in Derby locomotive works.

Main equipment in No. 4 bay included:

2 x 40-ton overhead electric cranes.

Equipment for fabrication work and testing of diesel fuel tanks.

Portable pneumatic drilling machines, welding/cutting equipment etc.

Erecting Shop – No. 5 Bay.

This bay concentrated on the conversion of wagons associated with the railways modernisation programme, namely drum wagon conversions for the 25kv overhead ac lines. Heavy repairs to brake vans, goods wagons and special bogie vehicles was also carried out.

Main Equipment in No. 5 Bay included:

1 x 40-ton Overhead Crane.

WHEEL SHOP

This shop concentrated on repairs to steam and electric locomotive wheels and axles, including new tyre fitting, this includes new tyres also for the carriage and wagon shops. Attention was also carried out in this shop for ultrasonic crack testing of axles. Repair work was also carried out to Hoffman and Timken bearing type axle boxes.

Main Equipment in this shop was comprised of:

Various types of wheel turning and journal lathes

Tyre boring machines

Journal grinding and turning machines in addition to a quartering machine with optical settings

Gas fired heating rings for tyre fitting to wheel

2 x 6 -ton overhead electric cranes.

COACH SHOP

The shop during this period was engaged in the wiring up of vehicles for the 25kVac overhead electrification programme. This in effect converting conventional coaching rolling stock. Conversions included, Office and mess coaches, equipment/tackle vehicles, generator coaches, ladder equipment vehicles and pantograph vehicles. Also, motive power breakdown train conversions as well as hostel coach conversions were carried out.

This shop was also used for the overhaul of the Manchester/Hadfield and Glossop 1500 volt dc Electric Multiple Unit stock, though occasionally this stock would sometimes have work carried out in the main erecting shop.

The shop also had a section where polishing, trimming, and coaching furniture repairs were carried out, also a small plumbing section was incorporated. Another section/bay had the sawmill.

Outside the shop on the south side was a timber yard approximately 50 feet wide with an overhead gantry electric crane of 3-ton capacity. A rail line connected the timber yard to the sawmill.

Output of coaches, averaged three per week.

WAGON SHOP No. 1

Repairs that were carried out during this period were on a progressive repair system for the repair of heavy wagons. The main rolling stock repaired here consisted mostly covered goods and fish vans. This area also had a jobbing sawmill.

Rolling stock output was approximately sixty heavy wagon per week.

The main equipment consisted of:

An electric traverser (outside the building) approximate 56 foot wide (feeding all lines between the Coach Shop and Wagon Shop).

A Smithy section

Equipment for vacuum break testing.

4 x journal and tyre turning lathes

A Lifting Bay comprising:

1 x 5-ton overhead electric crane.

1 x 15-ton overhead electric crane.

A traverser inside the shop approximately 20 feet wide for conveying heavy components (wheels/axles etc) from all the shop bays to the lifting bay/wheel lathes

Sawmill.

LOCOMOTIVE PAINT SHOP

The Paint Shop in close proximity to the Carriage &Wagon shops was (at this time a two road shop – formerly four roads)

Preparation, painting and sign writing of steam and electric locomotives to full specifications.

The paint shop was provided with roof steam heating panels throughout the shop.

WAGON PAINT SHOP

This shop occupied the former tender shop following the closure of the Carriage &Wagon Works at Dukinfield.

All wagons were prepared for and painted in this shop following repairs. Sign writing as necessary was also carried out to the wagons.

Output, approximately fifteen wagons per day

Main Equipment:

1 x 15-ton overhead electric crane.

1 x 10-ton overhead electric crane.

Wagon 'Tipplers' for under vehicle paint spraying (wagon tilting equipment)'

ELECTRICIANS SHOPS

The Electricians Shop carried out all electrical repairs to machinery in the locomotive, Carriage & Wagon and Motive Power Departments (running sheds).

Included in those repairs were switchboards, switch breaker, underground and overhead electrical reticulation repairs. New installations maintenance of electrical welding machinery and all lighting in the shops and yards.

Equipment included:

1 x 1½-ton overhead electric crane

Lathe for armature winding purposes

Electric motor test bed.

MAIN MILLWRIGHTS' SHOP

This shop was fully self contained to be capable of carrying out maintenance and repairs as well as installations to all heavy engineering machinery that was in use at that time.

The list of repairs carried out included, but were not confined to, overhead cranes, high pressure water pumping equipment, capstans, compressors and compressed air equipment throughout the whole of the Gorton Works complex and running sheds. Also maintenance and overhauling steam and diesel cranes in addition to turntables and water columns etc. This work also included working on other equipment from outside the works from the Eastern and North Eastern regions of British Railways. Also maintenance and repairs carried out to the Gorton coaling tower over at the running sheds yard.

Equipment included:

Fully self-contained workshop. Full range of heavy tooling equipment.

1 x 15-ton crane.

TRACTOR SHOP

The tractor shop was located at the north east side of the works near the spring shop and maintained all the works internal transport vehicles, i.e. fork lift trucks, tractors, trucks and trailers.

The works transport system worked on an outer and inner circuit.

The Outer Circuit:

Conveyed items from one area of the works to the other, this made instances where the crossing of the main yard became necessary and also having to cross the main public roadway (Widnes Street) to the C&W Shop.

The Inner Circuit:

Was used for conveying items from one shop to another in the same workshops area.

Equipment used included:

Hydraulic quick-lifting jacks

Battery charging units

Tyre repair, vulcanising plant.

JOINERS / BUILDERS SHOP

The building department carried out all work of a civil engineering nature including all structural work within Gorton works as well as the maintenance to walls, flooring, temporary structures together with water, oxygen and gas services. The department undertook all major installations requiring building materials of all types including foundations work and brickwork that was required in connection with the three Lancashire boilers, incinerators, drains, furnaces and sanitary requirements that came under and covered by the Factories Act Regulations.

The Joiners' section carried out all work involving repairs to partitions, doors, floors, cabinets, windows, wooden archways and cupboards etc.

The shop had a small wheelwrights' section that carried out repairs to ladders, trailers wheel barrows etc.

Equipment in the shop was mainly associated to repairs and maintenance to wood machinery in the Pattern Shop.

PUMP HOUSE

The main pump house delivered high, medium and low pressure water services throughout the whole of the works including the running sheds. The pumps were capable of delivering 40,000 gallons of water per hour supplied from the Canal Depot filtered reservoirs. The maximum pressure was 60 psi. The water pumps were of the vertical-throw type with 13-inch rams, being driven from 65 hp motors dc supply.

The water reticulation system for the works fire hydrants was also delivered from this supply.

BOILER HOUSES – STATIONS

The principal boiler installations were at three locations.

1. The largest boiler station contained three large Lancashire boilers. This was located at the north end of the main workshop complex for supplying heating and steam for the smithy hammers. Two of these boilers were fitted with chain grate feeders. The third boiler was hand fired. All boilers worked at a working pressure of 80 psi.

2. The second boiler station had two stationary ex-locomotive boilers installed. One of the boilers was fired by an underfeed stoker. The other boiler was coke fired and supplied high pressure water for heating purposes. The boilers supplied most of the steam for the north side of the workshops.

3. The third boiler station was for supplying heaters and process steam to the C&W workshops with two boilers installed. One boiler was an 'Economic' type boiler with an output capacity of 10,000 lbs. per hour. The second boiler was an ex-locomotive boiler and was used as an incinerator burning waste wood giving heating and process steam.

ELECTRICAL SUB STATIONS

Two sub stations provided electrical reticulation to the whole of the works. These being supplied at 6000 Volts ac and giving an output for the works at 440 Volts ac at 50htz 3-phase, and, rectified in some cases to 230 Volts dc, this transformed to 110 Volts, 50 and 50 Volts for hand tooling purposes.

Sub Station No. 1 Supplied power for the principal workshops of the main works.

Sub Station No. 2 Supplied power to the Motive Power Department and C&W Shops.

COMPRESSOR HOUSES

There were four compressor houses.

1. Main Compressor House. Located near the smithy. Installed were two compressors able to produce 750 cubic feet of free air per minute each.

2. This Compressor house had two compressors installed. One compressor capable of delivering 1,000 cubic feet of free air per minute and, one dc compressor giving 800 cubic feet of free air per minute.

3. No. 3 Compressor house was capable of delivering 300 cubic feet of free air per minute, and was situated at the Permanent Way shop.

4. No. 4 Compressor house was capable of delivering 400 cubic feet of free air per minute and was situated at the C&W Shops

Note: All of the compressor house air supplies were interconnected to supply compressed air to all of the departments of the whole complex at 100psi. All connections for hand tooling were standard throughout the works.

CANTEENS

The works had two canteens. One canteen was in one of the Canal Depot buildings on the opposite side of Cornwall Street adjacent to the Main Offices, this canteen was housed in the building originally built by the Manchester Sheffield and Lincolnshire Railway (MSLR) as a school for the companies children. The second was on the west side of the works between the Locomotive Running Sheds and C&W workshops. This canteen was originally part of the works paint shop, the paint shop was remodelled from four roads to two and the shop rebuilt into two separate sections.

EMPLOYEES WELFARE

The British Railways Staff Association (BRSA) had their premises in the old Canal Depot on Cornwall Street opposite the main offices. The BRSA provided all social functions and indoor activities. Outdoor activities and sports were carried out on the sports fields at Woodley in Cheshire, this included the Crowning of the 'Railway Queen' whenever this event was carried out.

OLD IRON FOUNDRY

The old Iron Foundry (Main iron foundry and plate foundry both of which were fed by four centrally placed cupolas) was by this time shut down and was used mainly for storing obsolete, and surplus machinery and machine tools. The foundries were built on the site of the former Steel Foundry and Rail Rolling mill of the late 1860s.

It was also inside the Iron Foundry that ex GCR locomotive No. 506 (BR No 62660 *Butler Henderson*) took a well deserved rest before it entered the erecting shop to have its restoration carried out to its former GCR glory prior to it going on public display at the British Transport Commission Museum at Clapham. Since its Clapham days it has been returned to running condition on the preserved Great Central Railway at Loughborough and has also been on public display at the National Railway Museum.

TEST HOUSE

The Test House was located in the two storey building at the east end of the boiler shop buildings. The work that was carried out there covered the testing of all lifting beams, hooks, slings and loose lifting chains for all departments in the works and also for some areas of the North Eastern and Eastern Regions.

The machinery used could test chains of all sizes up to a capacity of 100 tons. The department also carried out work involving hardness and bend testing for all production and workshop purposes.

FIRE STATION

The Fire Station was situated close to the works main entrance near Lawton Street and was manned full time during the works working hours.

The station contained all the necessary equipment for fighting fires and had facilities for refills necessary to keep fire hose cupboards and fire points operable at all the distribution points throughout works and yards.

There were two part-time fire brigades which were 'on call'. One was to cover the Locomotive and Road motor department and the second to cover the C&W departments. The two brigades worked closely together to cover the locomotive running department.

AMBULANCE ROOMS

There were two fully equipped ambulance/first aid rooms in the workshops. One was located close to the works main entrance and the adjoining the canteen at the C&W workshops. The centres were staffed by fully qualified nursing staff who were capable of rendering first aid and administrating medication etc as was necessary. There was also an ambulance man who was on duty to accompany patients to home or hospital as was necessary.

Note: It was due to the fact that Gorton Works had its own fully qualified nurse on duty at the time of a gas cylinder explosion in 1946 that the nurse was able to carry out immediate emergency treatment.

MAIN OFFICES

The Main Offices were situated at the East end of the works on Cornwall Street. The offices were divided into four administrative departments and included the works managers office. A separate office block housed the drawing office, method study office and the planning section of the production department.

The Site Today

Photographed from the corner of the bridge on Chapman Street and Railway Street looking in the direction of Manchester Piccadilly Railway. Of the four lines, only two tracks are in regular use. The works site is now the new Manchester Smithfield Market with a section at the far end occupied by a division of Greater Manchester Police. If travelling past the site on the train, one would not recognise going over the four bridges that formed the Priory Junction or the parapet wall that supported the Birdcage as it joined the now long gone footbridge, and is now completely overgrown with foliage.
The view below is looking along Cornwall street towards Ashton Old Road at the point where the Tank's main offices were situated. All was demolished around 50 years ago and the embankment grassed over. The trees are indicative of the length of time that has elapsed.
both Author

Above: Directly across the road from the previous photograph was once the canal depot. Close to the nearest houses the Railway Staff Associated Club had their premises. Further along was the enginemens barracks, once the MS&LR childrens school. Corner of Lawton Street and Press Street. The streets now remodelled.

Below: Viewed looking across Lawton Street, the Works entrance was approximately between the bill board and the lamp post. Turning off to the immediate right is Press Street. The road leading off into the distance is new and would have hit the works' boundary wall.

both Author

BIBLIOGRAPHY & SOURCES

Great Central Vol. 1; The progenitors, 1813-1863, George Dow, London, Locomotive Publishing Company, 1959
Great Central Vol. 2 Dominion of Watkin, 1864-1899, George Dow, London, Ian Allan, 1962
Great Central. Volume 3: Fay sets the pace 1900-1922, George Dow, London, Ian Allan, 1965
Steel wheels and rubber tyres Vol. 2; A General Manager's journey, Geoffrey Hilditch, Usk, Oakwood, 2004
The LMS and LNER in Manchester, R. Eric Rose, London, Ian Allan, 1987
Woodhead, Scenes from the Past, Part 1, E. M. Johnson, Stockport, Foxline, 1996
Woodhead: the electric railway, E. M. Johnson, Bredbury, Foxline Limited, 2001
Steam over Woodhead, E.M. Johnson, Nottingham, Book Law Publications, 2013
J. G. Robinson : a lifetime's work, by David Jackson, Headington, Oakwood Press, 1996
The Harmonious Blacksmith Robinson, A. C. Hancox, Stephenson Locomotive Society, 1995
Yeadons Register of LNER Locomotives (various volumes), W. B. Yeadon, Nottingham, Book Law Publications
Locomotives of the Great Central Railway. Vol.1 1897-1914, E. M. Johnson, Pinner, Irwell Press, 1989
LNER 4-6-0s at Work, Geoffrey Hughes, London, Ian Allan, 1988
LNER Locomotives, 1923-1948, H. C. Casserley, Truro, Bradford Barton, 1977
The Great Central in LNER Days, David Jackson and Owen Russell, Ian Allan, 1983

The Railway Magazine various issues
Great Central Railway Magazine 1905 to 1923
LNER Magazines 1927 to 1938
The Railway Gazette various issues
British Railways, various booklets concerning Gorton
The 'Green Books', various numbers
Great Central Railway Society magazines

National Railway Museum, York
The National Archives, Kew

POSTSCRIPT

A personal final tribute

Just before the works closure, all the workshop apprentices and other personnel were given a choice of which depot or workshop they would like to be transferred to in order to finish their apprenticeship and continue working on the railway (if they wished to do). My own choice was for a transfer to Doncaster locomotive works, geographically this was not possible, the next best choice was for a transfer to Crewe locomotive works, so this is what I opted for. Several other apprentices also decided on Crewe, others for Derby and several others for railway maintenance depots around the Manchester area, Longsight, Newton Heath and Reddish etc. Amongst the apprentices transferred to Crewe were, me, Eric Bond, Jeff Newton (Spike), Bill Ashton, Peter Hodgson and David Miles-Jones. On completion of our apprenticeship we all went our separate ways. I obtained a transfer to Reddish Electric Traction Depot on the day I came out of my time. Eric Bond stayed on at Crewe. Eric Bond and I formed a very close friendship, both within and out of work, along with Denis Wilde. Eric lived in Droylsden, ten minutes on a push bike from my home in Bowness Street, Higher Openshaw. Denis lived in Glossop. Glossop being fourteen miles away, meant that slowly our meet ups with Denis unfortunately diminished and eventually over time we stopped contact. Eric Bond and I kept our friendship up for a number of years until Eric's family moved down to the South of England with Eric moving there also. I did speak to Eric about ten years ago, he now lives in Alicante in Spain. On our final day at Gorton, soon before the closure came along, Eric Bond and I went to the machine shop offices to say our farewells to the shop foremen. The machine shop foreman at that time were Bill (Batty) Batters, Tommy Hagan, Freddy (Micky) Mitchell and the head foreman, Bill Grundy. Bill Grundy was a very well liked and respected man. A true railway foreman of the day, immaculately dressed in suit and waistcoat. Looking at Mr Grundy (in those days, everybody was Mister), you knew he was the main man, a person admired by all in the works. I forget now how many of the four foremen were in the office that last day, but, Bill Grundy was certainly there. Eric and I told Mr Grundy that we had enjoyed working in the machine shop under him and our time at the Tank, we bade our farewells and wished them all the best for the future (Bill Grundy must have been nearing retirement age - so hopefully he could continue working or retire earlier than anticipated and be able to reach his goal in life). Mr Grundy said that he also wished us all the best, for our continued apprenticeship and employment on the railways, and, as we shook hands, his final words to us were:

"*Don't let the name Gorton Tank down when you get to Crewe*".

After fifty odd years, (Mister) Bill Grundy is no longer with us but I will simply add:

"*Mr Grundy, I don't think that we ever did let the Tank down*".

The enjoyment I have had in compiling this book is testament to the fact that I never forgot what he said.

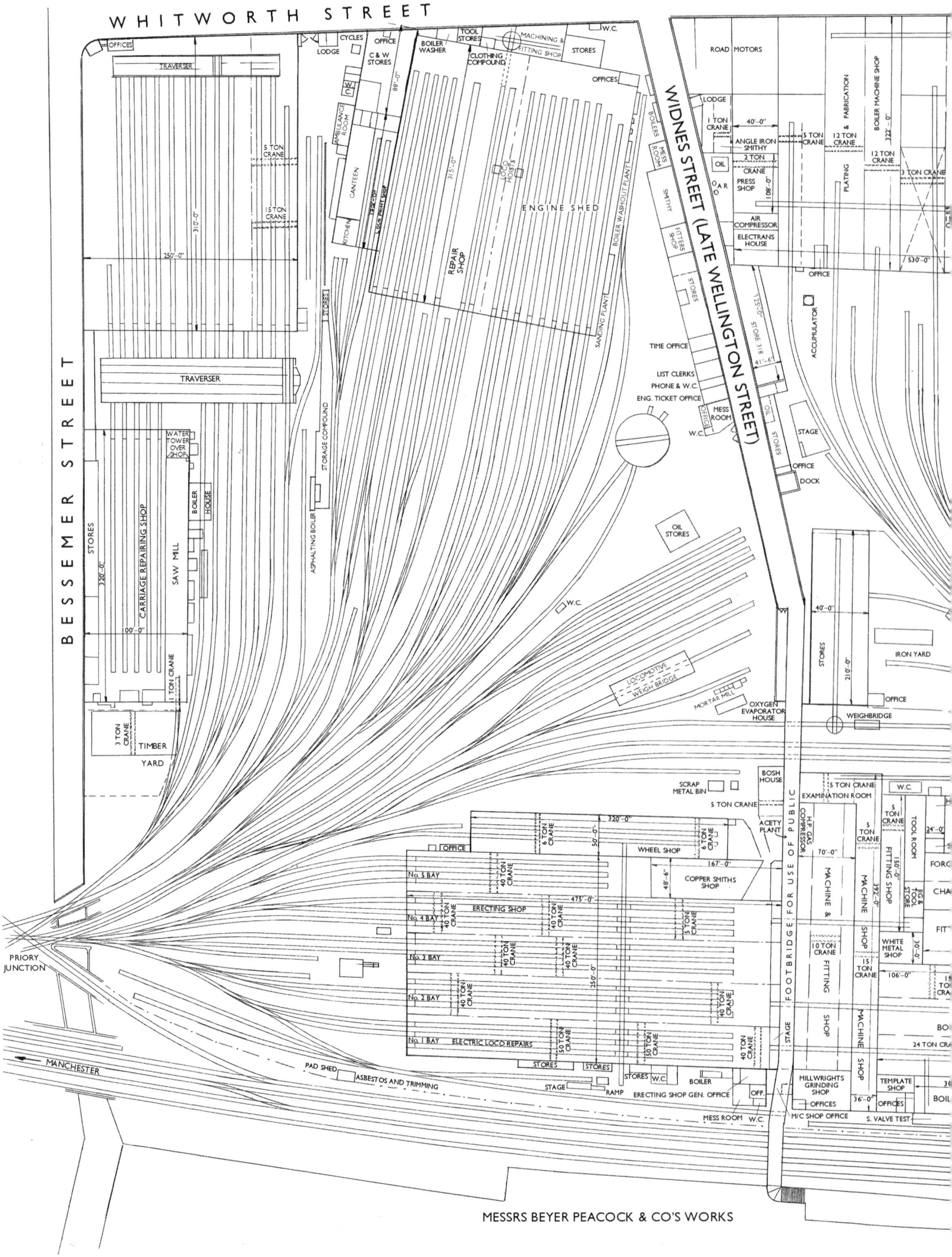

MESSRS BEYER PEACOCK & CO'S WORKS